An Introduction to Ethics for Nonprofits and NGOs

Craig Hanson

An Introduction to Ethics for Nonprofits and NGOs

palgrave
macmillan

Craig Hanson
The School of Arts and Sciences
Palm Beach Atlantic University
Palm Beach, FL, USA

ISBN 978-3-031-23076-9   ISBN 978-3-031-23077-6 (eBook)
https://doi.org/10.1007/978-3-031-23077-6

© The Editor(s) (if applicable) and The Author(s), under exclusive license to Springer Nature Switzerland AG 2023

This work is subject to copyright. All rights are solely and exclusively licensed by the Publisher, whether the whole or part of the material is concerned, specifically the rights of translation, reprinting, reuse of illustrations, recitation, broadcasting, reproduction on microfilms or in any other physical way, and transmission or information storage and retrieval, electronic adaptation, computer software, or by similar or dissimilar methodology now known or hereafter developed.

The use of general descriptive names, registered names, trademarks, service marks, etc. in this publication does not imply, even in the absence of a specific statement, that such names are exempt from the relevant protective laws and regulations and therefore free for general use.

The publisher, the authors, and the editors are safe to assume that the advice and information in this book are believed to be true and accurate at the date of publication. Neither the publisher nor the authors or the editors give a warranty, expressed or implied, with respect to the material contained herein or for any errors or omissions that may have been made. The publisher remains neutral with regard to jurisdictional claims in published maps and institutional affiliations.

Cover illustration: gremlin

This Palgrave Macmillan imprint is published by the registered company Springer Nature Switzerland AG
The registered company address is: Gewerbestrasse 11, 6330 Cham, Switzerland

For Paul, who held down the fort.

Contents

Introduction: A Framework for Analyzing Moral Situations   1
Ethics, Naive vs. Nuanced   2
The Is/Ought Distinction   3
Relativism   5
Deontological Ethics: Duty and Law   7
Teleology: Judging Cases by Consequences   12
Insights from Medical Ethics   15
Virtue Ethics and Feminist Ethics   17
Practical Tips for Instituting Ethics in Your Institution   20
Conclusion   24
Bibliography   24

From Theory to Action   27
Ethics vs Law   27
Demanding the "Right" Answer   29
The Informed Argument   32
Applying Moral Theories   33
Collating Our Observations   47

Boards and Oversight   51
Covid-19 Vaccine Policy in a Medium-Sized NFP   57
The Helpful Board Member   59
When Democracy and Mission Collide   60
The Employee with Family on the Board   63

Social Enterprise vs. Social Service	65
The Board Member's Pet Project	68
Regime Change and the Perils of Being a Hero	70
The Possessive Major Gifts Officer	72
When Personal Problems Threaten the Mission	75
References	77
Moral Dilemmas in Executive Leadership	**79**
Meltdown in Monrovia	82
Cutting Vital Services	84
Changing Staff's Job Descriptions	87
Child Sponsorship in the Afterschool Program	90
Accepting Crypto Donations	92
The White Savior in the Dark Continent	93
Internship or Exploitation?	95
Graft at the Top	97
References	99
Money, Finance and Fundraising	**101**
Misallocation of Resources or Unreasonable Donor?	104
Lean or Starving? On the Tyranny of Low Administrative Cost Rates	105
That Time When Your NFP Became his PR Crisis Response Plan	108
A Successful Event	110
Missing Money at the Group Home	111
Bribery or Just Doing Business?	112
Coalition Building or Finder's Fee?	114
Inheriting an Albatross	116
The School for Civil War Orphans	118
The Best President We Could Ever Dream Of	120
The Post-Mortem "Take"	121
Missing Money?	123
"Give Me a Child You Don't Care About"	124
References	126
Intercultural and Cross-Cultural Ethics	**127**
Short-Termer Headaches	137
"Hire a Young Woman"	139
In Our Country They Would Be Married	140
What Counts as Diversity Numbers?	142
Vaccine Resistance in Vulnerable Communities	144
The At-Least-Somewhat Racist Missionary	147
Later that Evening, in the Same Town	149

Nurturing African Entrepreneurs	151
The Successful West African Recycling Entrepreneur	153
Bibliography	154

Ethics in Program Operations 155
Ethics Committees	155
The HR Department	156
Staff-Training and Grassroots Ethics	157
The Protective Guardian	158
Dealing with Noncompliance in Syracuse	160
Putting Nationals in Harm's Way	161
Another Feeding Program Begins	162
What Could Go Wrong?	163
Land Title Woes in Sub-Saharan Africa	165
Microfinance, Interest and Islam	168
Indian Nationalism and the Foreign NGO	170
Lying to the Police	171
Closing the Orphanage	174
Professorial Malfeasance Abroad?	176
References	180

Digital, Online and Cyber Ethics 181
Archiving a Nation's Text Messages	183
Where There Are no Government-Issued IDs	185
Political Disinformation, Community Outreach and Vaccine Drives	187
Election Season and Viral Online Videos	189
Revealing the Location of Vulnerable Women	190
Child Porn, Revenge Porn and Non-Fungible Tokens	192
Bibliography	196

Appendix I: Discussion-Leader Tips	197
Appendix II: Structuring an Ethics Discussion	199
Appendix III: Evaluating Ethics Argumentation	203
Appendix IV: Assessing Written Case Analyses	211
Appendix V: Discussion Guides to Each Case	219
Bibliography	269
Index	275

Abbreviations

AP	Accounts Payable
BAM	Business as Mission
CDC	The Center for Disease Control and Prevention
CEO	Chief Executive Officer
CIA	Central Intelligence Agency
CSR	Corporate Social Responsibility
DEI	Diversity, Equity and Inclusion
FDA	Food and Drug Administration
FGM	Female Genital Mutilation
GAAP	Generally Accepted Accounting Practices
GO	Governmental Organization
GPA	Grade Point Average
HIPA	Health Insurance Portability and Accountability Act
IRB	Institutional Review Board
M&IE	Meals and Incidental Expenses
MHA	Ministry of Home Affairs
NGO	Non-Governmental Organization
OSHA	Occupational Safety and Health Administration
PSA	Public Service Announcement
ROI	Return on Investment
SDN	Specially Designated Nationals
UNHCR	United Nations High Commission on Refugees
USAID	United States Agency for International Development

List of Figures

Boards and Oversight

Fig. 1   NFP Evaluation structure   54
Fig. 2   One of several possible communication structures   55

List of Tables

Money, Finance and Fundraising

Table 1	Paws and purrs annual gala budget	110

Intercultural and Cross-Cultural Ethics

Table 1	"Ousmane's Budget"	153

Appendices

Table 1	Teaching modalities	201
Table 2	Facts vs judgments	204
Table 3	Good and bad writing prompts	205
Table 4	Good and bad analyses	207
Table 5	Informal fallacies	208
Table 6	Le buget d'Ousmane	257

Introduction: A Framework for Analyzing Moral Situations

This book begins by providing tools for moral reasoning in Non-Governmental Originations (NGO) and Not-For-Profit (NFP) leadership, then proceeds to present a number of real-life cases which illustrate various facets of moral issues which occur, and recur, in NFP and NGO operations. It is intended to be a discussion book for new and seasoned professionals whether in university education or within NFPs or NGOs themselves.

It is often the first course of action when confronted with a complex moral issue to proverbially "shoot from the hip." But such an approach often produces more heat than light. Anarchic moral processes are often resolved by the loudest voice, the most belligerent personality or the most empowered individual declared the victor. This is to be avoided. I will therefore introduce a series of frameworks which professional ethicists have used as a common starting-point for the analysis of moral issues. The extent to which these frameworks are of use is very much up to the reader, and I personally endorse no particular ethical starting-point. But what I can say with confidence is that the ideas contained within this introduction are those the professionals use and reuse when tackling the most difficult moral issues found in human civilization.

An exhaustive treatment of this centuries-old literature would require much more than an introduction to a book. It would (and actually does) require a significant amount of background reading and analysis before we ever arrived at the stage of applying these insights to real-life moral problems.

I therefore propose an unhappy compromise: in the remainder of this introduction I will outline a variety of moral insights that have gained traction over time in professional ethics literature. I will omit most of the history and reasonings behind them. But I will pay for that transgression by providing a bibliography to the reader should the reader decide to conduct further investigation. This is then followed with an "applied" section in which I demonstrate how to use these frameworks in real-life situations.

Ethics, Naive vs. Nuanced

The insistence that ethics matters to organizational leadership is not new. Hippocrates (460–370 BCE) did not argue that above all else we should make sure our measurement instruments are calibrated. He argued that one should "above all else, do no harm." Since this time it has been a longstanding principle of professional behavior that it is essential to not merely perform actions that promote certain technological or scientific ends, but to do so in a way that respects moral confines.

Professional ethics is sometimes portrayed as an endeavor in which the would-be ethicist is asked to "figure out" which possible course of action is the right one, given the dubious assumption that once we figure that out we will invariably do it. But all too often this is not so. What is right is not always obvious. And it is far from certain that even if it were that we would do it.

The problem before us is deeper than just the intellectual challenge of deciphering the right from the wrong. Because while it is a comparatively easy matter to choose the right over the wrong, it is much more difficult to make a choice when no course of action seems right. If the reader of this book were to reflect upon the variety of decisions they have undertaken with significant moral consequence, I would wager to say that most do not so neatly fall into the "right vs. wrong" category.

I propose a distinction (of my own invention) between "naïve" and "nuanced" ethics. Naïve ethics rests upon the belief, unsupported by human experience, that the world always and invariably divides into the right and the wrong, that the right and the wrong are always knowable in advance, and that anyone who comes to know what is right will consistently do it. Readers who have subscribed to what I call "naïve ethics" will be disappointed with this book. I take solace in the fact that such a reader would be unlikely to read it in the first place.

While describing naïve ethics in the manner I have just done makes it appear impotent *ipso facto* its description, it would be wrong to underestimate its ubiquity and influence. Western democracies are witnessing powerful forces which exert strong pressure upon persons to adopt naive ethics. Political polarization increasingly bids the population to view the world as neatly divided into two camps, one of which is right and good the other wrong and evil. Religious forces from time-to-time do the same. Indeed, a hallmark sign of naivety in moral reasoning is the view that on moral issues it's "us versus them."

Conversely, "nuanced" ethics is murky. Such an approach to moral reasoning requires that the ethicist be prepared to discover that there are more than one or two ways to understand a moral situation. It requires that the thinking, reflective person take seriously the possibility that their initial impressions might have been wrong. Equally, it requires that such a person take seriously the possibility that their friends or peer group are wrong. It requires a thoroughness and humility that is not often socially praised. It requires that the deliberate thinker be prepared to side with political enemies against ideologically like-minded friends. And above all else it requires the virtues of carefulness, thoroughness and courage.

Does this mean that the work of the ethicist is that of a lone gunman on a wild moral frontier of ideological lawlessness? Hardly. As it turns out there are a number of helpful tools that have been painstakingly articulated over the many centuries of human learning. Some were written on papyrus sheets 2600 years ago and others on computers far more recently. No introduction to a case study textbook could ever adequately cover them all. But enough can be said in these pages to offer the reader some tools which have helped many ethicists in a variety of situations to tackle seemingly intractable moral problems. In what follows I will briefly outline these tools.

The Is/Ought Distinction

David Hume (1711–1776) was a Scottish Enlightenment philosopher. He is also often categorized as a skeptic—someone who thinks that what most others take to be knowledge is actually not knowledge at all. In an era when the abilities of modern science and technology seemed to be unstoppable he cast a wary eye upon the intellectual underpinnings of such endeavors in nearly every way—the nature of scientific laws, the abilities of people to acquire new knowledge, even the existence of individual persons. It's not at all the case that he was anti-science. Rather, he thought that one of the things that science teaches is that what passes for knowledge often isn't. Of importance to this work is his observation which in retrospect we call the "is/ought" problem.

This problem is a simple one. The problem is that we never strictly speaking perceive what *ought* to be the case. At best we only ever perceive what *is* the case and then subsequently add to our perceptions any of a variety of moral properties or judgments. For example, I may *perceive* the intake staff at my NFP speaking to incoming clients in a particular tone of voice. That perception is merely that—a perception regarding the tone of a voice. Yet quite apart from my perceptions I may have carried into my observation of the intake staff the belief that "anyone who talks to people that way is rude." The point is not that my antecedent belief that speaking to people rudely is a false belief. The point is that my application of my moral appraisal was not "contained in the perception." I added it to my perception. That addition may be correct, incorrect or somewhere in between. But it is an addition nonetheless.

Hume's point is that "adding" moral features to empirical observation is as suspect as adding new civil law at the stage of jury deliberations at trial. Hume therefore asserts his characteristic dose of skepticism—he questions the validity of all moral judgment. If knowledge is rooted in the empirical and morality is divorced from empirical observation, then the moral enterprise is suspect.

Whether or not the reader agrees with Hume's point is a matter for the conscience of the reader. But his observation offers an important word of caution for those who dare to engage in the moral life rigorously: the fact that something appears morally obvious does not show that it is. Because the fact that something appears morally obvious may have more to do with the psychology of the observer than of the persons or situations being observed. This is why, in ethical decision-making, it is essential to surround one's self with persons with a wide range of different experience but who share a common trait: the sincere desire to responsibly think through difficult moral situations. Beware the ideologically driven zealot, be they true-believing progressives or died-in-the-wool conservatives. Beware the passionate religious zealot solely motivated to preserve the faith and the passionate anti-religious zealot solely motivated to preserve theirs. Zealotry is the enemy of ethics because it blinds the zealot from their own prejudices. And it does so in the most pernicious of ways: It prevents the zealot from detecting the bias they build in at the level of their own observation.

Relativism

Taken to an extreme, the preceding reflections seem to imply that all moral judgments are intrinsically suspect because they originate from persons who add their own moral judgments to situations that are not theirs to add to. Does this imply that we ought to jettison the moral enterprise and refuse to arrive at conclusions for fear of becoming a moral dogmatist? No, we should not. While the dangers of naive, shoot-from-the-hip ethics are great, the implications of the opposite are also great. Admittedly, there are many philosophical positions which argue that the very project of ethics is impossible, I will focus on one nebulous one: the challenge of moral relativism.

Moral relativism can enshrine itself in many forms—too many to cover here. I will detail just two blanket forms: individual relativism and cultural relativism.

Cultural relativism, however we parse it, is a thesis that asserts that cultures call the moral shots and that there is no more truth to moral claims than whatever it is that cultures assert is true. Furthermore, and perhaps most crucially, cultural relativism implicitly asserts an incommensurability thesis: that it is not appropriate to cast praise or blame from the standpoint of one culture when appraising that of another. Hence, one activity in one culture could end up morally appropriate for partisans of that culture, but the "same" action would be inappropriate in another.

Individual relativism is much more radical. The Individual relativistic schema asserts that the standards of moral appraisal vary from person-to-person, not just culture to culture. Therefore, the legitimacy of moral judgments varies depending upon each individual person.

What is wrong with this manner of thinking? After all we certainly do perceive cultural differences in ways that seem to matter morally. And don't we prefer for each individual to live life as they see fit? It turns out that there are a great many problems with moral relativism, running the gamut from intellectual inconsistencies to grave institutional consequences. We will see that if we are to avail ourselves of relativist insights, we must do so with a significant degree of savvy not embodied in the two preceding forms. Let me now show why.

Let us begin with a criticism of cultural relativism. Whether it be the mountains of West Virginia, the tribal areas of Northern Nigeria or Midtown Manhattan, are we to believe that all persons within the geographical confines of those areas invariably think and believe the same? Certainly not. We have ample reason to think that a simplistic cultural relativism is false. The reader of this book is probably aware of people raised more or less in the same circumstance as theirs but who diverged from dominant cultural "teachings" on key points. Stated perhaps more provocatively, what other than ignorance could make a person think it obvious that not all one's neighbors think the same, but that groups in far-off places are morally monolithic?

There is another problem with regard to cultural relativism. On the face of it, the thesis of cultural relativism implies that moral reformers are by definition immoral persons. They are immoral persons because they oppose dominant cultural values. Suddenly Martin Luther King Jr., Gandhi and Jesus rank as the most immoral persons in the history of humanity. Because if what makes things right and wrong is the fact that a culture does or does not approve of it, then persons who disagree with cultural ethos are immoral.

Neither I, nor I suspect many others, are willing to embrace that position!

Furthermore, cultural relativism threatens to collapse into Individual Relativism. We are all aware of persons who were raised in one allegedly identifiable culture but which in several respects disagree or object to some of their own culturally taught values. It seems absurd, if not ignorant or immature, to assert that cultural objectors are intrinsically immoral solely because they differ from their neighbors. Arriving at such a conclusion seems to undermine the right of persons to their own consciences. If we concede this point then we have reason to think that matters are much more complex than the cultural relativist depicts them. Perhaps moral codes are more varied than just the number of cultures that happen to exist. Perhaps they are as numerous as the number of persons on the planet. Hence gone is the view that each culture creates moral values, and in comes the view that each person does. But if the dangers of cultural relativism are significant, the dangers of Individual Relativism are much worse.

Many have experienced or witnessed cases of religious, gender or sexual orientation bigotry. One of the most striking features of such cases is that persons who engage in such bigotry are often convinced that their behavior is morally acceptable (even citing the power of their conviction as justification of their moral position). But if Individual Relativism were an adequate way of understanding morality, then in each of those cases we would have had to conclude that the accused were blameless. Because if individual conviction settled the moral matter, then the bigot would have been blameless. The institutional toll of such moral permissiveness is almost incalculable, running the gamut from legal liability to fundraising impact to employee morale and beyond.

The NGO or NFP must resist the swan song of carte blanche relativism. There really are moral standards of behavior, and violating them, no matter the reasons, is not appropriate. The bright dividing lines that delineate morally acceptable behavior from morally unacceptable behavior must be articulated, disseminated and reinforced.

It is important to point out, before moving on, that the problem with relativism as discussed here is not that it is entirely false. Rather, the problem is that it is an abused theory which if left imprecise makes all ethics impossible. We will encounter cases throughout this book, including in the next chapter where we apply theory, which give us reason to think that cultural attitudes matter and that individual beliefs matter. No serious ethics analysis should ever dispute this fact. Rather, it is important to not resort to relativism as a way to make troubling moral situations disappear. Doing that has the propensity to make moral problems escalate, not dissipate.

What are we to make of the preceding two considerations—that the is/ought problem makes us think twice about making moral judgments but the problems with moral relativisms require that we make those very same judgments? In what follows I will outline a variety of tools, some new and some very old, which have been successfully used in institutional ethics situations. It will not always be the case that all of them are used in every situation. But they have survived the test of time and have proven to be useful for professionals in a wide variety of situations.

Deontological Ethics: Duty and Law

The Greek word "deon" from which the word "deontological" stems means "duty." Deontological ethics views the moral life as resting upon a bedrock of duties—duties to follow the moral rules.

Religion-based ethics is often viewed as deontological, only one example of which is the Mosaic law. While probably an oversimplification, the religious ethicist might understand the relationship between persons and ethics in the following way: On the one hand there is the law and on the other hand there are human persons and their behavior. Whatever human persons think or say or do, this has no effect upon what the moral law is. If one follows the law then one is morally right for doing so. If one breaks that law one is wrong. If God has said that "honoring your mother and father" is right and if a person proceeds to treat their mother dishonorably, then what they have done is wrong. We may need to wade into the tricky waters of attempting to understand what it means to treat someone honorably, but none of that discussion will change the moral law. It will clarify it.

The possible institutional problems associated with implementing religiously based ethics into NGOs or NFPs are many. On the one hand there are religiously based not-for-profits and on the other hand there are those that are non-sectarian. Neither of the two has an easy path when it comes to religiously based ethics.

The religiously based NFP or NGO must take great care to articulate in advance what the moral confines are within which they do their work. Will Mennonite NGOs require women to wear long skirts? Will a Jehovah's Witness food pantry permit a line-worker to volunteer who has had a blood transfusion? Will an Islamic micro-bank permit interest to be charged? After those confines are articulated they must be disseminated in advance of employment and in advance of client participation.

Furthermore, sectarian NFPs and NGOs must be aware that not all religious convictions are protected, and that even if they are in one country they may not be in others. For example, a Jehovah's Witness organization has a well-established protection in the United States against the use of certain vaccines, rooted in their interpretation of Levitical law. The legal protection for Jehovah's Witnesses' approaches iron-clad when it comes to the prohibition of at least certain vaccines and other medical procedures. But a Southern Baptist homeschool group will enjoy no such legal protection in the courts, no matter how vaccine-resistant its members may be, even if their reasoning for their position were identical to that of the Jehovah's Witnesses.

Matters become even more thorny for the religious NFP or NGO regarding certain issues such as LGBTQ+ concerns. It is a difficult position to defend which states that opposition to certain orientations is embedded within one's millenniums-old faith tradition when no such position could be found in any institutional document before the year 2022.

Finally, religiously affiliated NFPs and NGOs need to understand that there are vast generational differences to be found among your staff, donors and clients. These differences impact attitudes toward both ethics and faith. The Christian NFP cannot count on the 20-something arriving at their employment door to be a card-carrying Republican Conservative. The Islamic NGO must anticipate that their youth were brought up in a very different psychic world than that of their grandparents. If it is your decision to take a "hard line" on any of several cultural, political or moral issues, then it would be dishonest to attempt to have your cake and eat it too. The ruse often played of being a conservative to your board and a liberal to your staff is doomed to failure on many levels. The best course of action is to come to a reasonable compromise with every stakeholder committed to your mission.

It would be a mistake to think that the non-sectarian, non-religious NFPs or NGOs need not think about such issues. As the French jurisprudential tradition has robustly illustrated, *laicité* is a position, not an anti-position. It is essential for non-sectarian NGOs and NFPs to understand that many of your employees work to fulfill your mission in part because they perceive that it is consonant with their own religious faith. Religion for such employees is not oppositional to the NFP mission, it is an ally of the mission. Therefore, messaging a purge of religion, whether from corkboards, watercooler chats or post-it-notes messages could convey to employees that the mission of the institution is secondary to the ideology of its leaders. While some NGO or NFP missions might be fundamentally adversarial to faith, the vast majority are not. And in a world of increasing animosities and rivalries, it is best to not multiply enemies beyond necessity.

A similar point must be stated to the religiously motivated worker at a non-sectarian NFP or NGO. Such a worker needs to understand that they have voluntarily sought employment at their institution. They have not been coerced or forced into indentured servitude. It is therefore deeply inappropriate, no matter how passionate one's faith, to use one's position to endorse an ideological line which lies outside the mission of the institution one works for. If it should come to a point at which such an employee perceives that they must choose between faith and employer, then it is probably time to seek employment elsewhere. And luckily for such a person, there are ample opportunities to serve in religiously oriented institutions where they will likely be more comfortable.

Finally, the non-sectarian NGO or NFP should be aware that many values which are portrayed as benign secular humanist values are anything but. Many axiomatic policies and ideas which dominate the NGO and NFP landscape have robust religious origins. Understanding this will go a long way toward understanding which ideas fundamentally influence you and will go a long way toward creating a truce within your institution. The examples of this are innumerable. I will illustrate just two.

First, institutions increasingly are adopting strong non-violence standards within their employee handbooks. Such standards increasingly tend to label "violence" as more than just laying a hand on another person. It can include many other forms of violence from speech to hostility and environmental factors. Labeling as "violent behavior" more than physical violence is wise. But it is also fraught with difficulty. And related to the point just made above, it is also not new. The Quaker religious tradition has worked on this very issue for many more years than your NFP or NGO has existed, and has done so at a very high level of ability. Those adopting non-violence standards would serve themselves well by looking at this literature. Quakers have thought about these issues for quite some time, probably at a higher level of ability than you have. Why not consult it?

And secondly, it is common practice to offer struggling employees an "improvement plan" rather than being sent to the curb on the first infraction. Such a practice very directly stems from Jewish Levitical law. It was not invented by lawyers or HR specialists. Employers need to understand that extending such a plan to your employees is not a mercy offered by your administration but a moral standard, rooted in religion, to which your culture implicitly subscribes.

Obviously, this is not to say that improvement plans or "anti-violence statements" are religious acts. They are not. What it shows is a continuity between values often regarded as "secular" and those regarded as rooted in "faith." Good moral values have universal appeal, both to persons with faith and those without.

Let us now return to the main thread of this section on deontological ethics. As it turns out, religious ethics are not the only deontological ethics. There are other deontological ethics which require no subscription to any faith tradition at all. The most well-known example of non-religious deontological ethics is the work of philosopher Immanuel Kant (1724–1804).

Kant's life and writing career occurred immediately after David Hume's. Kant was deeply troubled by a great many things that Hume proposed and, in many regards, viewed his own work as a workaround. Much of this has no direct bearing upon ethics. But some do.

Kant envisioned ethics as being rooted in two universal laws. As he states them (here in English translation) they might appear complex. Let me first articulate them, complexities and all, then proceed to explain. His two laws are:

1. Act in such a way that you could consistently will the maxim presupposed by your action to be a moral law.
2. Treat all persons as ends, not as mere means.

The first of these two laws appears complex, but upon analysis looks quite a bit like the golden rule. The idea is that an action is permissible where it is the case that it would be possible to do it in a world in which everyone does the same. If upon analysis it turns out that a world in which everyone behaves similarly is not a *possible* world, then your action is impermissible.

For example, let us assume that your fundraiser is in a situation in which they could receive a large gift if only they lied about how the gift would be used. This first law asks us to imagine a world in which every fundraiser at every institution always lies about how every gift would be used. In such a world, Kant asks rhetorically, would donors give money to fundraisers? No, they would not. Word would spread quickly that fundraisers are always liars and that whatever it was that donors gave money for, it wouldn't be used for the stated reasons. Fundraising would collapse. And because fundraising would collapse were everyone to behave in this way, it is therefore morally wrong for any one fundraiser to behave in this way. Fundraising would not be *possible* in a world in which fundraising was always rooted in deception.

The second Kantian law is much more intuitive. It asserts that it is immoral to "use" people as a means to an end. So robust is this conviction among Kantian ethicists that his moral theory is often referred to as the "Ethics of Respect for Persons" or "ERP" for short. Let us illustrate this law with another case.

Imagine a case in which a service recipient appears before the board to report on how the services provided affected them, presumably making their lives better. Not only is this unobjectionable, but it is good practice. Boards are the NFP's most consistent donors, volunteers and supporters. As such they derive immense satisfaction from seeing the impact of their labor and generosity. It is good practice to share these success stories with your board and with others. International NGOs should consider video-conferencing with recipients of services. And, of course, observe all confidentiality requirements that apply.

But consider a very different situation that might look the same on the surface. Imagine a CEO that knows that the board will give to a cause for which there are only marginal benefits to clients. So the CEO enacts a plan to manufacture a success story by selecting one articulate client to receive disproportionate benefit from a pilot of the program. The CEO then brings this manufactured client before the board to extoll the benefits of the program. In such a case the CEO is in clear violation of the second Kantian law. They are not bringing the client before the board for the purpose of illustrating how clients benefit. They are *using* the client for their own ends—accruing donations. In fact, the CEO is doing the very same to the board members. Those board members are being *used* for their financial contribution.

As we close this section on deontological ethics, let me offer a few summative comments regarding the two versions mentioned so far. Deontology has the strong benefit that it is rooted in rules. And rules are good things. They are regulative and stable. If the reader believes in the existence of inviolable human rights, then the reader shares a common belief of deontologists. If the reader believes that there are certain boundaries that could not in principle ever be crossed no matter how good the consequence, then the reader shares a belief of the deontologist.

But there are drawbacks. And those drawbacks are the flip side of the benefits. While immutable moral rules appear useful, their inability to change often draws criticism from their detractors. One's moral rule might say that lying to people is wrong, but what does one say to the child trafficker at the door of the orphanage looking for his escaped "investment?" Theft from a department store might be wrong, but it is poor strategy to begin with this fact when counseling clients. Our rule might say that we should respect the decisions of autonomous persons, but that standard is strained when confronting the case of autonomous racial violence.

Teleology: Judging Cases by Consequences

A very different moral universe can be found among the "teleological" camp of ethics. Again, etymology is of help. The Greek word "telos" means "aim" or "goal." The foundation of all teleological ethics is that one judges the rightness or wrongness of actions on the basis of the consequences that the actions produce. If an action "aims" at a good end and hits it, then the action was good. If it misses the mark then it is wrong.

There are two broad forms of teleological ethics, one of which is currently suffering from widespread (perhaps justified) unpopularity and the other exactly the opposite.

The broadly unpopular teleological view is that of the egoist. The egoist assesses the rightness or wrongness of an action as a function of how the action affects the person performing the action. If a person benefits from doing something then the action was right, and if not then it was wrong. It probably will not take the reader very long to think of the potential problems with this line of moral thinking. The current popularity of criticizing capitalist ideologies is very much rooted in the well-documented problems with the egoist moral universe. Profit-seeking entities acting in reckless abandon of the interests of others have the propensity to cause suffering, not eradicate it. Likewise, those solely motivated to look out for themselves are seldom viewed as morally virtuous persons.

Another facet of the egoist school of thought is not moral at all, but empirical. The egoist thinks that not only *should* people act from their own self-interest but that also this is what they invariably *do*. What separates the successful egoist from the unsuccessful egoist is the degree to which they can think about their interests with sophistication. The self-interested person seeking short-term gain is typically less sophisticated than the one thinking about long-term gain. The self-interested person who burns social bridges might derive satisfaction in the moment but often pays a social price that is higher than their momentary gain.

Such a theory often leaves a bad taste in the mouth of the reader. But it would be a mistake to dismiss it for this reason. Because thinking like an egoist can help to explain many of the moral neuroses of institutions. Indeed, from Thrasymachus as found in Plato's *Republic* until today there have been a great many egoists doing professional ethics. And none of them advocate for a world of egoistic agents run amok. Rather, they take egoistic thinking as brute to humanity and view the moral challenge to be to create institutions which mitigate against the worst forms of egoistic action. This matters to NFPs and NGOs.

Consider a fundraiser who has a yearly fundraising number to "hit." At the end of month 11 of the fiscal year they are behind and need to catch up. If they perceive that they will be solely evaluated on the basis of that number, then they may consider doing things which under different circumstances they would not. They may elect to solicit funds from persons without the ability to give, from persons whose money would be better put to use elsewhere, from persons badly in need of positive PR for their own private indiscretions, or any number of other sources which under more normal circumstances would not be pursued. If we do not want our fundraisers to solicit funds from such persons, then we probably shouldn't incentivize them to do so. This is why it is always a bad idea to evaluate fundraisers solely on the basis of dollar amounts received. Because incentivizing in this way opens the door for egoistic abuses. So also is it foolish to evaluate service providers on the basis of billable hours or teachers on average GPAs. Such evaluative measures breed corruption. So before casting judgment on those who commit what appears to be immoral egoistic actions, it is good to ask a self-reflective question about your institutional policy: Are there institutional dynamics which reward this behavior?

NFPs or NGOs should review institutional policies, especially evaluation and compensation policies, and ask hard questions regarding what is and is not incentivized. Such a study can be revealing. If an NFP is unhappy with the rudeness of its client intake staff, are those standards reflected in the way the staff is evaluated? If an NGO is uncomfortable accepting funds from convicted felons, does a policy against this exist? If an organization wouldn't want the state to investigate the way that client services are coded, then study the incentive structure of the accounting department.

Egoism is just one kind of consequences-based ethics. The other broad category, diametrically the opposite in many regards, thinks that the rightness and wrongness of actions is rooted in the consequences for all persons, not just one. This view of ethics is called "utilitarianism." Like most theories we can see its roots in antiquity, but unlike the others discussed up to this point its popularity is much more recent. Its modern popularity stems from the nineteenth-century philosopher Jeremy Bentham (1748–1832) and publicly championed by his student John Stuart Mill (1806–1873). It arguably dominates all political policy debates in the western world. If you were to watch deliberations in your own Parliament, Senate or House of Representatives you would be very likely to hear the language of utilitarianism spoken.

To quote Bentham, the utilitarian admonishes us to create "the greatest good for the greatest number" (Bentham, 1988). When it comes to thinking about which policy, which rule or which direction your NGO or NFP should take, the only morally salient point is to forecast the (potential?) impacts of that policy/rule/direction on all persons that are affected by it. The right choice to make is the one that makes things the best for most people. The wrong choice is that which does not.

Any NFP or NGO who has heard the language of "impact" or "scale" has heard the language of utilitarianism applied to your activities. Both of those terms implicitly bid your organization to increasingly maximize the good consequences of your services to the greatest extent possible.

The utilitarian way of thinking is powerful, albeit challenging, to institutions. The following is just one of a great multiplicity of possible utilitarian moral analyses: Imagine an established not-for-profit whose model originated during the NFP boom of the 1960s. Whereas their economic model may have sufficed for some decades, adjustments were not made in light of a changing legislative and financial environment. Consequently, many decades later the failure to pivot causes a significant decrease in program outcomes. The utilitarian in such a case would admonish the NFP to change its model. This may require programming changes, administrative changes and even mission changes. Faithful employees might have their duties altered or even eliminated. But on utilitarian grounds this would all be not only justified, but positively *required*. Because if an institution has the ability to bring about better consequences and fails to do so, then the institution is to be morally blamed.

More generally, the utilitarian analysis constantly bids the NGO or NFP to ask "how can we do this better?"

But like every theory discussed in this chapter, there are known objections. One common objection is that utilitarian analyses have difficulty accounting for concepts that to many seem to be essential. Chief among these is the concept mentioned earlier: human rights. If all that matters are consequences, then we risk finding ourselves in an "ends justify the means" scenario. If by marginalizing or mistreating a certain group makes your bottom line better, then the utilitarian analysis positively requires you to do so. It probably is true that some evangelical Christian institutions could increase their donations through vitriol against LGBTQ+ persons or that progressive Political Action Committees could do the same by increasing its vitriol against Evangelicals. But should they? If there is a difference between program outcomes and moral rightness, then there is reason to be suspicious of utilitarianism.

Finally, of direct relevance to the NFP and NGO, it is important to point out that utilitarianism is flatly incompatible with issue advocacy. By definition, issue-advocacy philanthropy begins with the assumption that the mission of your institution will be to advocate all and only your own issue. This includes scenarios in which your funds and labor could be put to allegedly "better" use elsewhere. If, for example, a social scientific study reveals that your women's employment funds would cause better outcomes were it allocated to land rights, the utilitarian view would require that you cease your work on women's employment and allocate resources to land rights.

This very issue rushed to the forefront with regard to the popularity of the "Effective Altruism" movement. This movement is Bentham-style utilitarianism applied to philanthropy. For example, MacAskill details in his book the resources that are spent upon issue-advocacy issues in sub-Saharan Africa produce positive outcomes. But the amount of funds that they draw from other much-needed philanthropic areas create a sub-optimal situation. Resources are disproportionately bestowed upon popular, lower-net-utility endeavors and not allocated to more impactful higher-net-utility endeavors. But summing up the will to resist the political temptation to fund low-impact programs we can create a world with more effective social services.

Insights from Medical Ethics

We have now discussed four moral theories—two deontological theories (religious and Kantian) and two teleological theories (egoism and utilitarianism). I have presented this information to give the reader analysis tools when navigating moral difficulties. But beyond the confines of philosophical theories regarding the fundamental nature of ethics, there are also useful apparatuses which can be of great help to the professional working in an NFP or NGO.

One is an apparatus which has increasingly found popularity in the medical ethics community.

Because ethics can be so nebulous, and because life-and-death circumstances so pressing, the medical community has seen fit to adopt an ad hoc system which has proven to be helpful when analyzing moral situations. Following Beauchamp and Childress, we might adopt a fourfold approach to analyzing moral problems (Beauchamp & Childress, 2019). Beauchamp and Childress endorse the view that when confronting moral problems there are four values, sometimes competing, which we must consider. They are:

1. Nonmaleficence: We ought not cause harm to persons.
2. Beneficence: We ought to create benefits for persons.
3. Autonomy: We should respect the decisions that people make for themselves, and endeavor to fortify the capacities of those who lack autonomy.
4. Justice: we ought to treat persons and allocate all resources with fairness (Beauchamp & Childress, 2019).

Admittedly, quite a bit is packed into each of these terms not the least of which is the term "justice" for which there exists a robust literature spanning back several millennia. But this much can be stated in this introduction: This fourfold value set strikes a compromise between the deontological and the utilitarian perspectives. The first two are arguably teleological and the latter two arguably deontological. Furthermore, and of much greater value, is the fact that agreeing upon these four concepts creates a common vocabulary for moral analysis thereby limiting a shoot-from-the-hip ethics. Much in the way that the United Nation's Sustainable Development Goals creates a unified means of discourse, this artifact from the Medical Ethics community likewise creates a streamlined path for moral communication.

Another important point regarding these four values is that they are intrinsically *defeasible*. This means that we acknowledge in advance that there will be situations in which providing benefit might impinge upon autonomy—seat-belt laws are such a case. In other cases beneficence might be sacrificed in order to adhere to the principle of nonmaleficence, an example of which is to not release new drugs known to cause some benefit until it is certain that undesirable side-effects don't occur.

The examples to which this method could be put to use are innumerable. But so as to offer applicable examples, here are a few:

1. Participation in an NFP's program may have maximized benefit for the NFP's clients in the past. But as facts and social circumstances change, so

do client needs. In such circumstances, it is easy to unintentionally exclude clients who might benefit from NFP services. This *prima facie* stands in contrast to the principle of justice.
2. It is easy to measure effectiveness with confirmation bias—that is, to declare the mission a success on the basis of whether those that participated saw benefit. But what of those who do not participate? Could they be captured as well, thus increasing total benefit? This points to the need to follow the principle of beneficence.
3. Many NGOs and NFPs work with vulnerable populations who have diminished capacity to act autonomously. This could be due to educational deficits, cognitive deficits or intellectual deficits or others. Clients may suffer from addictions or compulsions. They might be under-age or incapacitated elderly. The principle of autonomy therefore implies that one must take special care to ensure that autonomous decision-making occurs with all program participants. It is one thing to satisfy one's legal requirements, but another to satisfy moral requirements?
4. Foundations demonstrate a tendency to fund new and bold initiatives. This typically involves a situation in which a clever program provides a new benefit to those who have never had it, or a benefit delivered in an innovative way which had not been thought of before. But changing social systems with a program can cause unintended secondary consequences. This points to the need to adhere to the principle of nonmaleficence.

Virtue Ethics and Feminist Ethics

The four theories mentioned in the initial section of this chapter and the medical ethics section mentioned just previously hardly constitute the bulk of the enterprise of ethics. In this final section I would like to briefly illustrate to the reader two additional perspectives which have likewise proven the test of time in terms of usefulness and fruitfulness.

The first stems from Aristotle, winds its way through the Roman Catholic tradition, and most recently finds its way into the work of Alisdaire MacIntyre. In his immensely influential book *After Virtue*, first published in 1981, MacIntyre proposes his view that moral value is neither a consequence of actions (teleology) nor the nature of rules (deontology). In his view ethics is the art of embodying virtues. Examples of such virtues might include charity, humility or generosity. Whatever the list of virtues ends up being, the point of the ethical life is not so much to analyze cases as it is to become a particular kind of person. Specifically, it is to become a person whose life embodies the virtues (MacIntyre, 2022).

For the virtue ethicist, right actions are the reliable result of persons who possess virtues, not the definition of those virtues themselves. Correspondingly, the path to moral probity will never be a matter of creating the greatest good for the greatest number or of ensuring that all persons are treated as ends. The moral life will be a matter of individual discipline, practice and attitudes. This is arguably messier than the theories previously discussed. But it has nonetheless demonstrated great usefulness.

Here is a practical application of this theory. The moral tone of an NFP or NGO comes from the top. If employees perceive that upper management is cut-throat and Machiavellian, then it should be no surprise that service providers follow suit. If upper management is lazy and uninvolved, then it should come as no surprise that service providers emulate this behavior. If the good-cop manager empowers a bad-cop disciplinarian, then it should be no surprise to find that a caustic personality has taken power at a lower-level of the institution. NFP and NGO leaders must do more than implement a technique. They must model a way to live and behave within the institution. Publicly practicing fairness, collegiality and humaneness goes a long way toward eradicating moral problems. And this just shows that virtues (or the lack thereof) direct the moral tenor of institutions.

Another feature of Virtue Ethics is that it is far more *personal* than other moral theories. Whereas a utilitarian or a Kantian are able to analyze moral situations by appealing to their proposed principles and axioms, for the virtue theorist the moral life will always be embodied in persons. This feature of Virtue Ethics explains the interpersonal judgment calls that we make about persons in tricky moral situations.

Take, for example, a case in which the "right" thing was done callously: say, an unqualified employee is rejected as an applicant for a position by a manager who in the process of rejecting the applicant yells out "Go get some real job skills!" While the judgment to reject the applicant may have been justified, we still take a dim view of the manager for their callousness. We think that even if their judgment was justified, the *kind* of behavior they exhibited was repugnant. This just goes to show that the Virtue Ethicist's insight is essential. While *what* we do is important, so also is the *kind of person* that is doing it. This will become an important insight in the next chapter when we assess how to use these theories in practical situations.

And finally there is the ever-evolving circle of scholars working in an area which we loosely call "feminist ethics." This area of research is so large, so expanding, that it is difficult to assert one single commonality between all of them with the possible exception that nearly all such scholars agree that gender issues matter morally. And they matter at every stage of the moral process, from what we perceive to how we deliberate and what we finally judge. At risk of oversimplifying, I make three observations about this literature.

The first is that it is far too easy to respond to feminist ethics with tokenism. Creating an ad hoc women's empowerment initiative risks providing lip-service to this pressing social need. And ultimately it will harm the cause of women's concerns as "women's issues" are forced to become the affairs of a special interest group, not an issue with which humanity ought to be centrally concerned.

The second is that one of the most commonly repeated assertions across all feminist literatures is a structural observation, not a moral one. Namely, it is the observation that women fail to be included at important points in the decision-making processes of institutions. I would urge all NGO and NFP leaders to survey the board room and management team and ask hard questions. If there were a pressing moral issue affecting women, would the executive team be aware of its existence? And beyond the issue of women's perspectives, yet taking cues from it, if an NFP serves persons with disabilities does it also include persons with disabilities in leadership? If an NGO serves refugees, are there any new immigrants on the board?

Thirdly, the most common methodology of the Feminist Perspective is to approach a moral issue by probing the *engendered* facets of the case under analysis. How a situation arises, how we deliberate about it and what we think is the right thing to do can sometimes be influenced by latent gender ideas, sometimes in unexpected and surprising ways.

A well-conceived example of this can be found in the work of Madilyn Frye who has written on the "door-opening ritual." Frye argues that women often face a "double-bind" situation in which alleged options are in some sense available to women, but all of them propose a situation of oppression or censure. This happens in the cultural tradition of the west when a man and a woman approach a door and the man perceives an obligation to open it for the woman.

Defenders of the door-opening ritual might say that this is a "nice" or a "polite" thing to do. But Frye thinks that it reveals a double-bind situation which affords the woman no "right" choice. On the face of it, the ritual seems to imply both that women are incapable of opening doors themselves and also that what they most need is a man to do it for them. Hence for a woman to acquiesce to the ritual is for her to condone these presuppositions. But for a woman to request that the man not open the door is for her to be viewed as opposed to civility—she violates cultural rules of politeness and decency. Neither option available to the woman is one which empowers her. She is in a "double-bind" situation.

Frye and other Feminists think that this case has parallels in a great many other ways—in domains ranging from politics, to religion and every other facet of our social worlds. Making the new "Female VP" speak for all women at the board meeting is an example of a double bind. If she refuses she is "wrong" because she refuses to speak for women, but if she agrees she risks being wrong for failing to live up to the preposterous demands of speaking for all women.

Practical Tips for Instituting Ethics in Your Institution

It is one thing to learn from the valuable collection of moral theories that have been articulated over the course of the millennia, but quite another to put that theoretical work into practice. It would be tempting to search for a magic moral wand which, when waived, implements a perfect moral protocol into an institution. If the IT department can deploy a patch which fixes a network issue, then why can't we unleash a moral equivalent which does the same for moral ends? The reason we can't is that neither ethics, nor any of the core endeavors which humans value, are easily universalized. Correspondingly, there is not one single way to apply the previous subject matter to your institution. There are many. That's probably good news. The next chapter will be devoted to the implementation of the theories just discussed. But before entering into those applied waters some wide-angle observations will be helpful.

A significant choice that an NFP or an NGO needs to decide is whether or not a formal ethics procedure is required. Such a procedure might include an independent committee or someone operating in a hybrid capacity of ombudsman-ethicist. It also might include a process that runs through the Human Resources department. There are plusses and minuses to this approach, and institutional leaders must consider the consequences upon their institution.

In the plus column is the fact that large NFPs (like universities and hospitals) already have the resources to operate within these sorts of apparatuses. Universities have Title-IX offices and it is now standard procedure for a Hospital to have a formal ethics committee to hear cases. Another plus is that the members of this committee can be chosen formally and institutions can exert control so as to ensure broad gender/ethnic/professional diversity. This method also permits large NFPs to ensure that those on such a committee or deliberative body have the requisite training. Medical institutions should only select as members those with formal training in biomedical ethics or, alternately, those with extensive experience in situations that call for ethics deliberations. Likewise, non-medical entities should ensure that the members are not agenda-driven or ideologically like-minded, effectively creating moral blind-spots within your ethics apparatus. Finally, it is always good practice to review any guidelines of relevant professional bodies regarding the use of ethics in your institution. Some professional bodies require such an apparatus and provide their own standards, others suggest it, and still others take no position at all.

The safeguards just mentioned point to the problems with institutionalized ethics processes: They can be dangerous. Rogue ethics committees with pre-established agendas can coerce the moral compass of an institution in ways that may clash with the stated mission. This may involve religiously or politically oriented factions seizing control of such committees, or factions of establishment or anti-establishment committee members doing the same. Agenda-driven ethics committees, especially those with no member term limits, are to be avoided at all costs.

Another potential problem with institutionalized efforts such as committees is that they create a culture in which ethics is the responsibility of an isolated department, not of all employees. This makes ethical decision-making an institutional obstacle much like processes for expense report receipt submissions. Plus, when situations become morally complex employees outside the committee will begin to approach the committee with their situation in an effort to shift the burden of decision-making to the committee rather than the professional. This is common in medical institutions. Such committees should not be in the business of delivering an opinion which states "We judge treatment in this case to be futile" but rather "If you conclude on the basis of the evidence before you that treatment is futile, then you are within your professional rights to advise cessation of treatment." Because if an ethics committee colonizes the territory or moral verdict there will be no end to their colonial activity. In fact, staff outside the committee would be strongly incentivized to never make a moral judgment themselves on pain of contradicting your committee. This observation leads to another best practice: implement ethics in a way that prevents controversies from blowing up in the first place and avoid measures which merely relocate those controversies. Staff that know how to detect and remedy moral controversies go a long way toward protecting the interests of your institution.

The case of local and regional government is a special one. Some municipalities have resorted to creating ethics committees which are chartered in such a way as to create a body which is empowered to independently review grievances of various kinds. Typically this happens after known instances of public corruption followed by citizenry outrage have surfaced within municipalities or counties. But such committees exist within such a wide range of power dynamics that articulating one model for the charter of such committees is difficult. Knowing how to do so requires a significant degree of legislative and bureaucratic savvy. Nevertheless, the following provide some guidelines.

First, consider the creation of an ad hoc committee with an expiration date to deal with a specific problem rather than a committee which exists in perpetuity. Secondly, political leaders need to think about how to fortify civic engagement within their own municipalities. Nothing has a more swift, brutal and targeted effect on political behavior than electoral defeat. Finally, governmental ethics committees are especially threatened by increasingly common state statutes requiring that all deliberations of all recognized state bodies be public. Such committees are commonly fed information that should not be a part of the public record, and requiring them to be on the record at all times makes for significantly imperiled decision-making. This creates a lose-lose scenario and constitutes strong incentive for people not to approach the committee.

Finally, establish an advisory committee which broadly represents the interests of the citizenry and which simultaneously contains policy and governmental experts.

A very different approach to creating a culture of ethics within an institution is to interweave it into the hiring, training, evaluation and advancement practices of the institution rather than to create a special committee for it. Most NGOs and NFPs have no other option than doing it this way. The creation of committees would be too burdensome for them, whether financially or managerially. But there are a lot of benefits to a more "grass roots" approach to ethics in an institution. For starters, problems are resolved before a formal committee is needed in the first place.

Broadly speaking, there are two sorts of emphases that most NFPs and NGOs need to attend to when it comes to institutionalized efforts to train ethics *en masse*: those that pertain to money (whether fundraising or accounting) and those that pertain to your mission. The former are somewhat universal and the latter as numerous as there are NFPs.

On the financial end, NFPs and NGOs should ensure that their accounting department knows and abides by generally accepted accounting practices (GAAP). In the likely event that staff are credentialed accountants, they already know these rules. Therefore, ensure that a member of your accounting department is at the table when making strategic decisions for the institution. An accountant or CFO will have insights that could prevent errors.

Another financial consideration is to ensure that the fundraising activities have well-understood confines. Ask the hard questions, collectively agree on policy, then abide by the policy. If the NFP or NGO has agreed that it does not accept gifts from convicted felons, then a policy should reflect this decision. Do not penalize a fundraiser who passes on such gifts. And do not apply indirect pressure on fundraisers to get them. Yearly quotas or commission-based pay are *de rigeur* in the for-profit world. But they could be a veritable moral disaster in the fundraising world.

One final note on fundraising ethics is worth pointing out. There is already much work on ethics specific to fundraising, and standards of the Association of Fundraising Professionals have already been articulated. Adopt those principles.

As noted earlier, some moral values or moral positions are embedded within an NGO or NFP. Just which ones this might be are numerous. NFPs that serve the needs of the LGBTQ+ community must institute moral principles regarding human sexuality at a more central level of their professional environment than, say, the NFP created to build a gazebo in the town central park. One such difference is that the NFP servicing needs of the LGBTQ+ community would be well advised to ensure moral standards of full support from all staff and donors, while the NFP that creates the gazebo is *ipso facto* within their rights to receive funds from any community member whatsoever.

This just points to the intensely *local* nature of ethics. Savvy NGOs and NFPs are uniquely prepared to handle this and quite likely are already staffed with professionals who understand the real-world implications of the mission, including moral implications. Use the wisdom of seasoned professionals within the NFO or NGO to train the incoming workers, whether they be volunteers or employees. Just because your much-needed volunteers might be coming from a university or a well-regarded NGO does not mean that they are prepared to do the work that you do. Never outsource ethics.

Finally, nearly every NFP and NGO has an institutionalized method for employee training and development. Often times it is the relevant professional bodies or NFP accreditation bodies that demand this. Consider instituting ethics training into that curriculum. Doing so is inexpensive, easy and fun. Contact a university near you with an ethicist on staff who specializes in "applied ethics" and ask them to give a presentation. Meet with them in advance of that presentation to help them better understand the unique nature of your mission so that they can craft a curriculum that meets your needs. At board meetings, begin with a quick case study and let board members talk. During executive sessions do the same. Use the cases in this book as a discussion-guide. What you hear might surprise you. My experience is that what you end up building from such sessions is not just a moral foundation, but a dialog of trust.

Conclusion

I have now offered the rudiments of several theories of morality and offered institutional tips for implementing them. It is now time to look at some cases.

Each of them are real, not invented. Most are anonymized versions of cases I was personally involved with. Others adapted from discussions with colleagues. My intention is to offer them as discussion pieces for deliberation among professionals. Each of them concludes with some guiding questions which prompt discussion.

Bibliography

Beauchamp, T. L., & Childress, J. F. (2019). *Principles of Biomedical Ethics.* Oxford University Press.
  This book is often cited as *the* seminal work of biomedical ethics. Its central four chapters on nonmaleficence, beneficence, autonomy and justice have taken on a special place of their own among both professionals and ethicists in other areas of human activity.
Bentham, J. (1988). *Bentham: A Fragment on Government.* Cambridge: Cambridge University Press.
Frye, Marilyn. (1983). *The Politics of Reality: Essays in Feminist Theory.* Crossing Press.
  Frye's book is a foundational work in feminist ethics and feminist explorations of western society. This is the work which first proposes the concept of a "double bind," but also presents to the reader the core ideas which would become the feminist ethics movement.
Hobbes, Thomas. (2021). *Leviathan: With Selected Variants from the Latin Edition of 1668.* Hackett Press.
Hume, David. (1993). *An Enquiry Concerning Human Understanding: With Hume's Abstract of a Treatise of Human Nature and a Letter from a Gentleman to His Friend in Edinburgh.* Hackett Press.

This edition contains both Hume's *Enquiry* as well as other works of significant importance. His discussion of the "is/Ought" distinction can be found in III.I.i of the *Enquiry Concerning Human Understanding*.

Lindemann, H. (2019). *An Invitation to Feminist Ethics*. Oxford University Press.

This text is a comprehensive introduction to the many, often times competing, facets of feminist ethics.

Macaskill, W. (2015). *Doing Good Better: How Effective Altruism Can Help You Make a Difference*. Guardian Books.

Macaskill's book is an example of the aggressive moral stance, sometimes viewed as too aggressive, adopted by the utilitarian. See especially his argument that some forms of issue advocacy must be abandoned because resources allocated to them could cause greater good elsewhere.

MacIntyre, Alisdaire. (2022). *After Virtue: A Study in Moral Theory*. University of Notre Dame Press.

MacIntyre's book is probably one of the most significant contributions to Philosophy in the twentieth century, not just philosophical ethics. In this masterpiece MacIntyre argues that moral language has been lost in modernity and that recovering it will require a different understanding of the basic grammar of moral language.

Rachels, S., & Rachels, J. (2019). *The Elements of Moral Philosophy*. McGraw-Hill Education.

Rachels' book is a classic introductory text in moral philosophy, used in state universities, professional societies and in the US government.

Singer, P. (2013). *Ethics*. Oxford University Press.

Singer's text is a fine compilation of the most important historical works in ethics, beginning in antiquity and ending with contemporary readings. The reader should know that these are primary sources and not secondary sources written in modern English.

Timmons, M. (2013). *Moral Theory: An Introduction*. Rowman & Littlefield.

From Theory to Action

We must now transform theory into practice. This chapter begins with a discussion of some false-starts frequently committed by those who engage in the practice of doing ethics, then illustrates ways in which the theories are typically implemented.

Ethics vs Law

When doing professional ethics, it is a mistake to confuse the law with ethics. While the two might (and hopefully will) often indicate the same course of action, this will not always be the case. That, and there is a considerable mismatch between the concept of a "moral obligation" and a "legal obligation."

We can see this mismatch clearly when we review extreme cases. For example, the city of Chicago in 1881 passed the "ugly law" which banned from public those who suffered from "diseased or maimed" states. This was a means of ensuring that persons with disabilities would be kept out-of-sight from a public that had expressed discomfort with their inclusion in society. Does the fact that a law existed which criminalized being disabled in public imply that it was morally wrong to be disabled in public? Certainly not. But notice that if all that there was to ethics was the observation of laws, then by this definition it would be morally right to seclude the disabled and morally wrong not to. This goes to show that the fact that a government can pass a law is morally unimpressive.

We therefore must be careful with the often-defended conclusion that our moral obligations are encompassed by our legal obligations. We demand a lot more from our co-workers, friends and family than just that they obey the law. We demand that, in addition, they be good and decent people. It's not illegal to harbor racist or sexist *attitudes*. Acting on those attitudes in particular ways could be illegal, but *having* the attitudes isn't. So the fact that hating a person because of their race or sexual orientation fails to be a violation of the civil law by no means exculpates such a person from being (correctly) labeled as having a moral defect. This, too, is because ethics and the law are different on a fundamental level.

This is why responsible NFPs serving vulnerable populations—say, a retirement home for low income persons—do more than ensure that they are staffing as per the federal or state guidelines. They attempt to make the living atmosphere pleasant and welcoming. They attempt to create a professional environment that is cordial and pleasant. The failure to do these things is no violation of the law. But these are the sort of actions that a morally responsible entity would undertake. This is also why NFPs accepting community donations for a variety of services (second hand stores, soup kitchens, etc.) express dismay when the public uses donation boxes to dispose of worn-out, dirty or useless objects. Such an action is not *illegal*. But what it says about the moral character of the donor is not good.

Professionals working in the international arena, especially on development projects involving the issue of permits, will constantly face the collision between legal and moral obligations. A foreign law may state that permits must be acquired in advance of construction. This lends an appearance of sameness of regulatory environments both "at home" and "abroad." But in many foreign localities, and sometimes nations, the system for issuing permits has never been used despite the fact that the law states that it must be. I have gone to the counter of the municipal government of several different nations in search of a permit only to receive a blank stare from the department head. Many such offices do not know what the permit looks like, what it should say, or what the procedure is to get it. In one instance in which an NGO was *required* by the US federal government to nonetheless receive permits in advance, the staff at the NGO had to design a foil stamp in the states for the foreign government's office to use on its permitting documents because that foreign governmental office had never had to use the technology. The NGO also designed the government application forms and the legal procedure for signoff. The irony of this situation is that the US federal government's requirement to attain permits necessitated the violation of international law: namely, the requirement that US entities not operate as agents of foreign governments!

Typically, in such countries, the real-world procedure for developers or builders is to design and then immediately build whatever it is that they want to. If the developer is lucky the amount of the fine levied after construction can be negotiated in advance. Many NGOs can negotiate a fine of exactly zero dollars if they are careful. Doing it this way is simpler, faster, cheaper, more predictable and it is what the local government prefers developers to do. Asking for the permit is positively aggravating for them.

The point of this vignette is to show that the categories of "legal obligation" vary in different cultures in ways that defy those same categorizations in the other nations. Maybe it is wrong to build first and receive the fine later. Maybe it is not. But it would be a factual error to assume that foreign cultures use the category of "legal requirement" the same way that other cultures do.

In a similar case, I observed the work of a man who had built a career as a real estate developer. He became wealthy and successful. His invariable procedure was to build first then pay fines later. He was well-aware that the wealthier he became, the larger the fines were. Some such fining documents contained an itemized "gratuity" line in on it. But a religious conversion instilled in him the belief that this situation was wrong—that it was no longer morally acceptable for him to violate the laws of his nation. He would seek the permits first and when doing so never pay a bribe. He then decided to pivot his business model and focus on projects that benefitted his people, not just the wealthy elite (like himself). He designed an orphanage, a worker training center and a very large recycling plant. But once he made it clear that he would refuse to pay fines or engage in public corruption he found that the entirety of his business ground to a halt. He was nearly bankrupt within three years and has now fled the country.

Demanding the "Right" Answer

Another temptation which must be resisted when doing professional ethics is the temptation to view ethics the way one views simple arithmetic. In arithmetic, there is always a right answer, and this right answer can be known by anyone. If there is a dispute, the dispute is settled easily. It only takes the use of a calculator.

Ethics is not and never will be this way.

Yet it is common for someone, troubled by a vexing situation like the situation of the building developer with a religious awakening to say "let's just look at the outcomes. What is the sum total of the consequences of building first then paying the fine versus not building until the permit is issued? Whichever one makes things turn out the best is the right thing to do."

But notice that this approach *just is* to say that utilitarian analyses are correct. But if there were agreement among ethicists that adopting a utilitarian theory was the "objectively correct" way to do ethics, then none of the other theories discussed in the previous chapter would exist. We would all be utilitarians and that chapter would have contained only one theory. But the other theories do exist, and for good reason. They provide important insights into the nature of morality. Recognizing this fact does not help to make the activity of doing ethics easier. Quite the opposite. But it would be an error to brush aside pesky theories because the muddy waters preferred to be kept clear. Some waters just are muddy.

The persistent desire to figure out the "right" answer is also an implicit rejection of the concept of moral disagreement. This is a serious matter. When we say that there is a "moral disagreement," we presumably mean that there exists one issue upon which two (or more) parties differ in their moral analysis. The thought that there is a "right" answer which resolves the disagreement in such a circumstance is just to say that at least one party of the disagreement is wrong in their position. Perhaps one party has their facts wrong, perhaps they reasoned inappropriately toward their conclusion, or perhaps they suffer from a deficit of rational capacity. The demand that all moral disagreements be resolved *just is* to say that someone is invariably "wrong" when a moral disagreement occurs.

This view does not survive the impact of reality, especially when it comes to ethnically and economically diverse populations.

I once spoke with a doctor who had served for several decades in practice in the sub-Saharan bush in a rural hospital. Many residents of the region had never attended a school. There were no western religious traditions present, and hence no vestiges of their ethics. One farmer brought his eight-year-old daughter into the hospital with a serious infection in her leg, apparently after suffering a traumatic injury some weeks earlier. The doctor quickly realized that only amputation would save the girl's life. Without the procedure, she would die within a few days and this death would be agonizing. Upon hearing this diagnosis and the recommended treatment the father refused to permit the surgery.

This proved troublesome for my doctor friend. An important principle in foreign medical ethics is that where there are two moral systems in competition, one must always act to enforce the principle with more restrictions rather than the one with less. A common example of this is that when doing research involving children it does not matter that a foreign government does not require IRB approval. Since the US government does, then even though the research is being conducted abroad one must still acquire Institutional Review Board (IRB) approval.

This meant that while there was no provision in the law of the nation that required the doctor to respect the father's wishes, nonetheless the doctor's own training explicitly mandates the moral principle that a parent is responsible for the medical choices of the child.

The doctor spoke with the man in an attempt to convince him to permit amputation. The farmer explained that the only value that girls have in his village was their ability to carry water, do house chores and become married. If his daughter lived but without a leg, she would be a liability to the family. She could not carry water. She could not do house chores. And she would never be married. Her death was better for everyone.

I will let the reader decide on their own as to what they think that the doctor should do in this situation. But I suggest that the view that someone here is *simply* wrong is hasty. Such a quick conclusion does not take seriously the fact that westerners are enculturated into our own moral system and that this father was enculturated into his. Perhaps in the end we arrive at the position to override the father's directive. Perhaps in the end we arrive at the position that we are to respect his directive. But this is a position to be *arrived at*, not begun with.

Compare this case to a very different situation—one to which we will make reference for the remainder of this chapter. On many an occasion, while approaching an airport in a developing nation, especially rural grass-strip airports, I have been approached by a mother asking whether I would take one of her children. The first time that this happened to me was many years ago when I was a significantly less experienced traveler. I was not ready for it. I stepped out of the land cruiser, tired after a very long, hot day trekking across the wilderness. In the ten meters between me and the iron gate of the terminal (which was just a shack with a corrugated tin roof), a woman rushed up to me through the crowd and shoved her baby into my arms. She then quickly withdrew down the road leaving me with my bags in one arm and the baby in the other. Meanwhile, the pilot saw that I had arrived and was ushering me into the terminal so that he could take off and finish his day.

I had a decision to make, and it had to be made quickly. I desperately needed to catch the flight. And bush pilots won't wait around while philosophers undertake moral deliberation. But in my arms was a human being over whom I now, unexpectedly, had complete power. This child had certainly done nothing wrong, deserved to be protected from harm, and I was now the only person enabled to make decisions that affected its future. If I set the child down and walked away it would perhaps become an instant orphan. To make matters worse, my act of setting the toddler down would be the cause (or "a cause") of such a situation. But taking the baby with me presented problems of its own.

Before proceeding to analyze this case in-depth, it is worth reviewing an assertion made in the previous chapter. It is easy to conceive of ethics as an endeavor in which we are to figure out how to choose between right and wrong. Thinking about ethics this way leads one to think that if there ever exists an appearance of "no right choice" then this implies that one hasn't thought hard enough about the situation. Because if ethics is about choosing right over wrong, then there *must* be a right choice in every moral situation. Probably, by "right choice" we would mean something like "known in advance to be right and emotionally comfortable with the situation." However, in situations like the one I found myself in with an unwanted child in my arms there are arguably no right choices of this sort to be made. I did not know what the right thing to do was, and no option felt comfortable. Whatever I did, something bad would happen—whether to me or to the child.

While it sounds like a slogan, it nonetheless is useful to conceive of the activity of doing ethics as one in which from time-to-time we are fortunate enough to be in a position of choosing a right over a wrong, but all too often find ourselves having to choose between a wrong and another wrong.

The Informed Argument

As we begin our analysis of what I should do with the unexpected baby, I propose a ground rule. That rule is that however it is that we analyze what I should do, the main tool of analysis must be an argument. More specifically, an argument that is informed by the high-quality moral theories discussed in the previous chapter. Because this is the essence of professional ethics. Consider an analogy from the law.

At trial it is rare for every part of a case to exclusively indicate guilt; or for it to exclusively indicate innocence. Even when the DNA on the murder weapon matched the DNA of the defendant, someone will make a statement to the effect that the defendant really is a good person underneath it all. The DNA points to guilt but the character reference points to innocence. That is, the evidence tends to fall on both sides of the balance of justice and it is the role of the judge or jury to decide which way the scales tip. Certainly, some evidence has more weight than other evidence. But the point is that it is rarely the case that *all* the evidence points to just one side of the case. Provided that the judge or jury uses the evidence and the law to decide, we are content to say that justice has been served when a verdict is reached. Following this legal analogy, the evidence in ethics cases are the facts at hand and the law is the moral theory we discussed in the previous chapter. Doing ethics well means taking facts seriously and thinking carefully within an enlightened apparatus of moral thought. Just like in trials, it will be rare for all of the reasons to point to just one conclusion, but that fact should not prevent us from making judgments.

Applying Moral Theories

Let us now take this previously mentioned case—the case of finding myself at an airport with a baby in my arms—and use the moral theories in search of the discovery of the right course of action. If only for the sake of simplicity, I will assume that there are only two options before me: To take the baby with me or to leave the baby behind. We will be bound to challenge this simplistic binary set of options, but will attempt to keep matters as simple as we can, and for as long as we can.

Egoism

The egoist thinks that right and wrong are prefaced upon the effects that an action has upon the person who performs it. It also predicts that what a person does will be indicated by some kind of reward. That is, what people do is predicated upon the benefit they think that they will receive and the pain they wish to avoid. We sometimes identify two sub-theses of the egoist project:

Ethical Egoism: One *ought* to do what is in one's best interests.
Psychological Egoism: As a matter of empirical fact, people do in fact choose what, at the time of choice, they judge to be best for themselves.

The picture that emerges is that a person's responsibility is to think as well as they can about what is best for them (we sometimes call this "enlightened self-interest") and then to proceed to do so.

The relevant question for the egoist to ask about my choice of what to do with the baby is "what would be the consequences for *me* were I to take the baby, and what would be the consequences were *I* to leave it behind?" Here is a brief attempt to answer this question:

> If I left the baby on the road then I am certain that no one would have blamed me. No local would have accosted me, there would be no outrage. The child would have sat there, probably alone for some time. Perhaps the mother would come back. Perhaps she wouldn't. But nothing would have happened to me. This was a town with a *lot* of abandoned children in it. One more abandoned child changed nothing. But bringing the baby with me would present a host of potential consequences for me, nearly all of which are negative. I would have to expend time and resources on the baby. I would need to transport the child across international borders. This behavior would likely be interpreted as child trafficking by authorities. Because arguably, that is what it would be.

It appears that if forced to choose between "leave" and "take," the egoist elects to leave the child. The consequences for my taking the child are too burdensome to me.

Utilitarianism

What of the utilitarian theory? How would it admonish me to choose?

A significant problem with utilitarianism—a problem that I have so far ignored—is that it places the agent on the proverbial hook for all consequences of their actions, not just the consequences they know about. So the fact that a person thought about (some) consequences by no means implies that they considered *all* the consequences. Yet a built-in problem of this case is that there is not much time to decide what to do. The decision must be made *now*.

For the moment, I will ignore this problem. But I will only be able to ignore it for a short time. It will return momentarily.

If I take the child with me then it is probable that I would be identified by authorities as a child trafficker. This poses grave consequences for me personally.

But as a utilitarian, one cannot think about consequences *solely* to one's self. It is also required to think of consequences for everyone else. If I were successful in smuggling the baby across international borders, the quality of life that the baby would have over the long run would be (likely) significantly greater than in the rural village it left behind. The baby would have education, healthcare, vaccinations, and access to the American Economy for the rest of their life.

Consequences for the mother matter as well. Whatever her motives, it is unlikely that she arrived at the decision to give her child to me out of a fully autonomous decision-making process. It is a virtual certainty that powerful social forces caused her to undertake this decision. If her situation is like that of others of which I am aware, those conditions include lack of access to employment, lack of support from her husband and economic hopelessness. Not having an extra child would significantly lift that burden.

While taking the child with me has significant negative consequences for me, the consequences for the child and the mother are positive—provided that I find a way to pull it off. Since my happiness counts only as much as the happiness of the child and the mother, it would appear at first glance that I am morally "outvoted."

But am I? Note that if I am stopped at the border and the baby is taken from me, then I suffer negative consequences, the baby suffers negative consequences (since it will in all likelihood become a homeless orphan), and the mother does not. This implies that I need to think not just about consequences, but the probabilities of those consequences.

While I have personally witnessed significant corruption in foreign airports regarding a number of immigration/emigration issues, I nevertheless believe that 100% of the time, were I to present myself and an African baby at the border, I would be stopped and questioned. So were I to attempt to engage in this (disturbing) case of child trafficking, this problem would need to be mitigated. Probably, I would need to arrange travel via a means other than commercial air. Such means include cargo ship or sailing.

Even if I invent a means of not being stopped upon exit in Africa, I still face the issue of being stopped upon re-entry into the United States. So it would be incumbent upon me to find a means of entering the states without passing a border checkpoint. This is easier than one might think. My years of work in Latin America have revealed the existence of a skilled industry of human traffickers. The cost to me for this service as of 2022 is approximately $600 if it begins in certain border towns with prices rising for longer distances of escorted travel (concierge service from some nations can run as much as $15,000). But there is also a degree of risk, as the methods used by traffickers are often unsafe, sometimes leading to the deaths of those trafficked.

If the reader is sensing that our real-life ethics case is transforming into a bizarre and uncomfortable thought experiment, they aren't wrong. But notice that for the utilitarian, I am responsible for the sum total of consequences of my actions. *If it is possible* to bring about positive consequences, then we have *a moral requirement* to do so. So if there exists a means to smuggle the child into the United States, and undertaking those means that the world is better for everyone than a world in which I don't undertake this elaborate set of actions, then I am morally required to do it.

Is this right? Does this mean that on utilitarian grounds I ought to smuggle the child?

Let us return to a point made at the beginning of this section—that this is a choice that must be made quickly. All of the preceding reasonings consonant with a utilitarian analysis takes time—exactly what I don't have in this particular case. In the actual circumstance in which I found myself, I had at most five seconds to think. If the best theory of ethics requires too much time to use in a real-life case, then it probably isn't the best theory in the world after all. Concocting an elaborate plan to smuggle a baby takes too much time. And this is not to even begin to mention the fact that the method here invented forces me to become a human trafficker!

It would be wrong to think that utilitarians have nothing to say about this problem. Often utilitarians distinguish between "act utilitarianism" and "rule utilitarianism." Both attempt to maximize the positive consequences of actions. But act utilitarianism would require us to ascertain consequences on a case-by-case basis while rule utilitarianism presents us with a subtly different "take." The rule utilitarian admonishes us to decide upon a set of rules—specifically, the set of rules which, when compared to any other set, maximizes total happiness. Then, in individual cases, we recall our rule and follow it. Perhaps rule-based utilitarianism will provide sub-optimal results in some discrete cases, but the net positive justifies the rule.

What are the rules that the utilitarian might adopt? On this issue, there is no consensus. But in regard to a case like the one under consideration, the following rule seems easily justifiable on utilitarian grounds: Do not engage in human trafficking. This rule might have the negative consequence of preventing me from taking the baby with me, but the positive consequences to the world of everyone obeying such a rule overwhelmingly override this negative consequence.

Finally, it is worth asking whether this retreat to "rule-based utilitarianism" is theoretically justifiable. We might on utilitarian grounds adopt a rule that says "do not lie to other people." But circumstances will arise in which it becomes clear that telling a lie makes things better for everyone. In such a circumstance, we would then have to ask "which is better, following or breaking my rule?" And this is just to say that the utilitarian retreat to rules is not an altogether settled matter.

We will provisionally conclude that on rule-based grounds, the utilitarian will say that I should not take the child with me. But that check mark will have an asterisk next to it.

Kant

Kant thinks that there are two moral rules: The categorical imperative and the means-end principle. Let's review them:

- **The Categorical Imperative**: Act in such a way that you could consistently will the maxim presupposed by your action to be a moral law
- **The Means-End Principle**: Treat all persons as ends, not as mere means.

The "logic" of these two rules will be that any action which passes both tests is indicative of an action that is permissible to perform. But the failure of a proposed action of any one of the two constitutes grounds for asserting that the action is immoral.

Let us begin with the categorical imperative. I propose using three steps to implement it:

1. Identify the action
2. Create the maxim
3. Universalize and check for consistency

Let's begin with a test case to illustrate this method. Let us say that I want a new sports car but have no ability to pay for it. However, I believe that the salesman is gullible enough to give me the keys after I sign the loan documents. I, therefore, sign the documents, take the keys and drive away with no intent to repay the loan.

What is the action (step one) which I am contemplating? It surely cannot be my decision to shop for a car nor my decision to communicate in English with the salesperson. The issue regarding which we want clarity is the issue of whether it is morally permissible to borrow the money with no intent to repay. We have now identified the action:

1. "I will borrow with no intent to repay"

Creating the maxim is easy once we have identified the action. We just conjugate the first person singular into the third person plural.

1. "I will borrow with no intent to repay"
2. Everyone will borrow with no intent to repay

Now we arrive at the crucial third step. We imagine a world in which step two of our process is universalized—that is, a world in which every person acts (or tries to act) on the basis of the maxim. The key question will be "Would my action be *possible* in a world in which everyone else did it too?"

1. "I will borrow with no intent to repay"
2. Everyone will borrow with no intent to repay
3. In a world in which everyone who borrowed had no intent to repay, would the act of borrowing with no intent to repay be possible?

The word "possible" in step three is important to the Kantian. The issue is not in regard to whether we would like or dislike such a world. Neither is the issue of whether good consequences or bad consequences would happen in such a world. Good and bad consequences are the moral currency of egoism and utilitarianism, not Kantianism.

The point of step three above is to ask whether it would be *possible* to perform an action in a world in which everyone else behaves likewise. In this case of borrowing with no intent to repay, it would not be. No one would ever loan money to anyone in a world in which one was guaranteed that all loans would default. It would not be *possible* to get a loan in such a world because no one would give them. And because such an action would not be possible in a world in which everyone does it, it is immoral for me to do it in the real world. Put more succinctly and rhetorically, would you loan money in a world in which no one repays? Neither would anyone else.

Now let us turn to the case of the child in my arms referenced earlier. And let us recall the three-step process just noted. This process asks us to "identify our action." What is the moral choice that I am contemplating? This is a tricky question. On the one hand, I am considering "putting the child down" but on the other, "taking the child with me." Yet this can't be my *moral* dilemma. Because a world in which everyone refuses to carry a child with them on an airplane appears to be a possible world. Yet so does a world in which everyone carries their children.

Notice, though, that the assessment changes if I modify the portrayal of the action I am scrutinizing. Perhaps my choice is not so much whether to put a child down or to take a child with me as I am being asked whether I am obligated to protect this child. Let's test that proposal.

1. I will not provide for the needs of a child.
2. No one will provide for the needs of children.
3. Is it possible for there to be a world in which no one provides for the needs of children?

The answer to the third question is arguably "no, such a world is not possible." Because in such a world in which no person cares for the needs of any child, there would be scarce few children who make it to adulthood. And hence no world.

Is this correct? Does this settle the issue? The reader may have a nagging suspicion that at issue is not whether it is right or wrong to care for the needs of a child, but whether it is appropriate for a stranger to be given the responsibility for doing so on the part of someone who arguably more than any other has that obligation—the child's parent.

We might see this more clearly by looking at the second of the two Kantian rules—the means-end principle. This principle requires that we not treat people as means to an end. So, for example, being nice to someone solely because we want their money is a case of the violation of the means-end principle (professional fundraisers should pause to think about this). Likewise, treating others with rudeness or meanness in order to coerce from them something one wants is likewise a failure of the means-end principle.

Now observe how we might analyze the behavior of the mother in this case. She is not handing her child to a random stranger in the crowd. There were other people in that crowd she could have chosen. But she chose me, probably because she profiled me as a wealthy white westerner. She probably wanted that child to have a better life and in her judgment, a life spent with a wealthy westerner was preferable to a life spent with her or anyone else in her town. Quite probably, her own life would be better off too.

This is a clear violation of the means-end principle. The mother was using me in order to accomplish her own ends.

The following may or may not help Kant's case much, but he did discuss a case quite a bit like this. He imagined a case in which a homeowner was asked to shelter a would-be victim of a murderer in their home. Kant reasons that doing so is the right thing to do. Then Kant proceeds to imagine the murderer appearing at the home, asking the homeowner whether they know where their victim is. Can the homeowner lie? Kant states that because lying constitutes a violation of the categorical imperative (a world in which everyone lies is a world in which no one communicates), it is therefore immoral to lie to the would-be murderer.

We have a reasonable analogy in the case at hand. We earlier saw that the mother committed a violation of the means-end principle by giving me the child. So my accepting the child from a mother who immorally thrust it upon me would be participation in her immorality. Hence it is wrong to take the child with me.

Feminist Ethics

Cases like the one under consideration cry out for a feminist analysis. And as stated before, that analysis will be embodied in a set of structural and moral observations.

Feminist ethicists explore the way moral issues are "engendered." That is, they explore how concepts of gender make their way into moral reasoning or deliberation, sometimes in surprising and unpredictable ways. And with regard to the case of my finding myself in front of the airport with a baby in my arms, we are presented with a situation that significantly involves a host of feminist issues. Notice that a reasonable person wants to know more about this situation than just what a visiting westerner should do. We want to better understand the motives of the mother. We want to understand the conditions of the town. And we want to understand how those two things are interrelated. These kinds of questions are what a feminist analysis does.

The feminist does not deny that the question upon which our entire discussion so far has been predicated (the question regarding whether I should keep or leave the baby) is illegitimate. But the feminist ethicist will simultaneously insist that the thought that this question could be considered in isolation from gender issues is both factually incorrect and quite likely leads to continued moral wrong.

A discussion I once had with a professional sectarian translator illustrates this point. This person had been serving in a remote ethnic minority group for many decades and was in the final process of translating the Jewish and Christian scriptures into the indigenous language—not an easy feat since no written version of the language existed prior to their arrival. A translation dilemma presented itself when it came to the Hebrew phrase "as white as snow." On the surface, this was a technical problem. The local language did not have a word for "snow" since this equatorial region has never seen this meteorological phenomenon. However, there was a well-known colonial language in the region to the south which boasts many millions of speakers worldwide, and that language had a word for "snow." The question then became: "Should we use the colonial word, or use some other word in the indigenous language?"

This is a tough call. If the mission of the translation enterprise is to create a translation of a book into a new language that has never had the written form, then it appears to be an act of linguistic violence to smuggle a colonial language into the local language. But choosing a different word that already exists in the local language (they considered "coconut milk") would result in a deliberate mistranslation.

The following consideration proved decisive: There was a long and deplorable history of poor relationships between this people group and their colonial neighbors to the south. That history involved exploitation, manipulation, sexual violence and frequent killings. However, in the text being translated what was being washed "white as snow" were a person's sins. The translator (and her team) feared that using the colonial language in this passage would send a message to the ethnic group that the forgiveness of sins the passage was addressing was synonymous with becoming the colonizer. This paved the way for religion itself to be another chapter in the colonial debacle—something the translation team deeply resisted. They, therefore, reasoned that it was better to translate the passage into the following: "And your sins will be washed as white as coconut milk." Deliberate mistranslation was *better* than indeliberate colonization.

The feminist ethicist shares a similar "take" on the case of taking or leaving the baby. Like a translation team that thinks that the problem is deeper than that of using one word or the other, so also the feminist ethicist will insist that the real moral issue, in this case, does not consist in whether to take or leave the baby.

The feminist's first stop in the analysis, and probably the last stop too, will be to better understand the world of a mother who finds herself in a situation in which such an action is reasonable. To gain such an understanding we need to know more about her world. Here I can be of service.

In that town specifically, though that region generally, women have a social status not significantly better than that of property. True, the laws of the land, highly influenced by western democracies, have a language which guarantees them equal rights and status. But practice is a different matter than law. Cattle theft in the region is punished more severely than spousal abuse. Women in the town cannot own property, they cannot work, they cannot receive inheritance. If they derive income it is through selling small trinkets in the marketplace or the bounty of the fields that their husbands bring in. Their social lives are highly regulated and their ability to give voice to their hopes or dreams is minimal. In fact, I witnessed several NGO workers trying to run a program which gave the women of the town a congregating space to speak their minds in safety, but that project failed to gain participants since such a custom had not been practiced there before.

I have no knowledge of what this woman's marriage was like. But I can say with confidence that she was married given that she dressed in a way to signify as such. Previous social science surveys in the town reveal high rates of spousal abuse and male alcoholism. But I cannot say which, if any, of these problems was existent in her household.

It is in light of this much more rich set of social facts that the feminist ethicist can yield an opinion that is both rich and challenging. Quite likely, a feminist ethicist would assert that describing the moral situation at hand as resting upon the question of what a white male westerner should do is itself part of the problem. This is a case about women's liberty and the coercive and oppressive forces that limit it. It is not in reality a case about what a visiting professor should do with a baby in his arms.

If we were pressed to arrive at an analysis of what the professor in this situation should do, then the feminist would insist that the right answer to such a question pertains to which available course of action addresses the root engendered problems. Objections to the effect that this insistence causes the analysis of the case to become complicated is just, in feminist terms, to object to the facts being the facts.

For this reason, most feminists take great care to detail how and under what conditions a westerner should be appearing in a locality. Great care is taken to articulate the guidelines under which such research is to be conducted, and insistence that respect must be built into the otherwise innocent-appearing fact of a visit to a town.

If we were to request the feminist ethicist to offer an answer to our pointed question "Should I take the baby with or leave the baby behind" the most direct that the feminist would offer is that one should do what makes the conditions of vulnerable women better. And this is not an instance of avoiding the question. It is a method of answering the question rooted in a set of disturbing facts which an enlightened ethicist must consider.

Virtue Ethics

The virtue ethicist resists the implicit demand of many other theories to identify a property of actions such that, should an action have or not have that property, it is judged to be right or wrong. Consequentialists do exactly that—they assert that the property of human action that makes for rightness or wrongness are the consequences that the action produces. Deontologists do the same: They assert that rightness or wrongness consists in having the property of following or violating a rule. The virtue ethicist thinks that this is a mistake. To them what matters most is the moral character of the person performing the action, not the properties of the action performed.

Therefore, most virtue ethicists begin with a set of virtues which are acknowledged as being *the* virtues. We do not have the space here to reason toward them, but the most consistent candidates are virtues such as honesty, truthfulness, integrity, care, diligence and courage. There are likely more than just those.

So when the virtue ethicist is given a case like the one under analysis, their analysis would begin with the question "What would a virtuous person do?" And this is just to say "what would a person characterized by honesty do?" or "What would someone known for their courage do?" Or more generally: What would a person in possession of the moral virtues do in such a case?

Notice that this is an intrinsically inexact approach. At least utilitarianism and egoism had something resembling a procedure: count the consequences and do the math. Virtue ethics does not.

A reasonable first step is to begin with a virtue much discussed by the Greeks but not valorized today: imitation. Many people can think of someone that they morally admire. Perhaps it is someone one knows personally, or perhaps it is a historical or literary figure. It might be a spouse or an acquaintance. How would they act in such a situation? *And how would their action embody the kind of person that you know them to be?*

Of those people I know well and for whom I have a deep moral appreciation, not one of them would set the baby down on the dirt road and enter the airport unconcerned. Every one of them would risk missing the flight if by doing so they would make sure that the baby was cared for. More provocatively, most of those for whom I have the highest moral respect have the least respect for the egoist!

This attests to the power of the virtue of imitation. In fact, Aristotle, who was probably the first virtue ethicist, thought that it was the power of imitation plus human-kind's ability to live vicariously that constituted the reason why we love drama and story-telling so much. Because when done well it provides a way for us to vicariously live the felt-experiences of people who see the world differently or who face different pressures. We can learn important moral lessons through literature that would be too painful to learn any other way—such as how to act when love tears a family apart or how to behave in times of war. We can try on the moral psychology of the scoundrel or the saint and "see" what that life amounts to.

Returning to the question at hand—should I take the baby with or leave it behind—the virtue ethicist is not concerned with the consequences of the decision or with whatever rules a culture or a religion might require us to follow. They are concerned with how a morally mature person would handle the situation. Because ethics is never a matter of deciding what is right or wrong. It is a matter of what kind of people we will be. Therefore, any virtue ethics analysis will resist the question as asked and insist upon this sort of analysis.

The virtue ethicist, therefore, disagrees with the egoist who finds nothing awry at the prospect of simply abandoning the child outside the airport and walking onto the plane. What is wrong with this course of action is that it is the kind of thing that only a cruel-hearted person would do. It evidences a moral selfishness that morally decent people do not engage in.

What would we demand of a person who is not morally cruel? We would expect them to *do something*. We would expect them to try to resolve the situation in a way that evidenced care for other persons, that showed that they searched for a "third option." It is this search for a third option that evidences that the person making the decision is *virtuous*.

Anecdotally, this also shows the moral value of non-moral abilities. Entering rural communities with no language skills deprives the foreign worker of moral options. In this case, being able to communicate with other people in the crowd helps a lot. It makes being virtuous easier.

Biomedical Ethics

The apparatus of the biomedical ethicist is useful in the situation under scrutiny. Again, this system demands adherence to four values. They are:

1. Nonmaleficence
2. Beneficence
3. Autonomy
4. Justice

It is rare, as we said earlier, to be able to perfectly satisfy all four. So the methodology used in medicine is unlike the Kantian methodology according to which failure at any one point implies failure at all. Let us review these four features and analyze the case:

Nonmaleficence: Taking the baby causes me harm, risks some harm to the baby but also offers some benefit to the baby. Given the feminist analysis just performed it is difficult to say whether acquiescing to a coerced woman's demand is a kind of nonmaleficence or not. But there is an argument to be made to the effect that by taking the baby I am playing into a maleficent feature of a culture. Leaving the baby does no harm to me, but at least some harm to the baby and its mother.

Beneficence: Taking the baby with me gives me no benefit, the baby at least some benefit and the mother some benefit. Leaving the baby benefits me, not the baby and probably not the mother.

Autonomy: The principle of autonomy demands that we respect the autonomous wishes of other persons. Typically, children are not considered autonomous. And in the case described, I was not the person who made the choice to relinquish the child. This then leaves the mother's actions to consider. Would we say that the mother autonomously relinquished her child? Probably not. Whatever is meant by the term "autonomous" it would involve, as Beauchamp and Childress point out, a lack of "controlling influences." That is what the economic and social pressures are doing in this case—they are acting as controlling influences upon the choices of the mother. Since we are required to respect autonomous choices and the mother's choice is arguably not autonomous, I am not required to respect it.

Justice: Let us assume that by the word "justice" we mean "fairness." With such a definition, it seems plausible to say that I am being treated unfairly—I am being given an obligation which I did not seek. But what of the baby or the mother? Arguably, where there is unfairness, I am not the source of it. I am a means to alleviate the unfairness. So, again arguably, whether I take the baby with or leave it I am not committing an act of unfairness.

In sum, the principles of nonmaleficence and beneficence show that there is some reason to take the baby with and some reason not to. But the principles of Autonomy and Justice imply that one ought not take the baby with. Therefore, the medical ethics model implies that there is not an obligation to take the baby with.

Religious Ethics

Here we are confronted with a significant problem. Religious ethics are well-formed ethical modes of thought, sometimes with many thousands of years of intellectual history. Furthermore, there is no *one* religion, and even within families of religion categories (e.g., "Islam" or "Christianity"), there can be many competing strands of thought. A Roman Catholic view on LGBTQ+ issues will not be the same as a modern Episcopalian one. So it will be either a fool's errand or a very, very long affair to provide a religious ethics treatment of this case.

But this much can be said.

Religions tend to have what in the Roman world was called a *Scientia*. That is, a collected set of knowledge. This is rooted in interpretive histories predicated upon foundational texts and histories. The texts will not be limited to the Qur'an or the Hebrew Scriptures, although it will certainly include them. Those operating within a religious tradition would do well to make sure that you are aware of that intellectual tradition.

In some cases, that tradition will be rich, historical and rigorous. Examples of these are most Jewish nonprofits and NGOs, every Roman Catholic NFP or NGO, and every explicitly Islamic social service endeavor. These have moral systems which have been developed by learned professionals over the course of centuries, not decades. Persons of goodwill have invested precious time and resources thinking about important issues. If you work with or among such an entity, it is an essential job duty to become informed as to the moral foundations of these entities. Having that information will help the professional to understand why certain moral decisions are made and why certain features of moral situations are attended to.

Other religiously based NFPs or NGOs have a much less intellectually rich footing. Included in these are many Christian non-denominational NFPs and NGOs. Such an environment provides a less intellectually cumbersome environment, makes inter-faith participation easier, and provides the administrative benefit of not having to be linked to a theological party-line. But there is a price to be paid for these benefits. Moral reasoning in such institutions can resemble a philosophical wild west, and the lack of agreement upon first principles means that the moral choices of an institution are easy to manipulate by politicians, board members and donors.

No religious analysis of the case presented in this chapter can be done except when taking into account *all* of the religions. I will not take the time to do that here. Nevertheless, it would be a mistake to leave the impression that the inability to present one single analysis entails a lack of care for the kind of issue currently under investigation. Religiously based child care initiatives in the developing world vastly outnumber those of governments or non-faith-based NGOs.

Collating Our Observations

How do we proceed to package these observations together into a case?

One way to proceed (which will not get us very far) is to create an analysis matrix. We might list our theories on the Y axis and the available actions on the X. Such a chart would look like this:

	Leave	Bring
Egoism		
Utilitarianism		
Kant		
Feminist ethics		
Virtue theory		
Medical ethics		
Religious ethics		

But we must now address (at least) two problems: How do we fill in the matrix, and even if we can, what would the filled-in matrix tell us?

The former question—how to fill in the matrix—will be easy to address for some rows but harder on others. Following the preceding discussion, we might do so as follows:

	Leave	Bring
Egoism	✓	
Utilitarianism	✓*	
Kant	✓	
Feminist ethics		
Virtue theory		
Medical ethics	✓	
Religious ethics		

Earlier we argued that the egoist, Kantian and medical ethics system argued that we should leave the baby. We observed that for different reasons we could not come to a conclusion regarding the Feminist perspective, the Virtue perspective or the Religious perspective. And we agreed to place an asterisk next to the utilitarian position.

Shall we, therefore, conclude that since we have three definite "leave" votes (with a potential fourth) and no definite "keep" votes that therefore we are morally justified in leaving the baby?

Definitely not. This is for reasons similar to those which were used to defend the conclusion that confusing the civil law with the moral law is an error. Yes, we could devise a procedure which places each theory in a matrix (in roughly the same way we can devise a law in a country). Yes, we can then proceed to place check-marks on the matrix. We might even be impressed with ourselves for using the word "matrix." But why should the fact that we came up with a matrix permit us to dismiss the underlying reasonings of those positions which we declared to be the loser? It shouldn't. Matrices, like laws, are morally unimpressive.

To consider this point further, it is useful to reflect upon the feminist ethics position. We noted in our earlier analysis that the feminist ethicist would argue that insistence upon portraying this as a case in regard to what a visiting researcher should do was to locate our insistence where the real issue *is not*. The real moral issue, according to the feminist, is not whether or not a person should take the baby. The real issues are the social conditions that gave rise to the situation in the first place. Are we to brush aside this observation just because the feminist was outvoted on a matrix that we invented? Certainly not.

Perhaps we could modify our matrix and "weight" the check-marks. Very strong, clear verdicts receive greater weight and those with asterisks receive lesser. That means that the egoist check mark would be weighted heavily since that theory's verdict was swift, robust and determinate. The utilitarian check mark would be weighted less, and those without a verdict receive no weight at all.

But this does not pass scrutiny either effectively making the same mistakes but at a higher degree of complexity. If the underlying matrix approach has been shown to fail, then making the process more complex will not help.

What is left for the NFP or NGO ethicist is the articulation of an argument. As a social fact, this is best done in teams of trusted, informed people who have the freedom to speak their minds, sometimes taking controversial positions. The most elegant solutions to vexing problems are often done with executive teams populated by persons of both goodwill and varied backgrounds. Having voices present which reflect those you serve is immeasurable.

Let me share one final story which brings this point into focus. I have a colleague who is a researcher on healthcare issues in sub-Saharan Africa. This colleague became convinced that how people practiced religion had a dramatic role in healthcare outcomes. The hypothesis that my colleague pursued was that the religion that affected healthcare decisions the most was not a well-known organized religion, but a patchwork quilt of ideas derived from local religious traditions. He brought this hypothesis to the team of researchers he was working with and was greeted with considerable skepticism. It is important to point out that these researchers were all from western backgrounds and had earned terminal degrees at elite American institutions. None of them had ever participated in or practiced tribal religions. Nonetheless, with grant money behind them, they traveled for a surveying and canvassing expedition to several sub-Saharan countries.

In one interview, the team met with the director of a region's healthcare system—a region which encompassed five different countries. This director was a national of one of those countries and had traveled to the United States some years earlier where he had acquired his own terminal degree at one of the same elite American institutions. That is, he held the same high degree of educational preparation as every member of the visiting research team.

In one conversation, my colleague asked the regional director whether he himself visits the traditional healer before he goes to a doctor or a hospital. He answered that of course he does. Everyone does. And if that doesn't work he then goes to the doctor.

The other members of the research team were shocked. It would not have been wrong to accuse them of implicitly believing that education and religion were mutually exclusive affairs.

What arose from the conversation was a deeper appreciation for the way that religious beliefs play a role in the way that rational people make decisions. Group bias prevented them from seeing this until they let someone in with a different perspective. And quite probably, group bias prevents the groups from detecting the ways that they themselves have been shaped in their thinking.

I repeat the advice offered before: Ethics in NFPs and NGOs is best done in teams with diverse perspectives among people of goodwill.

Boards and Oversight

Just as there is no one single method to govern and administer the operations of a for-profit corporation, there is also no one single method for providing oversight for the nonprofit. But whether in the United States, United Kingdom, Australia or a great many other nations, one requirement of all nonprofits is the existence of a board which offers oversight. Who can serve on the board, how they are selected and for how long they serve is highly variable. Some nations posit citizenship requirements (India) while others list no qualifications at all (the United States). But is fair to say that when it comes to issues of governance, board activity is the starting point.

There is not one kind of board and there is not one single model that describes the interaction between the board, the executives and the operational staff. Unlike large corporations, it is common for the NFP to have a board member who also chips in on the front-lines of operations. An animal rescue organization might have a board member that helps out to answer the phones or organize a mailer, but it is unlikely that a board member of "Yum! Brands" will help to clean the fryer at a local fast-food franchise. This points to the areas of strength that NFPs have when compared with their for-profit colleagues. NFP and NGO boards, especially in small NFPs and NGOs, are populated by people who are very interested in what is happening on the ground. They want to know the status of operations in progress and are typically unafraid to offer to aid your efforts. They will likely be your most consistent volunteers, your most faithful donors and those most passionate about your cause.

However, these virtues are but one side of a proverbial coin with the other side being vices. NFP and NGO boards that constantly interact with operations can threaten to undermine professional decision-making processes. They can intentionally or unintentionally intervene in hiring and firing decisions. In fact, the amount of ways in which the free-flow interaction from board-to-operations can cause problems is likely as numerous (or more numerous) than the total number of NFPs and NGOs.

It would be helpful for NFP management and staff to understand the different *kinds* of boards that run organizations. Knowing the kind of board you serve undergoes a long way to understanding NFP and NGO decisions and actions. On the one hand, there are elected boards. Such boards are constituted by those who won an election whose electors are designated by the bylaws of the organization. A church's "members" might be the electors in a congregation or a community's residents might elect the community association board. Compare the elected board with the self-perpetuating board. A self-perpetuating board elects its own board members. Once a board member resigns or leaves, the board undertakes the task of finding a replacement. A third kind of board is the appointed board. Common in public-sector organizations, appointed boards are populated by board members appointed by a relevant office or body. An advisory board, as the name suggests, offers advisory oversight but not executive control. Finally, an NFP or NGO might be structured in such a way as to constitute a hybrid of any of the above (Boardsource, 2010).

It is wrong-headed to ask which of these models is the "best." Rather, it is more appropriate to ask which model best suits the NFP or NGO in question. Just what suits them will be a function of ethics, finances, mission and practical considerations. Here are two examples.

1. Firstly, an already-existing NFP might see a great opportunity in a new initiative which will require new leadership. A university, for example, might judge that programming a public policy lecture series could be helpful to the university's interests in a number of ways. While it is undeniably useful for the university to have its board members interested in the initiative, it might be more impactful to organize an advisory board whose sole task it is to offer guidance over this one initiative. This way the advisory board members who might not care that much about the allocation of undergraduate dorm space can focus on what they love without having to be tied to broader obligations that they don't want in the first place.
2. Or, secondly, a group of concerned individuals might elect to start an NGO that addresses the issue of immigration. Let us say that they live in

an area affected by the many challenges that immigration issues pose and desire to start initiatives in the home country of would-be immigrants. By selecting the self-perpetuating model they ensure that whatever becomes of their work that they will be able to ensure that the work stays on target. The "shoe on the other foot" principle applies here: If you were giving enormous amounts of time and financial resources to an NGO, would you want to have the ability to make the decisions that ensure that your time and resources were managed effectively and remained on target?

This matters when it comes to issues of management of NGOs and NFPs. If your board is self-perpetuating then it would not be surprising to discover that program managers or even the CEO doesn't have ultimate control over how or whether a program continues to exist. If your board is appointed by public officials it would be common to see governing methods and priorities change with the ebbs and flows of politics.

Boards also have responsibilities, and these responsibilities are a matter of law and legal precedent, not individual opinion. The Sibley Hospital case (Harpool, 1996) is widely recognized as having clarified board responsibilities. They are the responsibility of care, loyalty and obedience. They are to "care" for the institution by overseeing its finances and operations, they are to be "loyal" by putting the interests of the institution first and they are to be "obedient" to both the law of the land and to the mission of the NFP or NGO. These obligations are perhaps best illustrated via examples:

- EXAMPLE 1: A university board elects to invest a large portion of its endowment in a risky (unregulated) hedge-fund rather than an index fund because a segment of the board has learned that a colleague in the finance industry has recently had good returns. Exposing the endowment to such risk could constitute a violation of the obligation to *care* for the institution.
- EXAMPLE 2: A member of the community seeks and attains a board seat because doing business with the NFP would enrich him or herself. This constitutes a violation of the obligation of loyalty since the interests of the NFP are secondary to personal financial interests (This was at the core of the Sibley Hospital Case).
- EXAMPLE 3: The board of an NFP takes a course of action which implies a significant departure from the mission upon which it was established (Say, for example, an urban homeless shelter starting a Ukrainian relief fund). Such an action would constitute an instance of disobedience to its own mission. Other examples of "disobedience" might be cases in which boards fail to follow relevant legal guidelines.

One final note regarding the requirement for "obedience": just what the external guidelines might end up being is highly variable. So much so that it is common for boards to have a formal or informal requirement that at least one of its members must be a lawyer. Many NFPs need only ensure that they obey the Sarbanes-Oxley act of 1992 which requires that documents be kept and whistleblowers protected. And they must supply the IRS with form 990 every year. But it would be a significant error to think that legal requirements end there. NGOs and NFPs very frequently find themselves in an environment which requires other forms of legal compliance. Colleges and universities must comply with accreditation standards, medical NFPs will need to be aware of any state or federal guidelines relevant to their area of emphasis, and likewise, any NFP or NGO working with vulnerable populations (children, the elderly and those with disabilities) will certainly confront their own set of unique legal constraints.

A good source of the valuable board and governance-related information can be found in the professional fundraising literature, as it is with fundraising enterprises that many of these issues play a central role. I direct the reader to Barbara Ciconte and Jeanne Jacob's *Fundraising Basics: A Complete Guide*. This text, while containing quite a bit of information solely pertaining to fundraising, is an excellent source of basic information regarding the professional and legal requirements of boards and is used in their own conferral of CFRE credentials to members of the profession (Ciconte & Jacob, 2009).

One further responsibility of boards is to evaluate the CEO of the organization. More is packed into this previous section than might appear obvious at first glance. Here is an idealized institutional flowchart which makes the point more clear.

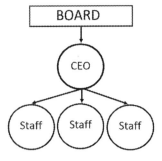

Fig. 1 NFP Evaluation structure

This institutional flowchart depicts an idealized evaluation structure. Here, the Board is responsible for evaluating the CEO of the organization and the CEO is responsible for evaluating the staff hired to assist in the execution of the mission.

Depicted in this way, matters seem simple. But in practice, it may become more complex. For example, the CEO appointed by the board frequently relies heavily upon a development or advancement officer to meet yearly fundraising goals, and meeting those goals might very well become an important piece of the evaluative structure of the CEO. Great pressure can be brought upon the CEO by the board in times of lagging donations, struggling endowments or budgetary shortfalls. Likewise, moral scandals committed in lower echelons of the organization could quickly become a board matter. So while as a purely formal matter this structure depicts an ideal evaluative structure, understanding how the directional arrows might become misaligned is important.

This can also serve to explain institutional miscommunication and misunderstanding. A CEO's new initiative might be as much the Board's idea as the CEO's idea. And a CEO might listen more closely to the grumbling of the board than to the grumbling of staff. The moral theory discussed earlier in this book called "egoism" offers an elegant explanation as to why this is so.

A common struggle for every NGO and NFP lies in how to manage information flow and decision-making between the board on the one hand and the executives and staff on the other. This points to the fact that Fig. 1, which was intended to show an evaluation structure, is far from reality on many occasions. Consider a revised figure one which shows the potential communication pathways within an organization.

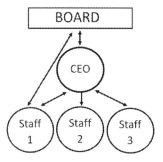

Fig. 2 One of several possible communication structures

What we see in this case, and admitting that there are an infinite variety of possible others, is that just as before the CEO and Board communicate with one another. But it also just so happens that "Staff 1" has a direct line of communication to the board, bypassing the CEO. Additionally, that same staff member enjoys two-way communication between themselves and the CEO. That is, this staff member has as much freedom of communication as the CEO! Meanwhile, Staff 2 only receives communication and Staff 3 enjoys give-and-take with the CEO.

This situation is dangerous, although often unavoidable. It is also endemic to a great many NFPs and NGOs. High-Dollar donors to an NGO will travel to sub-Saharan Africa just to speak with your staff and see how programs are going. Your staff will interact with your Board at fundraisers. Your fundraiser will send out mailings which include board members. Yet the moral of this story nonetheless remains the same: When it comes to evaluation, the structure must be like that of Fig. 2.

This begs perhaps the largest question of this section: What are boards and what should they do? There is not one single answer to this question, but many different answers. Michael Worth has summarized three models that have gained more traction in recent years in his *Nonprofit Management: Principles and Practice*. They are Policy Boards, Leadership Boards and Psychologically Centrality Leadership Boards. (Worth, 2020) A policy-driven board only works insofar as there is a need for policies constraining action. So, for example, a board in such circumstances would never decide to paint the lobby blue but they might articulate a policy detailing who is empowered to make such a decision or how such decisions are to be paid for. A policy-driven board keeps their hands out of operations. Leadership boards view themselves as setting agendas and priorities, not policies. This might mean that unlike policy-driven boards the board members *do* become involved in operational issues. Just how they do could be quite variable. But the most common form of such an interaction would be one in which greater institutional strategic advantage can be attained through the interaction than without it. The advocate of "Psychological Centrality" views the best relationship between the board and CEO is that of the CEO taking leadership over the NFP's action by providing leadership to the board members.

Hidden not so deep beneath the subtext of this discussion is the reality that board/executive/staff interaction is a common cause of problems in the NFP and NGO. Boards have the power to do a great many things in the institution they govern and this power is more than just legal. Often it is financial. The "customer" of the NFP, often referred to as the "client," isn't the one who pays for services. The donors do. And most of your largest donors are on your board. This creates a "judge, jury and executioner" problem that can be the source of inefficiency, chaos and mismanagement.

As we transition to the presentation of cases, I call the reader to four (fallible) principles which should be observed in issues of governance and leadership.

1. Boards must select executive leadership they trust, then empower that leadership to act. A board overseeing an NGO subject to leadership they do not trust is a recipe for disaster. This is what causes a great many cases of board-overreach. Relatedly, boards that make operational decisions risk communicating to their executives that they are not trusted.
2. NFP and NGO executives must embrace their middle position. They must recognize their accountability to the board and communicate clearly, precisely and frequently with them. Boards handle bad news far better than surprises. At the same time, executive officers must never forget what are likely their own roots—what it is like to be a frontline staff member. They must protect, encourage and develop the talents of the staff members of their organization. This is especially important for new executives who find it hard to walk away from frontline services.
3. Staff must respect the special relationship between the board and executives and neither invite nor tolerate intrusion. Staff report to program managers or to NFP/NGO executives, not the board. They are the frontline workers and have been placed in that position because they are good at their role.
4. Staff, Executives and the Board must understand that they work jointly with each other to fulfill the NFP's or NGO's mission.

Covid-19 Vaccine Policy in a Medium-Sized NFP

You are a part of the leadership team of a medium-sized not-for-profit that employs approximately 35 people. Of that 35, 5 (including yourself) are on the leadership team. Members are the CEO, the Director of Advancement, the Chief Financial Officer, the Human Resources officer and the Chief Program Director. It is August 2021 and the initial wave of Covid-19 infections has run its course while a new variant is rumored to be circulating.

Your not-for-profit serves children in the foster care system. You have three residential homes for them employing 12 of your staff as cooks, in-home house monitors and other support staff. Other employees are primarily occupied with welfare checks and integrating with the guardian *ad lidem* program in your area.

The three approved vaccines for the virus are currently available under emergency use and have not been approved by the FDA. The president of the United States has stated in press conferences that he expects that approval to occur "within weeks." Nonetheless, you have successfully organized vaccine drives for your group homes, as all of the children in your custody there are over the age of 12 (which is currently the minimum age set under the FDA emergency use authorization).

You were hoping to not have to decide on your own a Covid-19 vaccine policy, expecting your state to implement guidelines which you would then endorse institutionally. But the governor of your state has refused to create such a policy, electing instead to "let people decide for themselves."

In the absence of political leadership, you send out an email to all staff requesting that they elect to declare to you whether or not they have been vaccinated against the virus. After three weeks and two follow-up emails only 20% of your staff report full immunization with another 10% in process.

You wonder why 70% of your staff appear to be hesitant to receive the vaccine despite its widespread availability. Informal conversations lead to you believe that there is not one reason, but many reasons. Some of the younger female staff have resisted vaccination because they want to have children in the near future and fear that the vaccine might affect their fertility. One of them is currently pregnant. One person expressed reservation about taking the "Trump Vaccine" and another expressed hesitancy about taking the "Biden vaccine." Many of your program staff appear ambivalent about the threat of Covid-19 infection. And one member of your leadership team thinks that some are refusing the vaccine so as to continue to work from home.

Your business today is to decide upon a Covid-19 vaccine policy for your employees. Several policies are possible but none required since your state has refused to adopt a policy. Those policies include:

1. Do Nothing: Wait for state or federal guidelines to appear.
2. Mandate vaccines for all employees.
3. Mandate testing for the unvaccinated.
4. Mandate vaccines for residential staff only.
5. Mandate social distancing protocols for the non-vaccinated.
6. Declare to staff that they are "free to decide on their own" what to do.

Discussion Questions:

1. How can NFP leadership avoid the politicization of their own Covid-19 vaccine policy?
2. What are the effects of the politicization of healthcare policy?
3. Perform a cost-benefit-analysis. What are the pros and cons of demanding a carte blanche vaccine mandate policy in your NFP? And how would that be enforced?
4. To what extent do the reasons of your staff for not being vaccinated matter?
5. Do you believe that the Covid-19 pandemic is the last time your NFP or NGO will face decisions like this? Why or why not?

The Helpful Board Member

Much of the successes that NFPs attain are owed to the sacrifice of board members. They are consistent donors, committed allies and often times the most involved volunteers. John is no exception.

John made his money operating warehouses which temporarily house goods in a secure location as they are transported across our country. You don't know how many facilities he owns, but your boss has told you on many occasions that he is a big deal. That's odd because John never acts like he is a big deal. You know him mostly because of his constant and pleasant presence in the afterschool program for which you are the program director. You associate him with the role of the janitor, not the warehouse magnate.

John comes in early before the kids arrive to sweep the floors and take out the trash. He always asks whether there is anything else that needs to be done in addition to these basic custodial duties. And sometimes you do find things for him to do—a broken faucet here, a burnt-out halogen bulb there. He is usually on the premises 12 pm–3:00 pm, arriving before most of your staff do and departing just before the kids arrive. He once mentioned that he leaves at that time because he needs to prepare his warehouses for the night deliveries.

Recently, however, there has been a change in John's behavior. Now he is staying to greet the kids as they enter the building after school. He has been sitting with the kids while they do their homework, speaking with several of them in the tone of a kind and patient father.

You notice nothing improper about John's behavior.

You pull John aside one day and talk with him, hoping to better understand the change in his otherwise consistent behavior. John confides in you that his family life has been deteriorating and that he is looking to fill the void with something meaningful. He finds spending time with the kids to fill that void. He shares that he likes helping "the little one with the glasses" figure out her algebra homework. And he thinks that "that older mean looking kid" probably has a heart of gold if only there were a good male presence in his life to foster it.

As program director, you know that there are strict state guidelines for interaction with children. Background checks are mandatory and there are several trainings that must be undertaken with absolutely no exception. You never bothered to bring it up with John before, seeing as that he was an invisible presence up until recently. But now you wonder what to do.

Discussion Questions:
1. Is John's new level of involvement troubling?
2. Should you act to curtail John's involvement in your program?
3. What is the best way to address this situation? Who should be involved in any discussion that you might have?
4. How can your actions help to serve John's needs?
5. Is this a dilemma that the program manager should solve? Should someone else have communicated this information to John earlier?

When Democracy and Mission Collide

Alex was in shock. He had lived in this neighborhood for years. When he first bought his modest property, it was not the kind of place that anyone with any means would want to live. The prostitutes filled the streets all night long, drugs were common and the noise of police and ambulance activity was constant. It didn't help that the local fire station was just two blocks from his home so that at all hours of the night he could expect the roar of the sirens to respond to calls.

His neighborhood was one of the first to be built in his city and consequently the state. That state didn't see much change in its population between the civil war and 1920 when his neighborhood was built. The region never saw significant growth until air conditioning was invented by William Carrier. Growth thereafter went in spurts. There was a large expansion in the post-war years, another in the early 90s, and a massive, regional influx of new residents since the year 2010.

Nearly all of those new residents elected to live in the now numerous bedroom communities that surrounded his urban environment. He and his friends refer to those newly built homes as "McMansions"—a derogatory term that attempts to capture the cookie-cutter approach to creating idyllic suburban neighborhoods.

Alex had no desire to live in any of them. His friends at work endured an hour commute each way while his was about ten minutes. When events happened in the city center he could easily ride his bicycle there rather than driving and hunting for parking. When he needed to take a flight a rideshare trip cost no more than $20.

Alex wasn't alone. While Alex was among the first of the intrepid city-dwellers to desire to make his blighted neighborhood a home it did not take long for him and a core group of other neighbors to catch on to the same dream. They were an eclectic, friendly, bunch. Some of them were from young families that had themselves been raised in suburbs and did not want that experience for their own children. Others were recent immigrants who were more than happy to invest sweat equity into their property. And there were a great many members of the LGBTQ community who felt more at home in an urban city center than in the outlying suburbs.

At one-fourth of July block party that Alex and his neighbors began to think about what they could do for their community. That was when they created the idea for a neighborhood development association. That corporation would liaison with the city in an effort to identify blighted properties, articulate plans for the redevelopment of those properties, and to troubleshoot the several nuisances that still dogged their daily experience.

Their first big win was to convince the city to install a stoplight in front of the fire station that enabled the trucks to exit without sirens blaring. Having the mayor as an appointed board member was the stroke of genius that more than anything else produced that victory. The next win was to work with other members of his neighborhood development corporation to create design standards. Much of that work was thanks to his friend Mark and his husband Jack, both of whom were skilled designers and who worked *pro bono* to create a great many visual standards which would serve to guide the future of renovations in their community.

Structurally, Alex's NFP was a democracy with the exception of the Mayor's seat. This democratic nature was a necessary condition for any organizational project to have traction in his neighborhood. The neighborhood was a pluralistic place, not a monocultural isolate. It was and probably would continue for some time to be an exciting cross section of religiously, culturally and ideologically diverse residents. This meant that when the bylaws of the organization were created they stated that voting members of the board (whose proposals were then recommended to the city) served two year terms with at least 50% of those terms up for renewal every year. The Mayor served as a permanent member of the board and 6 elected community members served under the term limits. Additionally, a provision in the bylaws was insisted upon by community members who feared that they might lose a voice to this new association, provided that any motion from a community member during a meeting would become an official motion of the board if seconded by a board member. Finally, the term "community member" was defined as any person owning title to real estate within the boundaries set by the association and who declared that property their primary or secondary residence.

One of the "brownfield" development locations in the neighborhood was a large, prime spot within a stone's throw from the Atlantic Ocean. That spot was approximately 56 acres and its previous building had been demolished at the request of the association some years earlier. Removing that building opened up a large field which would go on to be a play spot for children of the community and an appealing spot of greenery with views of the water. Not in its entire history did his community have a park. But this land, while not technically a park, functioned like one.

Six months later Alex was shocked to read in the newspaper that the city had entered an agreement with a well-known developer to turn that patch of land into a high-income condominium complex for snowbirds, executives and high-net-income persons. At first, he couldn't figure it out. How could a 35-story condominium project go up in his neighborhood when there were clear guidelines regarding building and design standards? His committee had not seen any proposal at all. He and his team reviewed those standards after studying the news article, and it could not have been clearer that the association could veto the project effectively.

Nervous, he and his fellow board members approached the community center where their quarterly meeting was to be held to discover a scene unlike any previous meeting. They knew that something was up when they observed a parking lot packed with cars. Was there another event happening that they did not know about? But as they entered the room what they witnessed was not common for a quarterly meeting. Typically, there were as many board members as community members present. But what they saw was a small meeting room packed with several hundred people, most of whom they did not recognize. Reporters and news media were present.

As the meeting began an attendee raised his hand. As per the bylaws, he had to be recognized.

"I would like to recommend Bruce Berman to serve as board member" he chimed in.

The mayor of the city, a board member by charter, quickly chimed in. "I second the motion." He said.

Concerned about what he was witnessing, Alex asked (quite out of order) for the name of the community member who made the recommendation and where he lived. "I'm Noel Livingston. I purchased a condo in the new project that it going up just down the road. Because I hold title now, I and others like me are now voting members of this body." He answered.

It was then that the reality of the situation dawned on Alex. The association he had built was witnessing a hostile takeover. His democratic bylaws were being used against him. And by the end of the meeting, the board was stacked. With the decisive vote being the mayor's, the condo project was approved.

Discussion Questions:
1. What are the weaknesses of elected boards?
2. What could have been done within the bylaws to prevent this situation?
3. Is it always against the interests of gentrifying communities to see large investments in large projects?
4. Why did the mayor act as she did? What were her motives?
5. Boards need advisors and expertise. Who are the best representatives to be on a community development board?
6. What are the strengths and weaknesses of democratic processes?

The Employee with Family on the Board

Trevor is a bright employee in his mid-20s at your NFP that serves animals in need of shelter and veterinary services. He has a positive attitude, a commitment to the cause and is a diligent worker.

You, the executive director, hired Trevor for a lot of reasons, only some of which have to do with Trevor. Yes, he can do the job and yes, he makes for a good institutional fit. But the fact that his father, who sits on the board, asked you to consider him for employment didn't harm his chances of getting the job.

Trevor's work with you is good. In every way that an employee's performance would be evaluated, Trevor did well. But slowly over time a few red flags catch your attention.

Firstly, on several occasions, you overhear Trevor speaking to his dad on the phone talking about his day. Nothing of terrible consequence was overheard by you on any of those calls and you tried hard not to pry. They appeared to be simple conversations between a father and a son about what is happening in their lives. But something that very much caused you concern was an event that happened last week.

A few months ago you attended your board meeting to discuss NFP business, strategy and planning. These were always great sessions, albeit sometimes passionate and contentious. During that meeting, Trevor's father discussed a potential new strategy for the NFP which he couched in uniquely business-y terminology. He stated that the NFP needed to start a new initiative "tailor made to scale the operation" which would "leverage the social standing" of the NFP in the community. You couldn't help but notice that the proposed initiative would significantly alter the mission of the NFP. In the end, the idea was shelved for further consideration later on. This was of no consequence in and of itself. Exactly that scenario had been played out on scores of occasions with the board.

But a little while later, when you spoke with Trevor, Trevor pitched the same idea using the same terminology that his father had used in the board meeting. He stated to you that he thought the NFP "needed to leverage its social standing in the community to scale up the operation." You responded by stating that it was an idea that merited further investigation but that you were not ready to implement it at this time.

This happened more and more often. First, the father would mention an idea at a board meeting, and it would be shot down, whereupon the son would raise the same idea later on at work. You often wondered whether the father board member was feeding information to the son. Or vice versa.

At the next board meeting, the father brought up the same issue. You felt confident that the idea was not as fully developed as it needed to be. You were worried that it could expose the NFP to financial risk unnecessarily. You were concerned that there was not enough capital to get it off the ground. And you were concerned that implementing it could constitute the first step toward mission drift. And you stated all of these reasons in the board meeting. Once again, the idea is shelved.

Within 24 hours, you receive an email from Trevor, cc'ing all other board members in which Trevor declares his resignation. The letter is long. It airs every grievance he has about the organization, specifically identifies you as the reason why he is going, and makes for his immediate departure from the institution.

You immediately call a meeting with your CFO whom you trust with all sorts of difficult internal problems.

"It sounds like you have a real problem here. That board member is a generous donor to the organization. I'm showing $150,000 in cash donations this year alone." She says.

"Yes, indeed. But I can't get past how unprofessional this is." You add in frustration. "First there is the problem that one of my junior employees is in collusion with the board. I'm not OK with that. Then there is the problem that what they are colluding for is *not* in the best interests of this institution. Best case it throws us off mission, worst case it bankrupts us."

"I hear you about the collusion. I'm with you. Promise," the CFO states. "But what is the idea? What are they trying to do?"

"Trevor's dad wants to sell our physical facilities and position us to become an animal shelter *brand*. We then sell our brand to other animal shelters as a status symbol. They get to put a logo on their website and brag about it, I guess. That's about as specific as the discussions ever got. And honestly, it's not the first time this has happened. I go into those meetings all the time and have to talk the renegade board member out of a stupid idea that would wreck the place."

Discussion Questions:

1. What kind of interaction should there be between NFP staff and board members?
2. Should there be a policy against families of board members serving as NFP staff?
3. In this scenario, what are the responsibilities of the other board members?
4. What can you as the executive director do to improve your relationship with the board?

Social Enterprise vs. Social Service

Driscoll enlisted in military service because he believed in his country, because he believed in himself and because he wanted to be dedicated to a higher purpose. He admits in retrospect that he could not have possibly planned for what he saw in the battlefield. After seeing several of his squad members killed in action, his own number came up one day on a dusty road in the middle-east when his car struck an IED.

His road to recovery was by all accounts brutal. On the one hand, there were the physiological effects of the accident which left him permanently disabled. And on the other hand, there was the emotional turmoil that surrounded what he had seen and done while in service. All of this was met with a crushing futility as he engaged in his rehab back in the United States.

He could endure the physical therapy. At least, his ability to tolerate pain had never left him. But all of the stretches and weightlifting exercises didn't do the least bit to help him deal with the emotional issues that dogged him. Today we call it "PTSD." But he didn't have a word for it then.

Purely by accident, he discovered that creating pieces of visual art helped him to "articulate" the feelings that even he couldn't recognize with words. He had a hard time discussing the concept of survivor's guilt, but watercolor images of a barren landscape substituted in a tragic but therapeutic way.

His first few paintings became thirty. Then several hundred. He upgraded his apartment to one that had an artist's studio he could fit in a spare bedroom. And at some point, it occurred to him that he had discovered something that could possibly help other people in similar circumstances. At first, he invited others over to his place to talk. Then a few of those new friends started creating art with him. Very quickly, his new place wasn't large enough to house the people he invited in.

While his background and the origin of his trauma was rooted in military service, not all of his new "possee" (as he called them) had the same background. Some had escaped violent gangs. Others abusive childhoods. Just about the only thing that bound them together was the fact that they used art as their therapy.

But what Driscoll needed now was more space. So he approached a local vocational rehabilitation provider with an idea: Use the storage room in the back of his facility for his art classes. They were excited about the idea and gladly offered space in their headquarters for his art "class." But while they could offer him space, they couldn't give him a budget. And as Driscoll found out, buying watercolor paints on disability income is difficult. Driscoll created a 501c3 and recruited a board who were happy to offer what to them was a minimal investment for paint and canvas.

One discussion with a board member proved fateful.

"Why not sell your art online, Driscoll?" Mark asked.

Driscoll had never thought about it. His paintings were personal therapy whose goal was wellness, not profit. But after some coaching and clever branding he gave it a spin. Branding his art with a "Gritty Warrior Possee" logo, his online presence offered a paragraph description of his time in the service and the purpose of his creation of art. The other thirty or so pages on his website were dedicated to drop-shipped coffee-mugs and tee-shirts.

At first, word spread through his informal friend network. But a local TV station picked up the story and aired a three-minute piece one week. That was the match that lit the fire.

Ten orders a month turned into ten orders a day. Then twenty. Then a thousand a month. Driscoll couldn't believe what he was seeing. And he began to think, correctly as it turns out, that he needed to get ahead of the wave before it crashed upon him.

A few things worried Driscoll about his success. The first was that the branding, which he had spent no more than an hour designing, had positioned his work as art used as therapy for disabled soldiers. But the reality was that of the thirty men and women that attended his art classes, only four were former soldiers. The rest were dealing with similar trauma but from different sources. He had tried to make this clear to the TV crew, but they edited that part out.

The second was that he could see that his slim margin of profit could be made much larger if he stopped the drop-shipping and started controlling the manufacturing process himself. It would take a pretty minimal investment on his part for the equipment, then ongoing expenses for the staff to run it. But perhaps those expenses could be covered by his ever-increasing orders.

But it was not all concern. There was also an incredible opportunity for him. Just a few short months earlier he described himself as dead inside but that now he had a meaningful, impactful dream to live for. He could see success in his own life and in the lives of the people he met with every week. He didn't want that to end.

So he approached his board to discuss the situation. The board asked Driscoll a few questions which Driscoll wasn't able to articulate before that point. Those questions were:

Discussion Questions:
1. Do you think it is wrong to sell your art as therapy for former soldiers when that's not always true?
2. Do you have to be a not-for-profit anymore? Why not think about starting a business rather than continue being a not-for-profit?
3. Is there a goal that you are trying to reach that is best reached by a not-for-profit enterprise?
4. Should your online sales be a separate entity from your not-for-profit?
5. Have you investigated unrelated business income tax guidelines?

The Board Member's Pet Project

Phyllis is the longest-serving, most generous donor on your board. She and her now deceased husband were with your NFP from the beginning when they served as volunteers in the 1980s. That volunteerism and the rich experiences it provided her translated into additional services, generous gifts and principled support. Without question, her involvement has helped your NFP to offer consistent, safe, long-term housing for kids in the foster system.

Her help and the help of those she recruited translated into many millions of dollars over the years. And perhaps of greater value is the network of new allies that she was able to recruit over the course of her time with you. As you survey the roll of your current and past donors, you cannot help but notice that most of them stem from her presence with you. Most of them were Phyllis' friends or strangers that she subsequently converted into friends.

But none of that ever seems to help you cope with the piles of teddy bears that show up every December. You find yourself increasingly frustrated with them as the years go on.

Apparently, sometime before you arrived in your leadership position a plan was hatched in which community members were convinced to show their support for your NFP by mailing a teddy bear (and hopefully a check) to your offices. Pictures of the kids with their new teddy bears were then sent out in newsletters as a way of offering thanks. The success of that initiative paved the way for a sequel the next year. Then the next. And as the years went on the amount of teddy bears grew vastly. The mailed newsletter was replaced by website images. And years later those were replaced by social-media postings. Year after year the initiative only grew.

A regrettable downside of this growth was the ever-increasing piles of teddy bears—so many that each child they served could easily have had fifty allocated to them. Per year. With bears left over. Special delivery procedures needed to be negotiated with the postal service. The NFP had to remove several rooms from their operations every December to handle the mountains of bears, and quite a few staff hours were allocated to dealing with the onslaught. While other NFPs' greatest secrets tended to pertain to financial mismanagement and internal theft, yours was the fact that you shredded and disposed of several thousand bears a year in the dark of night.

This year, about 50% of the bears were sent without any financial contribution.

One day while confronting the visual testament of your frustration (one of three store-rooms piled high with stuffed bears) Phyllis appears. She wipes away a tear from her sincere, ever-passionate face and says "Isn't it just beautiful? Let's get even more next year."

The words hit you like a brick wall. If this program continued, then it would all repeat next year. You would have to ask 12 employees to leave their offices and take refuge on folding tables for a month. Once again you would lose at least three rooms in your headquarters And you would be showing up at the back door at midnight with the industrial shredder and a wheelbarrow.

You have a discussion with your chief development officer who knows Phyllis very well.

"This can't go on, Yveline. We've got work to do and for that we need space."

"I'm with you," says Yveline, "But if we kill the teddy bear drive we break Phyllis's heart. Now just think about it. Phyllis has been here for a long time. And except for this annoying yearly teddy bear tsunami, the relationship is great."

"Oh, that's true. But I'm coming to you because I want ideas. What can we do?"

After a moment Yveline says "Well, I've been thinking of some ideas. None of them are great. But here goes. On the one hand we can just say 'well, that's the cost of doing business. Phyllis wants teddy bears so she'll have the teddy bears.' I recon Phyllis has ten more years in her after which she won't be able to be active much more. So that makes for putting up with it for another decade."

The "I'm not thrilled" look on your face conveys to Yveline what you think of that idea.

"Ok, then. Idea number two. Phyllis agreed to stop the expensive mailer and move to an email newsletter back in the 2000's. That was a big deal to her. But she got over it and adapted. So maybe we convince her to adapt again. We enter the NFT market and create non-fungible token Teddy Bears. That would attract younger people anyway, and potentially limit the deluge."

"Maybe. But I'll admit that I'm nervous about the crypto markets. That and we would effectively be cutting out the now minority of folks who manage to send a check with the teddy bear."

"You and me both," says Yveline. "You don't just snap your fingers and make it so in those markets. I estimate we would need an entire crypto staff just for the initiative. And as of today we don't have the right kinds of people here. That and we couldn't afford them if we did."

"Other ideas?" you ask.

"Well, we could shift the burden. We could bring the problem to the board and ask for volunteers to house the teddy bears at their homes. But they don't have the shredder that we do so I'm guessing they will all make their way back here after a week."

"I'm still not liking my options. Any others?"

"The remaining options all involve getting rid of the bears somehow, or making Phyllis change her mind. Maybe we find some other 501c3 in need of teddy bears. Or perhaps we start an online teddy bear business that sells them. Maybe we put our foot down and tell Phyllis 'No More!'. But there are more reasons to want to stop the madness than just the space issue. Our community partners are giving us those bears with the expectation that they are used for the purpose of comforting children. Arguably, right now we are violating our moral obligation to deliver on that expectation since we accept the bears and proceed to shred half of them. That doesn't feel right."

Questions for Discussion:
1. Should the teddy bear program be cut?
2. If you were to retain this program, how could you mitigate against its institutional toll?
3. What are the benefits and demerits of long-serving board members?
4. Is this NFP ethically stewarding the resources that the community delivers to them?
5. Should boards have term limits?
6. Why is cutting a program more difficult than starting a program?

Regime Change and the Perils of Being a Hero

Robert was a technically minded worker at an NFP educational institution. Initially not assigned any duties related to proposal-writing, his precise, detailed writing skills were quickly identified by the Advancement Department. And just in time, as that department and the entire institution faced an increasingly difficult institutional forecast. At first, they allocated him the opportunity to write proposals related to just his own area of work. But after several noteworthy successes, Robert was recruited to write proposals on behalf of the institution, not just its individual departments.

Robert noticed that a large, internationally known foundation had just issued a request for proposals (RFP) which addressed social issues core to the mission of the NFP—urban youth educational opportunities. In his estimation, the NFP would have a little problem showing that it could meet the needs detailed in the RFP. Their only competitive disadvantage he could think of regarding the chances of success was the institution itself. It was

Boards and Oversight 71

not a nationally known player in the NFP scene. They were a humble, local, underfunded-yet-somehow-stable institution with a particular alacrity for work in the program areas specified. But Robert thought that they could do it. Robert proposed that he be given permission to write the proposal on behalf of the institution, pass it through the Advancement Department, and barring objections submit it to the foundation. He was stunned, given the large scope of the proposal that would inevitably result, that permission was granted within a business day.

The next three weeks, Robert worked tirelessly to craft the proposal. This required long consultations with program staff, writing and revising of budgets, clarifying reporting obligations and timelines, and quite a bit of writing.

He was curious as to the lack of attention being paid to his efforts by the upper-levels of the institution itself. This past month a new president had been named and accordingly a new staff in the Advancement Department. He thought it a collegial act to offer to deliver them a win, if at all it would end up being a win. But there was very little attention paid to his activities.

Six months later the award was announced. Robert's humble NFP that could had been given $5 million for the program which would last for five years.

Having created the program himself, Robert knew exactly what needed to happen to enact it. His tracking system had already been created at the stage of proposal-writing, and the timeframe for reporting was already in place.

Year one went as planned. He was able to begin the program and start the system of measurement and tracking. He was obsessed with the extent to which the program was working and the ways in which key indicators were showing trouble. But he was also curious about the fact that no one in the advancement department or the president's office bothered to check in on him.

It was at that point that some institutional decisions blindsided him.

The first was that positions within the institution specifically called for in the proposal were eliminated. In one case, an entire department integral to the program was cut and its staff was dismissed. Robert was unsure how to pivot given this unexpected reality and quickly sought meetings with the Advancement Department. But making that meeting happen proved difficult.

Robert and his peers were later on called to an all-staff meeting with the president and his advisors. During that meeting, the president shared that he had some great news. He had just recruited a "former NFL player" to be a part of the NFP team who would use sports as a way to help advance their institution. "Everything I ever needed to know," the president proudly declared, "I learned from football."

While Robert noticed that many of his peers were cheering the news, he couldn't help but wonder what this meant for the direction of the institution, much less his grant.

After the meeting, Robert decided to renew his work once again and made a stop by the accounts payable (AP) office to look at the balance sheet of his grant—a practice which he routinely and meticulously tracked.

"We're sorry." said Amy, one of Robert's closest friends and a longtime staff member in the financial office. "The remaining balance on that account is listed as encumbered. I can show you that amount, but until it becomes unencumbered we can't make any more payments out of it."

Robert quickly called the Advancement Department but was unable to get answers. So he went back to his office to think about what he would do next. Greeting him in his email inbox was a press release celebrating the commitment to build a new football field.

Robert was now in a position of needing to report on the activities of his grant program, but unable to fund any of those activities. Over the course of a few weeks, he was unable to have a discussion with any member of the administration about it, whether executive or fundraising staff. Robert did not know how to proceed.

Discussion Questions:

1. What are Robert's options?
2. What professional harm could Robert face in this situation?
3. If money has been misallocated, what are the consequences of that misallocation?
4. What institutional forces could have led to this situation?
5. What obligations does the NFP have to its donors, and what are the consequences of failing to uphold those obligations?

The Possessive Major Gifts Officer

"One day you're a hero, and the next day it's 'What have you done for me lately?'" Marjorie stated in exasperation. Marjorie had taken over as the Major Gifts Officer and director of the Institutional Advancement Department of her NFP seven years ago. Back then the department was in disarray. The staff, Marjorie would characterize it later on, were "idiots." The largest gift that she could find on record from a private donor back then was an unsolicited

$10,000 check from a local business. That had happened ten years before that and people were still talking about it. But $10,000 doesn't go very far when you're running a homeless shelter in the inner city. That amount could easily be spent on one client in one week.

Her efforts since then, made possible by carte blanch permission from the president, were both herculean and effective. They were also controversial. The first controversy was her decision to move into the ground-floor office space. That space had been used by staff for meetings and for clients for informal gatherings in the evenings. Marjorie was convinced that a well-appointed conference room was a necessary key to impressing would-be donors with the high degree of professionalism they offered. While staff hadn't had meaningful raises in at least a decade, she found a way to spend $50,000 on the renovation of office space and a conference room. This included locks on all the doors, the keys for which only she possessed. Even the president wouldn't have had access to those rooms.

Then came the creation of a new entryway in the back alley for the clients. That entryway subsequently became the entry for both clients and for staff. Marjorie believed that the donors to the mission did not feel safe entering the same doorway as the clients and that it was essential that they felt that the mission they were running was both safe and welcoming. "They don't give if they're scared shitless!" she once screamed at an objecting program officer. So while the executive staff and donors entered via the slick front entryway off the street, all others were required to use the alleyway entrance.

Significant gifts started to materialize approximately three years after Marjorie took the helm. First was the donation from a local businessman for $100,000. Then another similar gift. That caught the attention of others in the same peer group as those initial donors and their friends collectively engaged in a veritable bidding war for privileged status at the Homeless Shelter Annual Gala. The winner of that bidding war was "Mamette."

Mamette was the last living heir to a considerable old-money fortune. Gaining the fortune via her marriage to her now deceased husband, Mamette decided that she would do her best to "give back to the community" as best as she could. Marjorie was in a position to provide just such an opportunity.

Mamette's first gift was $500,000. Marjorie ensured that the gift was put 100% to operations. This pleased Mamette who felt confident that she could trust Marjorie to be a principled steward of her gifts. Nothing would be "wasted" on administrative overhead.

"You ARE a hero, Marjorie. You've done so much for us lately, and in the past, and I'm sure in the future. It's not that we're not thankful for your service." Said Mike, the CEO of the mission. "It's just that we need to do something more than spend the dollars coming in the front door. Have you considered setting aside 10% of all donations for an endowment? Because Mamette and her friends aren't getting any younger."

"Not going to work for us, Mike." Marjorie said abruptly.

Mike kept waiting for the "but" at the end of that sentence. Apparently a "but" wasn't going to work for Marjorie.

"There's real risk here, Marjorie. The programs we run are now dependent upon those donation dollars. If those dollars dry up, and they definitely will one day, all of the things that we have created here would be in serious jeopardy."

"Mammette gives to operations. Period." Marjorie stated, again offering no polite modifier.

"How about this," Mike said. "Why don't I meet with Mamette and talk to her about the durability of her philanthropy with us. I can show her how her gifts can be used for good deeds well beyond her lifetime. She can meet the clients and hear their stories. She can go in the back rooms and see how we operate."

"No way in hell!" Marjorie curtly interrupted Mike. "No one meets with Mamette without me present, and no one pitches ideas at her without my signing off. It would be disaster if she mixed with the clients and probably even worse if our staff tried to carry a conversation with her. This is a woman who grew up in Paris's first *arrondissionement*. She bought her perfume at Chanel in Paris at the *place vendôme*. The most culture our staff understand is whatever it is they streamed on Netflix last night or whatever idiotic superhero movie is playing right now. She reads Balzac in the original French and our staff don't read at all! She's not meeting the staff. Or the clients. Or anyone without going through me first. You and I agreed that I get to run my show the way that I want. That's the deal we struck five years ago. *MIKE*."

Discussion Questions:

1. Who is responsible for fundraising strategy at a healthy NFP?
2. What are the institutional risks posed by Marjorie's posturing?
3. Has the major gifts officer gained unhealthy power at the NFP? And if it is unhealthy, then why wasn't the issue addressed earlier?
4. What are the ways that Mike can respond to this situation?
5. Do you believe that the donor is being treated fairly?

When Personal Problems Threaten the Mission

There was never any question that Alan had what it took to do the job. You and your peers on the board of directors had enthusiastically selected him as the next president of your medical prosthesis NFP because of his unique set of skills. Having served first as a professional in the medical field then as owner of his own medical prosthesis firm, Alex understood the market dynamics, its regulatory environment and understood where philanthropy should be best targeted. This knowledge translated to a set of noteworthy wins over the first four years of his tenure with you. It probably didn't hurt that his large nest egg resulting from the sale of his business meant that he didn't need the small salary you offered him.

Starting about a year and a half ago you noticed Alan's demeanor change. He did not deal well with what he called "criticism" at board meetings. Confiding in you, he revealed his dislike of one board member—a member whom you happened to not like too well either. You offered him some advice on how to deal with it and resolved to keep a more watchful eye on the situation.

Then there was the board meeting last quarter. Alan ended the meeting halfway through the agenda and left the room. You couldn't make out what triggered such a response. Board members were debating the business of the day. But the tenor of the debate wasn't unusually hostile or contentious.

A week later you received a phone call from a former board member expressing worry for Alan and Ellen, Alan's wife. You learn from the former board member that Ellen has been suffering from mental illness for many years and that police have been at Alan's house on many occasions over the past year. Apparently, Ellen has been involuntarily committed to mental institutions throughout her life and the situation has worsened.

Then began to roll in several senior staff departures from the NFP. You wonder whether it is related to Alan's recent behavior. You do your best to make sure that Alan manages his staff at his sole direction and have never thought of intruding. But this hasn't prevented you from getting to know those staff members personally. They were good people with the skills relevant to the mission and they appeared to be enthusiastically committed to the mission. They had demonstrated professionalism and ability, and you and the board had high regard for them.

You stop for a moment and wonder what to do. Your first call is to the chair of the board, a colleague named Dawn whom you have known for many years.

"Are you aware of the departures from the organization?" you ask Dawn.

"I am." Says Dawn.

"Do you think that their departures are a problem…or a sign of problems?" you ask.

"It's hard to say," Dawn answers with concern in her voice. "A problem we have and will always have is that the people who work here have the kinds of skills that would land them great jobs in the private sector. It's not at all unlikely that they all happened to have found careers elsewhere."

"At the same time. All within six months of each other?"

"Right" Dawn concludes. Resuming the conversation, she adds "How would you characterize Alan's leadership lately?"

"So I see that you and I have been wondering the same thing. Yes, I've noticed a difference. And I think it is related to problems that he is having at home. His wife is not well." After a pause, you add "Look, I think that Alan is great. We're lucky to have him. But our duty is to protect the institution, not the institution's CEO. So if possible, what I want to do is to find a way to make sure the ship is stable and to make sure, if at all possible, that we help Alan."

"I'm listening," Dawn states intently.

"Well, I see two possible disasters looming. The first is that if he elects to take family medical leave then we are left with an operation with no chief executive. That can't happen."

"But officially," Dawn states, "We permit all of our employees to avail themselves of any federal provisions needed by the employee, without exception."

"Right. Officially. Another option is that we do nothing and hope that things get better. I can't say with certainty that this will or will not work. I haven't pried into his life and have no intention to."

"I hear you," Dawn says, "But my track record of 'waiting until things get better' isn't that good. So let me offer you another option. Why can't we appoint the CFO the temporary director, placing Alan on leave while he works on issues in his personal life?"

"That would be an aggressive move," you state, pausing to consider the waves this would cause in the institution. "We would have to be very careful *how* we do that. As you state, our obligation is to protect the institution."

Discussion Questions:

1. What are the obligations must the board meet in this situation?
2. If forced to choose, what does a board elect to protect: the institution or its executives?

3. Is it appropriate for board members to interview staff members in this case?
4. What are the first steps that the board should take?
5. If a leave of absence is arranged, what is the right way to go about doing this?
6. Is the private life of the CEO a board matter?

References

Boardsource. (2010). *The Handbook of Nonprofit Governance.* San Francisco: Jossey-Bass.

Ciconte, B. L., & Jacob, J. (2009). *Fundraising Basics: A Complete Guide* (2nd ed.). Burlington, VT: Jones and Bartlett Learning.

Harpool, D. (1996, Fall). The Sibley Hospital Case: Trustees and Their Loyalty to the Institution. *Journal of College and University Law, 23*(2), 255–283.

Worth, M. J. (2020). *Nonprofit Management: Principles and Practice* (Vol. 6). Los Angeles, CA: CQ Press.

Moral Dilemmas in Executive Leadership

Few aphorisms are more true in the NGO and NFP world than the one that exclaims that "it's lonely at the top." Executive leadership is accountable for every decision handed to them by the board and at the same time has a responsibility toward all of the staff of the organization as well as to those that they serve. This is no small feat.

NFP and NGO leaders face a panorama of moral difficulties that to their for-profit counterparts would never dream of encountering. A widget manufacturer does not have to think about the moral consequence of legal custody over its employees, but the NFP CEO running an employment center for persons with disabilities does. The manufacturer of legal notepads definitely needs to ensure its business model is successful, that it treats its employees fairly, etc. But they're never accountable for what ends up being written on their notepads. Compare this to the moral hazards of community counseling centers.

Neither will this situation ever change. Typically, NFPs and NGOs are created for reasons rooted in moral or cultural values, not technology or merchandisable products. This is not to imply that a for-profit entity offers nothing of value. But, rather, it is the case that executives, staff and boards tend to become involved in an NFP or NGO because of values-based commitments. And values are messy things to deal with.

Whereas there are learnable, validated techniques when it comes to mixing chemicals or sanding plywood, no such science exists when it comes to

© The Author(s), under exclusive license to Springer Nature
Switzerland AG 2023
C. Hanson, *An Introduction to Ethics for Nonprofits and NGOs*,
https://doi.org/10.1007/978-3-031-23077-6_4

human values. It is not possible to learn enough about ethics to be prepared for every scenario that will be thrown your way.

A vignette that I still think about from time to time occurred one day when I was in the office of a Manhattan-based CEO of a major pharmaceutical corporation. He had just been delivered a letter from a doctor in sub-Saharan Africa begging his company to stop sending anti-diarrhea medicine to his village. Apparently, locals thought that if one pill was good then twenty would be twenty times better. The consequence of this over-medication was lethal. Children who were once at risk of death from diarrhea were now dying more quickly from overdoses of anti-diuretics. Does he stop sending the medication knowing that children will die of dehydration, or does he continue sending it knowing that they will die of obstructed bowels? He turned to me and said "they don't tell you how to deal with this kind of letter in Business School."

He was right. They don't. But it is equally important to note that it's not possible to teach anyone how to deal with all possible letters from foreign physicians. Or all possible situations that could be thrown one's way. The best thing that executive leadership can do to hedge against the moral uncertainty and disasters that *will invariably happen* is to prepare as much as possible in advance of the storm.

It is worth surveying the literature at this point in an attempt to understand the unique nature of an NFP or NGO leader. What are such a person's job duties and what makes them effective or ineffective? I count several hundred answers to these two questions in the research literature. But Worth (2020) has condensed them into a short, uncontroversial list. Addressing the attributes of the effective leader he states that such a leader:

1. focuses on Mission
2. focuses on the Board
3. focuses on external relationships
4. shares leadership and empowers others
5. focuses on key roles and priorities
6. uses the "political frame"
7. Is the right person in the right place at the right time. (Worth, 2020)

This list is a tall order. I call special attention to item number seven of the list. One of the most difficult transitions an NFP can make is a change in NFP leadership. This is all the more difficult when the leadership transitioning out of power exercised their leadership via what is sometimes referred to as a "charismatic leadership" model. Readers interested in the nature of this form of leadership would be well-served reviewing Aviolo and Yammarino

(2013) who have provided one of the best texts on this unique issue. They point out that leaders who employ a Charismatic model can make much headway while simultaneously paying a price. Such leaders blur the lines between themselves and their institution, sometimes with great effect, sometimes not (Avolio & Yammarino, 2013). This combined with the fact that in NFP and NGO leadership fundraising can be rooted as much in a person as a mission can cause great problems for an institution should the day arise that a scandal occurs at the top.

This is especially pernicious for the faith-based NGO or NFP. Churches can be strongly identified with their clergy. International relief agencies are strongly identified with their CEOs some of whom may have descended from religion's equivalent of royalty. Boards must have the courage to ask whether, as charismatic as their leader may be, right now is the right time to have such a person remain in their position.

Returning back to the perspective of the executive leaders themselves, I offer some rules of thumb which may aid in the avoidance of or resolution to difficult moral problems which will inevitably befall your institution.

The first and most important thing the leader must do is to vet the integrity of the board that is hiring them. Do you trust their *values*? If you don't then run, don't walk. Imagine what decision-making will be like when a crisis strikes your institution. A board member that is a financially generous philanderer might come off as dislikable-but-useful in the best of times. But how will that change when you must deal with allegations of sexual harassment?

The second thing that an executive must do is to apply the same test to the other executive staff. The executive definitely needs performers and producers. But I have seen few larger threats to the NFP and NGO's continued existence than a moral disaster. Your NFP can recover from trojan horse attacks on your accounting software, but you might not be able to recover if local media uncovers embezzlement on the part of your accountant.

Selecting your executive staff is important in other ways. Ensure that your staff is capable of *seeing* problems before they arise. Make sure that there is gender, ethnic and religious diversity. Having that kind of diversity makes for a team with as few blinders as possible. Furthermore, think about the kinds of clients you serve and ask whether it is possible to have an executive team who has themselves dealt with similar issues. If you serve urban youth, for example, do you have any urban-area residents on your team? If you serve foster children, have any of your team ever fostered kids themselves? And do the profiles of your donors reflect the same commitment to diversity, equity and inclusion (DEI) that your programs do?

Another important element of moral leadership is to be well-read. Being a well-read individual has proven for millennia to be a game-changer for leadership. It matters less *what* is read than it does *whether one reads*. The ancient Greek philosopher Aristotle was the first to point out the truth that reading helps to teach moral lessons in ways that would be too costly to learn through experience. Some of life's greatest lessons aren't so much taught in schools as they are illustrated in works of fiction or history. If the only break you ever get from work is an entertainment news show or streaming sitcoms, you are loosing the opportunity to be better at what you do than you currently are. If the call to enlightened leadership is real, and I think it is, then it is time to experience some enlightenment.

Finally, by way of a practical institutional tip, make sure that you place ethics into your institution in methodical ways. When you have an executive team meeting discuss an ethics case from this book. When you do staff development exercises find a way to get them talking about a complex issue. Not only does this increase awareness of the importance of ethics, but as an added bonus it is a marvelous team-building exercise. One learns a lot of surprising things about one's colleagues when talk turns to values.

Meltdown in Monrovia

You are the national leader of an educational NGO based in Monrovia, Liberia. The services that you provide focus on primary school education for boys and girls. The model that you use is to send small teams of education coaches to cities throughout the nation. Those teams are equipped with a variety of supplies: materials to train teachers, classroom supplies, and a variety of telecom and medical supplies to facilitate the daily activity of your teams.

You are proud of the high-quality training that each of those teams received in Virginia during a crash-course in educational practice prior to their departure. While back home teams learned in 8 weeks how to use a variety of educational tools which have proven to be crucial in the successes of the American system and you feel confident that those who successfully completed that training will be able to disseminate that information to Liberians.

As a part of your job duties in Monrovia you receive reports from team leaders. Those reports contain a information essential to tracking and managing the resources allocated to you: several important data points ranging from community baseline data to numbers of children served over time and some educational outcomes. They also contain employee performance review material.

The data regarding your programming, with some exception, looks good. But you are drawn to the employee performance review data. Of note you read the file of "Christine" who is stationed at a southern coastal town across the border from the Ivory Coast. Initial reviews from a year ago seem to indicate that Christine was reserved and withdrawn yet happy to work on the initiative. Her classroom numbers and teacher preparation numbers look good.

You also note that about six months ago her supervisor stated that she reported late to her assigned school on several occasions and that recently she had been spotted at a local nightclub late in the evenings with a group of Liberian men. You pick up the phone to call Christine's supervisor.

"Hi, Laura. I'm reading your files and have a few questions about Christine. Do you have the time to talk?" you ask.

Laura responds nonchalantly "Christine? Well, I really don't know about her. She's doing the work, which is all I really care about. If you want to talk to her directly, I suppose you could call the Ghanan consulate down here. She's been hanging out there a lot."

"Does that worry you?" you ask, knowing that foreign relations have nothing to do with her primary job responsibilities.

"Not really," Laura answers, "What she does on her own time isn't my business. She's getting the work done. Mostly. That's all I really care about."

"Do you have any concerns about her welfare?" you ask.

"I really haven't thought about it." Laura responds. "We are working on the project, and what I expect of her are the reports that she has been compiling. Beyond that it's not my business. Who cares if she's messing around with Ghanan diplomats. Or whomever it is she meets at that club she visits."

"What do you mean by that?" you ask, trying to hide the concerns creeping into your mind.

"Oh, yea. Apparently she's quite the partier over there. She likes to hang out at the disco on the beach and drink the night away with the guys. Whatever. Not my business."

Questions for Discussion:

1. Is there any reason to be concerned with Christine's welfare? What further investigation should be conducted, if any?
2. Do the power-dynamics of romantic relationships change in foreign nations? Are sexual ethics different?

3. Is it appropriate to extend special welfare concern to women working abroad when compared to men, and is this a case in which gender roles influence the level of concern for the country director?
4. To what extent do program directors have an obligation to care for the emotional welfare of their staff?

Cutting Vital Services

From birth through the age of 21 services to persons with disabilities are typically handled by the public school system, whether through adapted classrooms in traditional schools or via services at charter schools specially geared toward the needs of persons with disabilities. But after the age of 21 when such persons "age out of the system" services availability is significantly reduced. Adults with disabilities who are lucky enough to have family members monitoring their needs might find themselves on a waiting list for services at a local not-for-profit. Those who are less fortunate face a much more dire circumstance which often leads to homelessness and indigence. This is not to mention the epidemic of sexual violence against the intellectually disabled (rates of violence against intellectually disabled men are 700% higher than the national average, and 1200% higher for women).

You are the CEO of an NFP that provides services to adults with disabilities. You serve approximately 500 such adults daily. There is no one single profile of your client. Some are the children of parents who are still living and who advocate for their needs. But others under your care arrive at your group homes as wards of the state and over whom your organization now has full custody.

Your organization was established in the 1970s when reimbursements from the state constituted 100% of your budget. But over the years not only have state dollars not increased, they have decreased. You note, for example, that 20 years ago the state reimbursed $12/hour per client for services in one of your programs but that today that number is only $8. This financial decrease shows in your facilities, employee compensation and programming. This financial picture is not helped by the fact that the state has legislated ratios of staff-per-client which prohibit cost savings by cutting staff.

You have no endowment. You do, however, have several parcels of land which were given to you by a donor at some point in the past. Those parcels are connected to your current property, but are not being used.

Fifteen years ago you invented a jobs program, aided by a minimum wage waiver, which services contracts to several local big-box retailers. You package cotton candy sold at the check-out aisle of a local grocery store, package honey for a local business and collate products for an events company. This infusion of cash has proven vital for your NFP. But now even that is proving to not be enough. Your facilities director informs you that the group homes need new air conditioners. Your cook staff reports that you likely will not meet inspection the next time the county drops in. You are told by your program administrators that the average amount of time direct services staff remain at your institution is 18 months.

You therefore engage in a financial study of your NFP's programs. You discover that one program which serves the needs of the most profoundly disabled is a significant culprit in your financial woes. State guidelines permit only two clients per employee in this program. But the state reimbursement for that client does not approach 50% of the employee wage, much less institutional overhead. That program services the needs of 14 adult clients with 28 corresponding staff. The program has a staff salaries budget of $1.8 million and draws in $500k in state revenue.

You understand what cutting this program means to the clients and their families. Clients with such profound disabilities have limited options. They will never work and need aid with the most basic of daily functions. Their families have correspondingly few options as well. Without these services at least one family member will have to be unemployed so as to aid the disabled family member. That, or they would have to finance private care which can easily cost $150k per year. This is not possible for most of the families of your clients.

You investigate lines of credit to make payroll. You investigate selling assets. You investigate renting space. But you wonder whether anything short of eliminating this program will help right the ship.

Before bringing your fears to the board you gather your executive team together and lay out the picture as you see it.

"What I want from you, from *us*, are solutions. At best, by selling assets, we will be able to hang on for three more years."

"We *cannot* close that program," Mitch, your VP for programs states. "Doing that would doom all of those families. It would be a complete catastrophe for them. All of them, and I mean *all of them* will go bankrupt. They all lose their houses, they all lose their life savings, they all lose everything."

"Right," Says your CFO, "But if we don't close that program then *every family at this facility loses their services in three years!* Where do we get off playing god and telling *all* the families that they lose just because we're not willing to tell some of them that they lose?"

"We're not the bad guys here," Lydia says, butting into the conversation. Lydia, VP for development has kept a keen eye upon financial needs given her requirement to engage in fundraising. "The state is the bad guy here. No one ever held their feet to the fire and they discovered that if they slashed the budgets to people with Downe Syndrome there would be no public outcry. I'd like to see them try to do that to other marginalized and disenfranchised groups. There'd be riots."

"Then let me be provocative," you add. "Why can't it be said that we're at fault? I've been looking over these books for months now. What I see is that for the past forty years no one has ever thought of pivoting. Or doing anything different at all. We've just done the same thing over and over. Everyone in leadership for decades simply held the course and did what their predecessors did. And here we are now."

After a moment of silence, you turn to Lydia. "Now, Lydia, I know that money doesn't grow on trees. That and people don't give to institutions that *have* needs. They give to institutions that *meet* needs. Give me your best case scenario. What would it take to see significant forward progress in fundraising revenue?"

"In short," Lydia states, "It will take about five years and a lot of work. Here's a rule of thumb: The larger the gift, the longer it takes. Neither I nor any other professional in the world is going to get a million-dollar gift this month just because we discovered that we need it. That said, I'd love to take on the challenge and to build the kind of ship that would attract those gifts. *That's what I do.* But we need to build that ship."

"And grants?" you ask.

Your CFO jumps in. "Grants tend to be for programs and usually exclude administration expenses. If we accounted for grants revenue the way that the grantors demanded, then the more grants we took in, the worse off we'd be."

"How so?" you ask.

"This happens because granting entities like starting new things, not funding old things. They like startup, not operations. And even with startup, there are things that they pay for and things that they don't pay for. They will pay for a new piece of technology we propose to use, but not for the person that operates it. Or they might pay for the person that operates it but not for the electricity bill. I estimate that our activities require somewhere between a 17% and a 25% administrative cost rate just to keep operations going. So the larger the grant, the larger the cost-rate gap we have to fill. Hypothetically, if we were to get a million-dollar gift, that million dollars could cost us $170,000 to implement. If we received a $10 million grant, that would put us in the hook for $1.7 million. Conservatively."

"And are there ways around this?" you ask, looking at your development director.

"Maybe. Of varying ethical levels of propriety," She says. "One way is to get two grants for every one program. Following the analogy just cited, we get one grant that pays for the technology but not the technician. Then another for the technician but not the technology. On each of those two budget proposals we list the portion paid for by the other grant as an expense we contribute to the project ourselves. That, or if not two grants, then two different funding mechanisms, the revenue from the one is accounted for as the institutional contribution on the other and vice versa."

"And that's OK to do?" you ask.

"Well...It's what's done. But before you get excited, I would like to point out that even if we come up with a plan that allegedly works, there are still drawbacks."

"Like what?" you ask.

"Like the fact that we have to keep the plates spinning. We won't recruit very good employees for programs if we tell them they have no guarantee of a job 12 months from now when the money runs out. Therefore we would need to create a lot of grant submissions, all at once, then in perpetuity. It can never stop since our client's needs never stop. And even if this plan is successful we wouldn't see a dime, I estimate, for at least 18 months."

"Or," you say, "We can just cut the program."

Discussion Questions:
1. Do you cut the program?
2. What options are there if you do not cut the program?
3. How could this situation have been avoided?
4. Would selling assets solve the underlying problem?
5. What is a development strategy, and how would such a strategy help to have avoided this situation?
6. Is the Development Officer's proposal to depict one grant's revenue as an institutional contribution to another grant application an instance of unethical behavior?

Changing Staff's Job Descriptions

"The secularization of the west has caused a tsunami of change in religiously oriented NGOs, including ours," President Steele said to the board. "It has been well-documented that the bedrock of philanthropy doesn't have nearly as much to do with political orientation as it does with religious orientation. A feature of western societies, which may not be much more than a quirk, is that secularists tend to see government as the primary vehicle of change while the religious do not. This translates to a lot of real-world consequences for us and others. We are a Christian refugee ministry, not USAID. Our donors give to us because of our sectarian emphasis."

President Steele looked across the boardroom to see nodding heads of approval.

"But the storm is getting worse, and the time to act is now. The first thing that we must recognize is that none of us are getting any younger."

This led to chuckles throughout the room. It was an often-repeated joke that this board, many of whom had been associated with this faith-based NGO for decades, was dominated by those well into retirement age.

"What gave it away?" said Myrtle, "Was it the blue hair?" she said with her characteristic self-deprecating humor.

"We have expended considerable resources to increase our donated dollars over the past five years," Mike continued. "There were some small successes, but from where I sit we haven't seen the forward progress from those initiatives that we should have. More often than not we're just fishing from the same pond." Mike could survey several nodding heads of agreement.

"So I want to explore another avenue of attack," Mike said. "I want to maintain the status quo with our fundraising activities on assumption that they will consistently decrease. In the future this may require cuts to that arm of our operation. So be it. But I want to respond to those anticipated losses with the creation of partnerships. On the one hand, I want to seek partner status with the federal government's United States Agency For International Development (USAID). They have a three billion dollar annual operating budget and keep giving to the same beltway bandits every year. But their office of faith and religious life consistently fails to find good candidates for funding. Invariably they turn to the usual suspects."

There was a murmur in the room at the suggestion. Many of the board had a principled stand against accepting federal dollars, fearing the mixing of government and faith.

"We don't do that, President Steele" one principled board member objected.

"I propose we debate the issue. But not before I finish. I recognize that I serve at your pleasure, not mine. But I do point out that this resistance to federal dollars isn't rooted in anything written into our faith. Our faith was founded well before the federal government of the United States even existed. Our resistance is a vestige of the Anabaptist tradition in our country. Those

Anabaptists arrived on our shores having fled government persecution. They were right to have their anti-government attitude. But our circumstances aren't theirs. Times change."

Mike could sense that there was uneasiness among his board. But he pressed on.

"And as a secondary measure, we need to avail ourselves more directly of the Christian and non-sectarian business community. For example, we spend about $1000 per family per month in some of our camps. For that money we get ground staff to acquire and distribute food aid, offer healthcare and provide other services. We need to think about linking with private businesses, pivoting from emergency aid and adopting a business-creation model. For example, the camps in Northern Uganda early on housed at most 100,000 people when we started operations there, but today have many millions of refugees. That's no longer a camp. It's a city. I propose we approach American businesses and pitch the creation of businesses, under our direction, to employ the refugees. Whether we work with their executive staff or Corporate Social Responsibility (CSR) offices will probably depend on the business. But what I am convinced of is that we need to get out of the operational expense nightmare of emergency aid."

The board went on to debate this idea in both this and in several subsequent meetings. But what began as a pie-in-the-sky idea started to look more real as time went on. Letters of support from American corporations came in, commitments from the "Business as Mission" crowd soon followed. And soon enough, it started to look like the idea had real legs.

After one board meeting, President Steele was discussing progress on the idea with his cabinet. The East African Region leader spoke up.

"Consider, President Steele, the following problem. I have in my hand the resume of our Uganda Operations officer. He has performed admirably. He has been in Arua for the past nine years with his family and is a reliable operational presence. There's not a single black mark in his file, and in every way that we have measured him he excels. He has an M.Div degree from Denver Seminary with an emphasis in Cross-Cultural studies. He has never started a business or run a business. He has never written, administered or tracked a federal grant. In fact, he has never entertained the possibility that we would ask him to do any of these things. We didn't hire him for that or train him for that. I'm confident that he can do the job he is doing right now. But do you really think that he, or any of the rest of us for that matter, can take on what amounts to a completely different job? Moreover, would that be a fair thing to ask of our employees?"

"I have some concerns too," said the Southern Africa director. "Our staff has been trained, indeed *selected* because of their commitment to and alignment with our current faith-based mission. I'm trying to understand how they would respond when they find out that in a board room 5000 kilometers away everyone decided that they need to stop everything they are doing and start a fast-food franchise instead. And knowing their economic situations, they might feel compelled to accept even though they might not be any good at it."

Discussion Questions:

1. When are mission shifts justified?
2. Why are some protestant Christian faith-based NFPs and NGOs reticent to participate in federal programs?
3. What obligations do NGOs or NFPs have toward their staff when the mission shifts?
4. How can NFPs and NGOs make changes of direction internally easier?
5. Should the NGO consider closing its doors?

Child Sponsorship in the Afterschool Program

Running a nonprofit is, to put matters mildly, a difficult business. Like any other legal entity there needs to be a revenue stream. But unlike a "widget" manufacturer, nonprofits tend to receive that revenue from activities which cant easily be "scaled." The growth that a for-profit business might be able to pull off with a simple savings account and ten years of time could take an equivalent nonprofit fifty years.

Pierre's afterschool program is just such a nonprofit. By all accounts he is successful, impactful and effective. He attends to the needs of the many new Haitian Immigrant children that are in his community, and their parents know, love and respect him for that. He and his staff are all either recent immigrants from Haiti or are the children of those immigrants.

His staff works in harmony with one another and he has very few management problems. His most pressing problem is financial. His primary revenue source—state dollars allocated for programs like his—is decreasing.

During an executive team meeting Pierre discusses the problem and the group spitballs ideas. Lots of them were great: seek corporate donations, foundation grants, alliances with churches, and other fundraising activities. It doesn't escape Pierre that all of those ideas would constitute additional job duties for him personally. But he listens anyway.

Jean, the program director, speaks up. He mentions that back in Haiti he ran a program with an American NGO that sponsored individual students. The donor was paired with a student in the school and was given the student's name and a photograph. This created a pen-pal relationship in which the student wrote letters to the donor and the donor was able to respond. That created a human connection that wouldn't have otherwise existed and proved to be instrumental in paying school fees and uniform fees.

The team spoke favorably of this idea. But Pierre was worried. He, too, knew about such programs. But he always uncomfortable with them. The organizational demands aside, he worried about commoditizing his students. He worried about giving donors access to privileged information (their names and photographs). He worried about the potential response of would-be private donors who themselves might not be comfortable with it. While not technically an accredited school, he always assumed that federal rules of privacy that universally apply in public schools applied to the kids in his program as well. Would creating a child-sponsorship program be an instance of child exploitation?

"So you would rather that the school close and these kids have nowhere to go?" Jacques stated to Pierre as Pierre raised his concerns.

"No, obviously not."

"Really?" says Jacques. "Because it looks to me that what we have here are the same difficulties but in a different place."

Sandrine, the child of immigrant parents but born and raised in the United States, speaks up. "I know that this is not popular, but I'll say it anyway. We scrape and save a lot of money every year to send back to Haiti. It's what, 20% of our budget? We're not a church. We're a school. And we have needs. Why can't we use those funds to support our school rather than just send them off to Haiti every month? Changing just this one practice would be more than enough to address our shortfall."

Jacques interrupts again "That is totally out of the question. Maybe you are used to life here where everything is so much easier. But we haven't forgotten our roots. We always send money back to Jacmel. Always!"

Thierry, the facilities manager, speaks up. "We could defer maintenance. A lot of the things on my list require purchases. If we don't make those purchases, then that would be a lot of money saved. And it would give me more to do around here keeping this place running!"

"What is on your list, Thierry?", Pierre asks

"Well, we have a broken toilet, there is a leak from the air conditioner in the back office, there's the peeling laminate in the teacher's bathroom. We will need a new flat roof on the back of the building within five years. The list goes on and on."

Pierre worries that if those items aren't addressed there could be problems with their occupancy permit. But the fact is that they need money today, not whenever the inspector comes.

Discussion Questions:
1. What are the moral challenges associated with child-sponsorship initiatives?
2. Are the children being commoditized in sponsorship initiatives?
3. Does a sponsorship program violate the privacy of student records? What cultural problems are posed by cutting the 20% donation earmarked for Haiti?
4. How do the experiences of immigrants differ from the first to the second generation in the United States? Does a first generation nonprofit worker make different decisions than an second or third generation nonprofit worker?

Accepting Crypto Donations

Your spam filter is pretty good. So the fact that it landed in your inbox meant that the message was probably written to you by an actual person. The content, however, raised flags.

A month ago you convinced your leadership to modify your webpage statement regarding donations to include the fact that you accept Crypto donations at your NFP. At the time this language inclusion was a minor point of curiosity in the meeting agenda. But the email message you just received meant that you had to decide whether you meant it.

"Dear Sir or Madam," the message stated, "We represent a group of crypto investors who have collected the proceeds of the estate of Ferdinand and Amelda Marcos. Pursuant to the law of the Philippines, 20% of this estate must be used to create endowments in nonprofit institutions. We are writing to you to inform you that we have selected your institution for this honor. Your commitment to providing for the medical needs of the poor is noble, and we have helped to create endowments at no less than 100 such not-for-profits worldwide. We would like to invite you to speak with us about this possibility at your earliest convenience."

Stories of unjustly deposed Nigerian Kings enter your mind as you read these words. But a lot of things about this email pique your interest. There were no attachments, no redirect links. The message seems to have been written directly to you by someone who knew what you did. Maybe it was a bad decision, but you respond back telling them that you would be willing to have a virtual meeting with them.

During that online meeting you were greeted by six Filipino-looking men, well dressed and in a highly professional office setting, who explain to you their investment model. They state to you that they have been given controlling interest over a portion of the estate of the Marcos family and have elected to invest that estate into Crypto Markets. Their gains on that estate had been strong, but their mandate to invest in nonprofits was proving difficult.

"We don't have a lot of stable nonprofits here in the Philippines," one man states to you. "Not like in the US."

"Then why don't you form one in the Philippines?" you ask with skepticism.

"We're financiers, not philanthropists." One of them responds.

"Well, you need to know that our Crypto Policy is to convert the cash to USD as soon as we take possession of it. We don't keep Crypto endowments *per se*."

This caused the Philippines to pause for a moment. Then one of them added "We might be able to work with that. But the terms that we would have under such circumstances is that you incur a 20% liability to us after the cash conversion, payable in USD."

Discussion Questions:

1. What are the potential liabilities to accepting Crypto donations?
2. The IRS treats crypto currency as property (which must be declared upon taking possession). How does this matter to the NFP?
3. Do you accept the donation?
4. What red flags are present in this conversation?
5. Should NFPs accept crypto donations, and what should the rules for those donations be? What special policy or staffing guidelines must be observed?

The White Savior in the Dark Continent

Your NGO that provides medical services in sub-Saharan Africa is heavily reliant upon donations to pay its bills. Those donations come from a variety of places. Professional societies and private foundations contribute an important portion of your revenue, but nothing compares to the contributions you receive from individuals.

An important tool you implement for solicitation of donations from private individuals is your year-end mailer. You invest heavily in it. You have purchased an address list from a professional medical association and send out approximately 50,000 solicitations at the end of November each year. The committee that creates that solicitation works for at least six months to craft it, drawing upon the archives of the year's on-the-ground photography and cold-hard data about the effectiveness of your work.

It is late November and your head of PR enters your office beaming "Here it is!" she says. She takes a seat and hands you the galley proof of the one-pager mailer.

On first glance it looks to be formatted in more or less the same way that many of your previous mailers had been formatted. The tri-fold brochure invariably had a quintessential image on the front, a description of your services behind it and the fundraising pitch at the end.

But something bothered you about the image this year. You recognize where it was taken—you had been there many times. It was at a clinic that you had started this past year in a rural African village. And it appeared to be in the examination room of the clinic. Depicted was a middle-aged African woman on her knees with her hands outstretched to the heavens, eyes closed and tears flowing down her cheeks. A child, probably hers, was clutching her leg and peering up at one of your hospital staff who was standing in front of the woman. That hospital staff member, a white westerner, was reaching out her hand to touch the kneeling woman on the head. It appeared as if the westerner was praying for the African woman as the wary child looked on. A dramatic shaft of light was beaming in through the open window illuminating the otherwise dark scene with its rays.

"Are you aware of the phrase '*the dark continent*'?" you ask your PR director.

"No, not really"

"It's a phrase that was used commonly in the colonial era. It was a term that was used to refer to Africa."

You see a look of puzzlement on her face and are not surprised to see that she hadn't heard the term and wasn't aware of its pejorative nature. So you continue.

"An idea much discussed and much written about when the western powers carved up Africa into what it looks like today was that of the enlightened west 'saving' hapless Africa with the might of its technology and beneficence. Authors described the whole of the continent as 'dark' to which we, the white westerners were to shed light."

You see the wheels beginning to work in your PR director's head.

"So while I cannot deny that it's a beautiful picture – heck, it's probably perfect on pure compositional grounds – I'm concerned that we are giving in to certain unhealthy cultural attitudes rather than eradicating them."

"To be honest with you, I'm not quite sure what to say," says your PR director. "Of all the images available to us, none of the others were even close. This image perfectly captures a motto that I've been training our staff to look for in our imagery. 'Us together with them.' And that's what the picture shows. It shows us arriving to Africa to be together with them."

Sensing that you are not convinced, she adds "Our donors give because they want to be the hero. They want to be the nurse in the picture. We are offering them that opportunity."

"I get that. But is it OK to convince people to give when their reasons for doing so might embody racially prejudicial ideas? Remember that once we release an image, we own it. All of it."

"Honestly," the PR director states, "Wasn't that always true? Last year and the year before? This never bothered us in the past. Why all of the sudden now?"

Discussion Questions:

1. Fundraising oftentimes creates "pitches" which position the would-be donor to become the hero of a story. What cultural attitudes are embodied in this common practice?
2. The term "development porn" is a pejorative term that is used by some professionals to refer to the use of suffering as a means of acquiring pleasure. That pleasure might be donor satisfaction or NGO revenue. Is this mailer an instance of development porn?
3. Do NGOs stand guilty of commoditizing suffering, and do donors stand guilty of colonialism?

Internship or Exploitation?

You are the new internship coordinator for an internationally known NGO in the faith-based sector working on areas of social justice policy. You understand that international NGOs, like the entire NGO and NFP sector, are subject to fads and popularity. In one generation primary education of impoverished children might be the *cause du jour*, in another the treatment of persons with AIDS, but in another it could be rural healthcare. You're just glad to be on the cresting wave of the current fads. As young people increasingly are attracted to issues of social justice and inclusivity you find yourself in the enviable position of having more high-quality internship applications than there are positions for those interns. They are college-educated, healthy, energetic, and eager volunteers willing to take a risk on something new.

Routinely making personal contact with prospective volunteers, you find that there are a number of questions about the internship experience that are asked with frequency. But you are unhappy with the quality of the answers you have been giving to those questions. You collect a list of the questions that they most frequently ask and endeavor to do internal research to find the best answers to them.

But the information you discover will not, you fear, be welcomed by your prospective interns.

The first thing that you discover is that most interns believe that by performing the internship they will have a better chance of becoming full-time employees. But your internal research reveals that almost none do. This is not because the interns don't ask, but because the conversion to full-time work isn't offered. Most of your operating funds go toward lobbyists, legal fees, administrative fees and reimbursements to locals in the variety of countries you serve. They almost never go toward the creation of new employee lines.

You also find that interns contribute a significant portion of the operating expenses of your in-country activities. The average intern contributes $18,000 USD per year of their own funds but incurs costs to your institution of only about $4000 (a number which slightly varies by country). And they pay for their own travel expenses. Many interns "live embedded" in communities and do not engage in operations. This would explain why they come and go on tourist visas rather than NGO visas. It is not much of a stretch to conclude that your internship program might just be a revenue-generating program onto which the term "intern" is slapped.

And it is armed with this information that you find yourself once again at the display table at a major faith-based conference with a horde of 20-somethings vying to earn your attention. One of them asks you a question.

"I'm trying to choose between going to graduate school in international development or perhaps just applying for an internship with you. They both cost the same. But all I want to do is development anyway, so do you think it would be a good idea to just go for the internship with you instead?"

Discussion Questions:

1. Is your internship program an instance of exploitation?
2. How ought you answer the question posed to you by the young person at your display table?

3. If you find anything to be wrong about your internship program, what ought you do about it?
4. Make two lists: One which constitutes criteria which would imply that an NGO/NFP is exploiting its interns and another that constitutes criteria which when met show that an NGO/NFP is not exploiting its interns. Which of those two lists does your NGO or NFP land on most?

Graft at the Top

It was bound to happen sooner or later. And there it is, before your eyes. You had tried to quell your suspicions for some time but the numbers never added up. And now that you have received the report from the outside auditor regarding the state of your finances it is obvious that there is a "leak in the ship." Money is disappearing.

But this was odd. Because while the report shows a leak, it also shows that revenues are up dramatically compared to previous years. Way up.

You suspect that the CFO has found a way to divert funds from your organization. The auditors you have just hired think, under analysis of their forensic accounting, that the skimming has been happening from the depreciation tables of your capital asset sheets. Sadly, that wouldn't be hard. Your NGO has several million dollars worth of heavy machinery that you use to fulfill engineering contracts around the globe. These range from excavators to long-haulers and boring equipment as you endeavor to perform the engineering contracts for major development projects globally. Your market differentiator has always been that you are an NFP, not a for-profit operation.

One problem that you face is that your CFO is a part of your public image. He was hired to show outside clients and donors that you are "the NGO with business sense." Coming from a fortune 500 company was the requisite pedigree that is prized by wall-street, so it was a veritable coup to have him come onboard. You were shocked when he traded in his Madison Avenue office for your headquarters in Atlanta. On more than one occasion your CFO has been identified by influential governmental and non-governmental organizations as a primary reason for confidence in your organization. In fact, his personal CV has contributed to your own past performance indicator rating.

But you have noticed over the course of the past six months some troubling behavior on his part. He has purchased several expensive cars. He brags about his many homes around the country. He keeps opened liquor bottles in his office. And at dinner parties it is not uncommon to observe that he has had more than his fair share of drink. His office is in disarray and you notice that his staff appears timid, even sheepish in his presence.

Your NGO's bottom line is good. He is most definitely bringing in the contracts. Your outside auditors confirmed this. Alleged graft aside, much of that forward progress is due to his presence. Your NFP is not in financial peril. In fact, quite the opposite. You have never done better.

But the report before you does not lie. There could only have been one source of the graft, and that person is the CFO.

You stop to think. Who are his allies and how do you proceed? You recall seeing him at a restaurant several times over the past month with your chief legal counsel and several board members. This had appeared not only normal but wholly appropriate. But now you wonder whether his relationship-building was part of his safety plan.

You also pause to consider what would happen to your public image if your highly visible CFO were to be dragged through the press. For starters, you conclude, your past performance indicator would take a hit. And the only way to resurrect it would be to undergo an outside audit. You already knew what that audit would find. The overwhelming evidence before you causes you moral outrage and motivates you to engage in a high-profile public "outing." But you also feel a responsibility to protect the institution and find a way to address the issue quietly.

Discussion Questions:

1. Which persons, and in what order, should you contact as you form a strategy?
2. It is known that on occasion NFPs and NGOs quietly dispatch scandals rather than admit them. What are the risks/rewards with regard to this approach?
3. Is there a moral problem with keeping this issue out of the public eye?
4. What are the implications of filing charges against the CFO, should it come to that?
5. Keeping the issue quiet almost always involves incurring financial loss which is never recovered. In what respects does this undermine your commitments to the donors of your institution?
6. What risk do you (the CEO) face in this situation?

References

Avolio, B. J., & Yammarino, F. J. (2013). *Transformational and Charasmatic Leadership: The Road Ahead 10th Anniversary Edition.* Bingley, UK: Emerald.

Worth, M. J. (2020). *Nonprofit Management: Principles and Practice* (Vol. 6th). Los Angeles, CA: CQ Press.

Money, Finance and Fundraising

Some of the financial obligations of NFPs and NGOs are well-defined outside this book. This includes common accounting standards, state-mandated reporting guidelines, and so on. This text makes no effort to elaborate upon such issues. But before passing over them, it is important to note that if your NFP or NGO is involved in activities requiring unique accounting and reporting structures it is obviously a prerequisite that you have expertise in your relevant area. This will be true of every NFP working in healthcare and/or with vulnerable populations. But it would be wrong to think that the list ends there. Counseling centers must have ongoing HIPPA training. Afterschool program staff must comply with background checks and undergo abuse reporting training, etc.

NGOs can face unique financial operations issues depending upon the foreign nations in which they do business. NGOs based in the United States need to be checking the IRS embargo list (IRS, 2022) and the Department of Treasury's Specially Designated Individuals and Blocked Nations List (U.S. Department of Treasury, 2022). Someone within your organization must be empowered to monitor and forecast changes to them. A best practice in this regard is to establish a weekly "sitrep" report which monitors any such changes.

Everyone from the lowest-ranking staff member to the CEO must understand that the NFP and NGO act to fulfill its mission, and that this mission probably doesn't make reference to finances at all. The finances are a tool to fulfill the mission, not the goal. Yes, it would be impossible to accomplish anything without the tool. But at risk of straining a metaphor too much, it would equally be strange for an automotive restoration business to tout its accomplishments by pointing to its collection of screwdrivers.

This is how frontline staff, middle and upper management need to understand their roles. Each is given a measure of authority to expend resources, whether by punching a clock or by buying medical supplies. It is wholly reasonable to expect accountability while doing so.

The first and lowest moral bar to pass when it comes to moral obligations regarding money is policy related: Do the policies exist at all? My experience with NFPs is that far too often they don't. And this is a significant moral hazard.

While it can be cumbersome to create policies for every possible scenario, too much policy is seldom the problem. Rather, alleged or real violations of financial propriety are often rooted in there not being any relevant policy at all. Review your financial policies and ask whether the following are reflected in them:

1. All expenditures are linked to budgeted items approved by the board.
2. Policy documents clearly state which expenditures are not legitimate.
3. It is clear from the policy document who is authorized to make financial decisions, and that document is reflected in the way that things actually happen in your institution.
4. Your policies are verified by internal control practices.
5. You plan for external audits.

Having well-defined policies does not merely prevent bad behavior. It encourages good behavior. Rational individuals in a policy-devoid environment are reasonable for fearing crossing an invisible line. But the program manager who knows they can rely upon a policy is thereby empowered to operate within it (Batts, 2017).

It also helps your staff to understand how dollars are translated to service. Your accounting department's 30% indirect cost rate might look like an internal graft to a frontline worker who doesn't have to think about workman's compensation insurance, the electricity bill or ongoing maintenance. Having a staff that understands the machine that is your NFP or NGO goes a long ways toward eliminating misunderstanding.

Finally, there must be transparency above all else. It is probably true that all responsible institutions need something like a "discretionary fund." But even if you dare to create just such a budget line it should never be the case that anyone in your institution can throw budgetary expenses into a financial black box. Everyone empowered to expend resources needs to know that they will be watched and held accountable for their decisions. Even if they are the most valued personalities of your institution.

One current financial issue of great importance to NFPs and NGOs is the difficulty in obtaining administrative funds. Often grants and funders specifically require that dollars go to "programs" or "new programs" rather than to ongoing operational expenses (Bragg, 2020). But it costs money to make good things happen and a 30% rate, despite what donors or foundations or governments say about the matter, is a wise rule of thumb. Just how your NFP addresses the current market dynamic is tricky. I urge NFP and NGO executives to dedicate serious attention to this problem, potentially altering the very methods by which you fulfill your mission, so as to have a healthy administrative cost rate. All the financial policies in the world won't help you avoid disaster if you can't pay someone to do the verification.

In sum, I propose three financial principles which I believe all NGOs and NFPs should observe:

1. Stewardship: Morally speaking, NFPs and NGOs are not possessors of their funds. They are given temporary custody over those funds so as to translate them into social value.
2. Transparency: NFPs and NGOs must institute a culture of financial transparency. And this transparency extends well beyond the filing needs on IRS form 990.
3. Accountability: Those with the ability to attract, manipulate and expend funds must be accountable for their financial actions.

Finally, a great many of the financial problems that NFPs and NGOs encounter can be found in the fundraising arm of your NFP and NGO. Fortunately, professional fundraising is a professionally guided institution. It is essential that NFPs and NGOs with fundraising arms review and adopt the "Code of Ethical Standards" of the Association of Fundraising Professionals. This code details standards of morally acceptable and morally unacceptable practices when it comes to the many ways in which fundraising can occur in your institution. The consequences of violating them run the gamut from egg-on-the-face to a mission-ending PR and operations disaster (Scharf & Tonin, 2018).

More than reviewing and adopting this list of "Ethical Standards" is the simultaneous requirement that NFPs and NGOs think about how their evaluation practices of the development/advancement department serve to ally or undermine these standards (Fischer, 2000).

It is easy for institutions to undermine the ethical standards of their fundraisers and equally easy for fundraisers to do so to themselves. While this could happen solely because an institution suffered the misfortune of hiring an immoral person, this is not usually the source of such wrongdoing. Often the etiology of moral disasters in fundraising is the institution's structures, expectations and above all else pressures that incentivize moral wrongdoing (Sargeant & George, 2021). For example, using your development department to make up the 30% institutional rate not disbursed by grants is not a reasonable or sustainable expectation. Relatedly, the development department should not ever be used to make up for the executive office's budget shortfall. This effectively shifts the year-end goals of the executive to the hands of the fundraiser raising the question as to whether it is appropriate to make the mistakes of one department become the obligations of another. Additionally, requiring year-end fundraising numbers as an indicator of raises, bonuses or continued employment will create a high-pressure environment which virtually guarantees that your most ethical fundraisers will leave and that those who remain will face pressure to land the gift regardless of whether they should.

Misallocation of Resources or Unreasonable Donor?

Those who have never done your job think that your primary job responsibility is to attend cocktail parties and weekend galas. The reality is that core to your job description is taking calls like the one you just received.

You are the Director of Development at a private university of 3500 students in the northeast. All fundraising obligations, from events to major gifts and PR, lie under your purview. A recent donor to your university, who made a considerable sum of money from their work in the medical sciences, has given a large sum of money to build a building within which is housed a degree program in the medical field that earned them their fortune. Both the building and several endowed chairs are named after various members of their families. A few yearly events which attract significant university contributions also explicitly bear the donor's name.

Grateful at the good fortune to have a new building, your campus room allocation plan has availed itself of unused space when the medical program is not occupying classrooms. This includes one section of an introductory French class, a couple of history classes and one philosophy class.

But one day the donor appeared on campus and observed that a French class was in progress in the building. He immediately calls you.

"Why are you teaching French classes in my building!" the donor bellows at you over the phone. "I didn't give you all of that money so that people can get useless degrees in French! I gave you all of that money so that people can have real jobs doing real things!"

"I apologize, Mr. Smith," you respond calmly. "That room wasn't being used at that time by the medical program so we thought we would put it to good use by putting the French class in there."

"Well, if that room wasn't needed, then why did you have me pay for it?" responds the donor angrily. The conversation goes on for several more minutes with no letup in hostilities.

As this is a high-dollar donor, you report immediately to the president of the university and explain the situation. She responds immediately "Get that French class out of there."

Questions for Discussion

1. Has the university misallocated funds?
2. Does the donor have the right to make this demand?
3. What are the internal implications of acquiescing to this demand?
4. What are the implications of not acquiescing to this demand?
5. A known truth of fundraising is that current gifts breed future gifts. If this relationship is hurt there may be impact upon future giving to the university. To what extent does this potential consequence matter?
6. How could this situation have been prevented?
7. How, in your opinion, did the donor learn that French classes were being offered in the building?

Lean or Starving? On the Tyranny of Low Administrative Cost Rates

Morgan's NGO began in the 1970s before she was born. So to say that she wasn't around when the initial decisions were made would be an obvious truth. While she was a toddler in the cornfields of the Midwest a generation of intrepid pioneers were dedicating their lives to creating healthy rural communities in Central America. She would never know that generation of visionaries personally, but she would inherit their work. And decisions.

Morgan became aware of the NGO while in college and almost instantly became a true believer in the cause. Even back then, living on poverty wages from part-time jobs, she sent small but sacrificial checks to them. Then as her senior year came around the NGO announced a new internship program and she knew what she had to do. She signed up and the rest was proverbial history. First she was a fundraising volunteer, then a fundraising staff member. Then she was a fundraising manager who was ultimately offered the job as the international director.

She never earned a salary from the NGO per se. Adopting the terminology from the modern Christian missions movement, she was "on support." This meant that every year she had to engage in long support-raising tours of the United States to earn the right to continue to serve. This was an important part of her work at the NGO. Their model prided itself upon the principle, in vogue at the time the NGO was created, that they directed all dollars toward operations and that no funds would be allocated to administrative personnel. All donations went directly to services.

That principle gave them a tremendous boost in the 80s when national rankings were invented through various charity information services which listed them as far above average "effective." Of every dollar received, exactly 100 pennies went to the charity's programming. When accounting practices changed, they slid to 97 much to the horror of NGO stakeholders.

Upon taking the reigns of the NGO Morgan embarked on a fact-finding tour of all of the international operations. She visited operations in twenty Latin American and Caribbean nations. In country-after-country she discovered that the problems she thought she was leaving behind by quitting her country directorship were replicated in every new country she visited. All of the schools, clinics and hospitals that they directed were run-down. The staff at them were just as beleaguered as she was when she left her national post for her new job. Concrete walls were cracking and mold growing through facades. Hospitals had poor lighting even in the surgery wards. Pharmacies had every kind of AIDS medication they could need but almost nothing else. Not even basic antibiotics. Kids still attended classes on dirt floors and the teachers were undertrained and underpaid.

Sometimes it was embarrassing. While visiting one country that had made great national developmental strides, she could not help but notice the juxtaposition of their downtown headquarters with the property next door. The visionary team decades ago had purchased the 10 hectares of land downtown when no one else wanted it and not much else was around. They built a school and a hospital on the land which at the time was probably the best in the nation. But there was no subsequent investment. Meanwhile the neighborhood became trendy. American investors built a western-standard mall on the property just to the east. It boasted five stories, glass observation walls, modern theaters and western franchises inside. Meanwhile next door the weeds grew at their compound, the roof leaked and the guard dogs were dutifully let out by the staff at 10 pm every evening.

Morgan didn't like what she saw. And she needed answers.

In the past the answer would certainly have been this: do a fundraising campaign. She knew that this was what the board wanted her to do. Because that's what they did at the NGO every year for the past 45 years. But that was also the strategy when every new fundraiser was for their next new location. They had never done a revitalization effort in the history of the NGO.

Upon returning to the international office she gathered her financial team (all of whom were "on support" themselves) and asked for options.

"Can't we set aside some of our operations budget to create a rainy-day fund?" she asked them.

"Of course we can" her trusted colleague said. "But we would have to get that approved by the board in the next budget. And that board wants all funds going to operations."

"But this NGO requires funds. Doing things this way is what has led to our being the most disgusting NGO in Latin America. It's embarrassing out there!"

"I hear you" her CFO declared. "But the budget is the budget."

After some silence the CFO added "But maybe there are some clever ways that we can build-in an institutional cost rate without calling it that. Since we allocate funds to structures with some regularity, maybe within the budget for each structure we can add a line for 'maintenance.' And maybe when we receive donations for our schools we can add an 'equipment' line. We could then use those funds as a de facto indirect cost rate. We would have to figure out how to then move that money around internationally."

Morgan's grant writer then chimes in. "This is a problem we had back in the states. We dealt with it all the time. What you do at the level of proposal-writing is to structure the budget in a way that lets you track the expenses like any other budget but that permits you more flexibility."

"How do you do that?" Morgan asks.

"Well, for example," the grant writer answers "When you know that a grant-funded initiative is going to take the accounting department about 10 hours a week to track, you create the line 'reporting' in the grant for a total of ten hours a week. You then don't hire a new accountant. You allocate those funds to the CFO's office to fund a portion of their staffing budget. Likewise, when it calls for a kindergarten teacher for 20 hours a week you don't hire a new teacher for 20 hours. You take the teacher we already have and assign her to those 20 hours and pay him or her out of the grant."

"Then what happens when the grant runs out?" Morgan asks. The grant writer responds "you get another grant."

The CFO then jumps into the discussion, stating "When I was back in the states at the University our policy was '30% off the top.' Period. We always budgeted a 30% institutional rate for everything that we did. It might sound crazy saying this here in this office, but back there we were competing with other universities for dollars when our competitor universities charged 50% for some of their science programs. I guess we're not in the university business here, huh?".

"No," said Morgan, "We are not."

Discussion Questions

1. How would the implementation of an administrative cost rate affect your operations?
2. What are the barriers to establishing a cost rate, and can they be solved?
3. How long can your institution remain stable without an administrative cost rate?
4. Have you ever been asked to sell assets because of a lack of operational funds?
5. Is it wrong to implement a savings plan without the board's approval?
6. Does it matter if the board is "wrong?" That is, even if their position harms the institution, is it not the case that they have the ultimate right to make such decisions?

That Time When Your NFP Became his PR Crisis Response Plan

You are the manager of a local safe house for exploited women. Many of your clients suffer from domestic violence, drug abuse and a variety of forms of exploitation. To service their needs, you offer an emergency home in an undisclosed lcoation which shelters women while helping them to extricate themselves from their predicament. You are meticulous and fastidious about serving their needs.

Money is, of course, a constant issue. You have known for a long time that there are far more women in need of your services than you have the capacity to help. On your desk you keep a copy of a plan to build another house which would increase your capacity by 30%. But that house will cost about $1 million to build. Your organization doesn't have that kind of money. But maybe some day.

You have also been following a local story which in some ways is related to your work. It relates to the recent arrest of a wealthy playboy under a cloud of sordid accusations. The newspapers have been reporting on his extravagance for some time now. It began with an indictment related to his professional activities at a large business he owns on the other side of town, but quickly descended into a catalog of indelicate stories regarding his private life.

Apparently, every weekend and most week-nights there was a stream of women who arrived at his mansion's gated entrance, all of whom were dressed suggestively. Neighbors had called the police tip line on many occasions but nothing seems to have been done about it. "The prostitutes never went away," a neighbor was quoted as saying on the local news.

Then reports began to trickle in about the drug use and private parties that raged all night long. Those same news outlets managed to find some of the partygoers and aired interviews with them over the course of the past six months. Exposes on his family depict him as a privileged playboy who inherited his parent's fortune only to use it to fund his excess.

Up until this point it was all just that—a local news story that might possibly become the *cause du jour* of the national press. But you have just received an unsolicited phone call from his lawyer who has approached your NFP with the offer of making a very large donation—so large that you can't find any record of any other gift coming close to it in the entire history of your operations. With a gift of this size, you could purchase several safe houses, not just one.

If you accepted this gift you could pay for all of your operations for at least a year *and* pay for the new home. That or you could create an endowment. But you wonder whether this would be a case of doing a deal with the devil. Were you being bought?

Discussion Questions

1. If you were to write-up a "pro's and con's" list regarding the decision to take the donation, what are the pro's and what are the con's?
2. In a similar vein, game-out the situation. If you take the gift what are you likely to do just after receiving the gift? What is the donor likely to do just after giving the gift?
3. To what extent does public perception matter to your NFP's operation?
4. Do you take the gift?
5. What is the motive of the donor, and does that motive matter?

A Successful Event

You and your team have arrived back at work the night after a successful annual event at a local country club. There was a band, a DJ and hors d'oeuvres were served with an open bar. The guests arrived early, stayed late and had a wonderful experience. Your nonprofit rescues stray animals and brings them to your no-kill shelter where the vast majority of your animals are adopted out thanks to a clever PR campaign you implemented a few years ago. This mission was universally celebrated at last night's event.

Greeted a hero as you walk into the door the next morning, you brush past the offering of high fives and handshakes and go to the president's office.

"Mark" you say warily, "we can't do this every year. We're losing money and losing ground."

Mark looks mystified. "What do you mean? It was an incredible night! We got to make a lot of new relationships, spread the message of our mission and reach out to the community. How could we possibly cancel this event?".

You then bring to Mark the executive summary of a spreadsheet that you have been using to track the costs of your event. You provide him with the following (Table 1):

"It looks to me like we made $39,000 from the event" Mark says. "That's a lot of vet bills we can pay."

"We did not make $39,000." You respond bluntly. "In-kind contributions are not cash in the bank. That's what we receipted the companies who gave products to us to be auctioned off by us last night. What we actually received for those contributions was just $10,000. In reality we lost $6000 last night."

Table 1 Paws and purrs annual gala budget

Paws and purrs annual gala—Executive summary		
EXPENSES		
	Venue Rent	$20,000.00
	Catering (@$70 pp)	$35,000.00
	Sound and Lighting	$5,000.00
	Auctioneer	$1,000.00
	Video Production	$1,000.00
	transportation	$1,000.00
	VIP Packages	$3,000.00
REVENUE		
	Ticket Sales (@$100)	$50,000.00
	Auction Revenue	$10,000.00
	In-Kind Contributions	$45,000.00
	TOTAL	$39,000.00

Mark looks somewhat taken aback. But after a moment responds, "OK, well even if that is true, losing $6000 on an event that gained us a lot of new friends and attention isn't really a bad thing. We spend more than that a month on our PR campaign."

"Well, Mark, $6000 was what we lost *last night*. But me and my staff have been working for three months to make last night happen. If you count our salaries and if you count the cost of not directing our attention to other fundraising activities the amount we lost was quite a bit more than that. We will never know the real number."

Mark pauses for some time and thinks about your point. He then says "This might be provocative, but if I can't say this to you then I can't say it to anyone. So here goes. Maybe we're wrong to think that we're here solely to help the stray animals. Maybe we're here both to help the stray animals as well as to host social events for those who like to think of themselves as supporters? So we put on our event, pay the DJ, buy the drinks and then use the other 11 months to get back in the black with the same donor crowd. What's wrong with that?".

Questions for Discussion

1. What are your criteria for a successful event? Make a list.
2. When performing the financial accounting for events, what should be taken into account? What counts as a cost and what counts as revenue?
3. Should in-kind contributions be accounted as revenue?
4. Should an event budget contain only the revenue and expenses of the day of the event or for the sum total of all revenue and expenses?
5. With regard to this event, is there a mismatch between the stated purpose and true purpose? Does that matter?
6. Should special events be a part of the fundraising budget or the PR and marketing budget?
7. Is there anything morally wrong about operating an NFP whose primary expenditures are social events for donors?

Missing Money at the Group Home

You are the director of group home that serves the housing needs of persons with mental illness. Your home offers an alternative to the homelessness of your clients, and you see every day the results of the newfound stability in their lives. They eat better, they have their medical needs attended to and over time you observe them begin to think about their futures.

Some of them have families, others not. Some of them have jobs but others cannot maintain stable employment. Some of your clients are capable of tracking their own finances but others are unable to do so. And for those who cannot, you have enacted an in-house banking policy. Clients with cash that needs to be safeguarded approach the home-leader and deposit into the home's safe. That deposit is counted, recorded in a ledger and available to the client at a later date.

Mark, a new resident at the home, has become angry. He states that someone stole his money again. You look at the ledger and see that Mark should have $75 dollars in his account. But Mark says that he should have $100 in that account. He is angry that someone stole his money.

You approach the house leader on duty and are reminded of your accounting policy. Money is received from the client whereupon the house leader counts it and banks it. You see that the ledger states that $75 was deposited. But Mark is stating to you that this is not correct. He gave "that other person" $100, not $75.

You discover that you are in a he-said/she-said situation. You speak to Mark again and to the house leader again but nothing that you say can resolve the issue.

Discussion Questions

1. How do the in-house banking practices help or hurt your ability to navigate this situation?
2. What policies would prevent this problem?
3. How do you respond to Mark?
4. The best resolution to a he-said–she-said situation is to avoid it in the first place. What processes and policies must be adopted in group homes with housing bank programs?

Bribery or Just Doing Business?

Mark worked for an orphanage in rural Haiti which he had come to know after he volunteered for a volunteer trip several years earlier. That experience proved to be life changing for him and for his family. Eventually, he left his life behind in the United States and moved himself and his family to Haiti where he helped to run operations on the ground.

Life was not easy in Haiti. But it was deeply rewarding. Back in the states his greatest accomplishments were measured by the number of subcontracts he gained in his construction business during a given month. But in Haiti those accomplishments were measured on the basis of how many kids were rescued from endangerment and exploitation. For Mark and his family, it wasn't even a close call as to which life was more rewarding.

One of his job duties was to travel across the border to Dejabon to the Dominican Republic to acquire food supplies for the orphanage. Conditions at the border crossing were chaotic and unpredictable. Day laborers gathered there early in the morning to cross and find work, sometimes (but not always) only to return home late at night. It could easily take him six hours just to get through the crossing on the way home.

That six hours was a significant problem for Mark for a number of reasons. For starters, this made for a considerable amount of lost time waiting in the queue just to move his truck a kilometer across the border. Worse than that, it also meant that the last part of his trip home would be conducted in darkness. This posed significant safety concerns. Nighttime driving is exactly the kind of thing that leads to crashes and kidnappings.

One day Mark tried something different. In his pocket was a $20 bill from the United States. Upon approaching the border, he accosted the guard whose name he knew well. Sliding the bill into the guard's hand he greeted the guard warmly.

"Another trip for food, I see," the border guard stated warmly. "Come on through!".

And with that Mark found that his six hour wait shortened to six minutes. Thereafter he never approached the border without two $20 bills in his pocket. One of them was used on the way in and the other on the way back. In exchange for his investment he acquired concierge border-crossing services and avoided what he thought was the most significant of all his safety issues—nighttime driving on rural Haitian roads.

One day the international director accompanied him on his border-crossing trip. It was the director's first time in Haiti and he wanted to see what a border crossing was like. As they approached Mark prepared his $20 bill. Seeing this the director exclaimed to his shock "What are you doing!".

It took Mark a minute to realize what had triggered the comment. "This is how you get through the border safely and reliably. If we don't do this it's the dark roads filled with bandits for us when we return."

"Mark," the international director exclaimed, "We have a policy. No government corruption, period."

"Is it really government corruption?" Mark dared to ask. "To them it's a service which exacts a fee. We're still going to show them our passports. What is the difference between this service and the USA charging members of the Global Entry program a fee of $110 for expedited service?"

"The difference is that this is a bribe! Do you realize that I have to face a board and donors who wouldn't be very happy with this situation? Mark, we can't do this."

"You're the director," Mark says "So if you're telling me that I can't do this any more I guess I will reconsider. But you do understand, don't you, that you're just swapping risks. By not paying the 'fee' as they call it we are deciding that I drive on roads with kidnappers and miscreants. Would the board and the donors like that?"

Discussion questions

1. Is Mark engaging in corruption? Is the guard engaging in corruption?
2. Is Mark's action wrong?
3. What are the potential consequences of giving the money to the guard? What are the potential consequences of not giving the money to the guard?
4. If corruption is morally permissible in this case, when is it not morally permissible?

Coalition Building or Finder's Fee?

You are the CEO of a NFP that helps to place high school graduates into jobs after receiving their diplomas. This activity serves a pressing need of the urban community you serve where college is rarely seen as an option and youth unemployment is high. You have recently engaged in an initiative which weaves your activities into that of the municipality's sports programming in local parks. Through the sports programming you offer your services to the young men and women who participate, linking them into your pre-established business network within the city you serve.

The initiative seems to have traction. But you underestimated the amount of manhours that it requires. It is not as easy as diverting a staff member for 30 minutes to make it out to the park and give a pitch. The information that you have is that for every 30-minute session you deliver at the park it requires about 6 hours of leave from your NFP. That six hours invariably is diverted from another program in need of labor.

Barry, an exuberant staff member in the new program arrives at your office door.

"You got a sec?" Barry says with glee.

"For you, any time!" you respond.

"You know I am good friends with Gene, right?" he asks. You nod that you indeed are aware of this. Gene is the donor from the community who gave a large sum of money to begin this new program. He is also a banker at the headquarters downtown.

"Well, I was talking to Gene the other day over drinks. And he and I got talking about the program," Barry continues with excitement in his voice. "We all see that this program could really work and get those kids into good jobs. But we also see that we need more people and more time and, well, that costs money."

"Correct you are," you state. "That's the problem that we have."

"Well, I was talking with Gene and he threw this idea at me. He is willing to place some of his own staff at the bank on the job. Gene says that he can have them reach out to their network of wealthy clients and look for the needed money. Gene says it probably couldn't be that hard. They're loaded. Gene says that the Bank just has to keep 4% as an administrative fee with 96% going back to us. That's less than half of what he charges anyone else for wealth management."

Not seeing a gleeful look on your face, Barry adds "Come ON! 96% of a million is way better than 100% of nothing! Which is what we have now!".

"True enough," you say to Barry. "But there is an ethical standard in fundraising that states that commission or finders fees in fundraising is unethical. When donors 'give' or 'invest' they have the expectation that the person asking them to give is not making that 'ask' just to receive a cut. This sounds to me like Gene is getting a cut."

"No he isn't," Barry bellows back. "He's eliminating all profit from the equation. It costs money to track money, and all that he is doing is making sure that the people who work to track that money get paid. Gene gets nothing and the Bank makes nothing."

"I don't' know," you say, "This still sounds unethical to me."

"But if *that's* unethical," Barry says, "Then isn't the United Way who gives us funds also unethical? They get donations all the time and pay themselves to track them, giving us less than the full amount donated in the first place. What's the difference if the Bank does it or if the United Way does it?"

Discussion Questions

1. All fundraising publications are in unanimous agreement that "finder's fees" or commissions are immoral. Is this a finder's fee and is it immoral?
2. Aside from the issue of finder's fees, what other problems does this scenario pose to the CEO?
3. Why are finders fees or commissions thought to be immoral?

4. What steps can be taken to prevent this situation or others like it?

Inheriting an Albatross

It is becoming increasingly clear that NFPs view each other as competitors, not as allies. That's why the call from Northern Industries was so surprising. For years you and Northern Industries competed for contracts from the State Government. Northern would land the toothpaste account for the prison system, but you would get the account for paper products for the capital building. Northern was then awarded the funds for a post-imprisonment re-entry program while you would get the account for collating and boxing disaster recovery supplies. Both of you employed persons on parole or just out of prison to provide services to your customers.

For years it seemed that you were racing each other to the bottom. And now you wonder whether Northern got there just before you did. Their legal representative informs you that Northern is looking to consolidate with another NFP in the same industry. And with the as-yet unannounced departure of their CEO now would be a better time than ever to consider the bold move.

The negotiations between your two organizations were tense. But you gained the upper hand by offering a management agreement with Northern as an interim measure. You agreed to manage the HR, payroll and AP systems of Northern. And you agreed to continue all staff management and evaluation needs. For this service you billed Northern an agreed-upon amount per month.

Your first gloss over the balance sheet of Northern Industries was troubling. Northern was operating at margins that were not sustainable. They were making a profit, but the margin was significantly lower than yours. They never seemed to have figured out that the state compensation would not be enough in the long term. Ten years ago when you took your job you made it a top priority to find solutions to this problem that avoided the Unrelated Business Income Tax trap. Finding new, more profitable products that still managed the re-entry needs of your employees was tough. But you did it. Northern Industries never did.

You reason that this explains why Northern folded before you did. And because you had solved the same problems at your own NFP once upon a time, you reason that you could do it again once Northern was in the fold.

You take over the management of Northern Industries and make some rudimentary changes which, while unpopular, turned a bleak outlook into a stable outlook. Profit margins, while not spectacular, were at least enough to keep the lights on over the short term.

Your lawyers look over the merger paperwork with great care. Negotiations proceeded. Oddly, however, members of Northern's board almost walked away once they learned that they would not be members of the post-merger board. Was this because of a principled commitment to the institutional mission of Northern which they desired to see continue? Or were there other reasons?

Another sticking point was Northern Industries' position that they would not dissolve into your NFP via bankruptcy, but would only consider a merger. Your legal counsel points out that dissolution would be tough in this case since Northern was not yet financially insolvent. You had fixed that problem under the management agreement. So the board at Northern probably had the upper hand on this point.

In the end, Northern's board agreed to the terms. Those terms were that Northern's board was allocated two seats on the new board of 12 and that all assets and liabilities of Northern would be jointly owned by the newly merged entity.

It took less than a month for the first lawsuit to hit your organization. This lawsuit had been filed by the previous CEO of Northern who claimed that bonuses had been unjustly deprived her during her time at Northern. It also claimed sexual harassment and a hostile working environment. Attestations in the suit included claims of an affair between her and one of the two board members you had placed onto your newly merged institution. The second was from a disgruntled donor to Northern who claims to have been promised profit-sharing at his packaging plant for services rendered. By the end of the month you were facing seven other lawsuits as well.

Discussion Questions

1. What fact-gathering needs to take place when considering mergers of NFPs?
2. When one NFP merges into another, what are the conditions that must be considered when conducting that merger?
3. What is your new board's role in this situation? How ought they respond?
4. What was the motive for Northern's Board demanding board membership on the merged board?

The School for Civil War Orphans

Peri's own story is intense by all accounts. Raised in an African nation during the height of instability, Peri managed to make his way out through the power of his intellect, the strength of his fortitude and not just a little luck. But he did make it out and managed to land a spot, tuition-free, at a prestigious American university where after three years he would eventually graduate with a master's degree.

While he was there a wealthy member of the university's booster club named "Pam" became sympathetic to his situation. At first she bought him clothes and took him out to dinner. But after some months Peri became a fixture in Pam's home where he would routinely gather around the family table and take part in the ordinary activities of daily American family life. It was probably the one factor more than any other that helped him to cope with his time in the States. He never could get used to the wealth that this heretofore strange and unknown family accepted as normal. But he managed. His newfound foreign adoptive family was kind to him and made his stay easier.

As Peri approached graduation he confronted a decision: Would he return to his nation or would he attempt to gain permanent residency in the States? Life was so much easier in the States. He had a degree that could land him a great job, probably on a foreign worker visa. But every time he thought of the benefit to himself for staying, he immediately thought of the situation of his family and friends back home who were not as lucky. He talked to friends and to the few other people at his university that were also from his country. Nearly everyone told him to try to stay in America. But that option never set well with him and he eventually made the fateful decision to return to his country in an attempt to give back to the community that had made him who he was.

At first Pam objected. She begged Peri not to go back home. It wasn't safe. He could do well in the States. But after several discussions, Pam finally said

"Peri, can I at least help you after you go back?"

Thus was born what would become a great many initiatives, the largest of which was the school for civil war orphans, named "The School of Hope." Funded by a nonprofit in the states at which Pam served as chair, Pam and her network were successful in creating a targeted educational institution located deep in the bush but which managed to offer one of the best educations in the region for primary and secondary school children.

It was not cheap. The school building for war orphans that they established would have cost about $500,000 in the states, but what with the higher prices for electricity, wire and concrete their costs more than tripled. Then there was the overhead needed to hire only qualified teachers. But every time an unexpected cost came up, Peri and Pam were able to rally friends and family from the states to give.

What neither Pam nor Peri predicted was that this school which was conceived as an option for those with no options would become the best school in the region. When word spread that it was an "American" school with good education prospective students came out of the woodwork.

At first this was a blessing. Finding civil war orphans for the school is a tricky business. Now Peri discovered that the town was bringing them to him. But that good fortune was short-lived. One afternoon a girl appeared at the gate of the school to ask if she could be a student there. Her parents had both died of disease and she was left with no educational opportunities since no one could purchase her school supplies or uniform.

Peri thought it wholly right to accept the orphan. But a few days later a group of wealthy American benefactors were on a tour of the facility and asked Peri about the profiles of the students in the school. Pointing to the new girl, Peri explained to the Americans that this was a local girl whose parents had died of disease and that this school was able to take her in thanks to the generosity of the donors.

A commotion broke out among the Americans, and it didn't sound good. This led to long discussions and ultimately a call from Pam.

"Peri," Pam explained with pain in her voice, "These people want to give to civil war orphans. Not to just any orphan. We have now raised several million dollars for your school and will likely be able to pay the operating costs for some time to come. But we have to make the tough call to stick with the mission."

Peri was disturbed by the call and quickly called in the School Headmaster. The Headmaster tensely responded "We have a duty to this community. We cannot say to one child that they can come here and to another that they cannot. And it shouldn't matter that the Americans see such a great difference between a child orphaned by war and a child orphaned by disease which couldn't be treated because the war destroyed the hospitals."

Questions

1. Is Peri's situation an example of mission drift?
2. How can Peri navigate the tension between the board and the school staff?
3. Who decides the mission of the NGO: The teachers or the board?
4. Should the girl be dismissed from the school?
5. How could this situation have (potentially?) been avoided?

The Best President We Could Ever Dream Of

Robert Newcomb was arguably *the* face of the university. He had risen to the presidency in the late 1980s after serving as the chief fundraising officer. At the time it was a controversy to even think of appointing as a president someone who held no graduate degree. But what Robert lacked in education he made up in charitable contributions. During the early years of his presidency he managed to brush off lingering hostilities and mistrust between him and the faculty, always justifying his position by pointing out to the board the large dollar amounts that he was bringing in.

And the gifts were indeed large.

Through his efforts, and in no small part because of the team that he assembled, the university between 1995 and 2005 was able to build two new dorms housing 5000 additional students, a new science building and a multi-purpose student life building with a restaurant, auditorium and road frontage which was rented out to local businesses. No tuition revenue was used for any of these projects. They were all funded by various fundraising activities spearheaded by President Newcomb.

Traditional on-campus enrollment, which directly translates to revenue, increased from 3000 to just under 10,000. While strongly resisted by the faculty, he also created a series of 100% online degrees which enrolled an additional 5000 students from around the world. Senior faculty members who survived the institution's instability in the 80 s joked that they remember when everyone referred to it as "Make-due U." But that moniker was a thing of the past.

No one on campus worked harder than President Newcomb. It was common for staff to say that they received an email from him at midnight before with the next email rolling in at 5 in the morning. His car was constantly in the parking lot at all hours of the day and the night. In fact, many people verbalized the thought that he didn't need a car at all since he never actually seems to have left the campus.

They were more right than they knew. When the most recent building went up he made sure that an "executive apartment" was built within quick walking distance from the president's office. The official planning reason for this was to house high-net-worth visitors when they came to campus. While records show that some external visitors did indeed stay there, the most common resident was the president himself.

There were also whispers of the unusual construction of the football stadium. That stadium was perched atop a hill owned by the university. Had that stadium been turned 90 degrees it would offer a dramatic view of the campus for all its visitors. But it wasn't. Furthermore, cloistered in the back of the stadium, facing a rugged wilderness appeared to be a hunter's blind built into the back of the stadium. Apparently, President Newcomb liked to deer hunt and the stadium's location was the best spot on campus for that. Not wanting to lose his spot, he had the blind built into the stadium's design.

But President Newcomb's behavior was starting to change. He didn't attend faculty events any more and was less and less frequent at many of the campus events. He missed the Parent's weekend entirely and was a no-show for homecoming. And it was about that time that the lawsuit came. Apparently, an external real estate investor was angry at not having been selected for a building project, and accused the university, naming Newcomb specifically, of racketeering. This lawsuit triggered a new scrutiny at the Board level than had ever been leveled in the history of Newcomb's leadership. It didn't take long to discover the presidential apartment and the hunter's blind. At the following meeting of the board, the board asked for President Newcomb's resignation.

Discussion Questions

1. Do you believe that the board had no idea of the work and life habits of the president?
2. Was it wrong for the president to use university facilities in the way that he did?
3. What blame, if any, does the board have for this situation?
4. How long is too long for a president to serve?
5. What safeguards could have been put in place to prevent this situation?

The Post-Mortem "Take"

"There is a reason most fundraising is done at a party," says John. "Because it's all about relationships, not causes. Money is the *last* thing you talk about."

That always stuck with you, and you weren't sure whether you were comfortable with it.

Ever since John said that you've taken a closer look at how he operates. On the one hand his contribution to your institution as its major gifts officer has been tremendous. You've never held him to a quota or calculated the institution's return on investment (ROI) on John, but it would not surprise you to learn that your institution receives 20 × salary out of him. But the way that he did it made for a strange working relationship.

While you were holed up in your office pouring over budgets, program designs and employee evaluations, John was out at the golf club. There wasn't a social engagement he would miss. If there was a cocktail party, he was there. He attended every wedding and funeral. He was a visible presence at the wealthy Episcopal church downtown. At every birthday, soirée and get together held by the town's elite, he was there. You had never seen him eat a meal at your NFP. Looking over his outlook calendar confirmed that he stacked his days, and most nights, with meals with donors. Neither did he choose NFP sides when it came to his socializing. Every other nonprofit in town could count on his purchasing a ticket to every ball, gala and party. You suspect that your NFP paid for those tickets. But so what? The donations were coming in.

One particular close friend of John's was Mildred. Mildred was the widow of a wealthy industrialist from your city, and she had no children. In fact, she had no other family that you are aware of. You had seen her at a number of events that you (and others) host, but never with family. She was always either alone or with her peer group of other women, most of whom were also the spouses of successful businessmen.

You did not know how old Mildred was, although you would have guessed that she was in her 80 s. That didn't prevent John, who was in his 50 s, from being her constant companion. Mildred would always save John a seat at her table, sometimes poking fun at herself "and the other old bags" who invited him into their circle.

One day, however, Mildred suffered a heart attack and attempts to rescue her failed. Following John's lead you made sure to attend the funeral and the wake. It was clear that John was more to her than just a philanthropic benefactor. John was a close friend and confidant. *Really close.*

The following Monday your chief council calls you into your office.

"Are you sitting down?" He says warily.

"Just say it, Marylin. Whatever it is."

"OK. I'll give you the good news and the bad news. The good news is that Mildred's will was just read and she gave your NFP 3% of her estate."

"And the bad news?" you ask with trepidation.

"The bad news is that she gave John 50%."

Discussion Questions

1. Is the 50% gift to John immoral?
2. What role did the CEO have in this situation?
3. What is the appropriate response of the CEO in this situation?
4. What should John do?
5. What would the public perception of this situation be?

Missing Money?

You have been given a new promotion in your not-for-profit that serves the needs of elderly patients with various transportation needs. Your program is clearly a vital one—85% of your clients have either had their driver's licenses revoked, suspended or voluntarily relinquished. But this fact does not limit their needs to go grocery shopping or make a variety of physician appointments. Without your services your client's medical needs and daily life needs would be left largely unmet. You take this situation seriously and strongly believe in your mission.

The road to your leadership appointment was typical. You were not the most senior candidate for promotion at your NFP. But it just so happened that when the position became available, the three people ahead of you "in line" had recently left to work with another local transportation firm leaving you as the most experienced candidate for the promotion. But you know that you are thorough, you work hard and you are committed to providing high-quality services to those you serve. You gladly accept the position.

On your first week serving in your new capacities you take it upon yourself to look under the hood of the finances of the programs for which you had previously served as a services provider. This is no small feat, occupying a great many hours off the clock.

One thing that you find is worrying.

You see that the state of Rhode Island has given your organization a grant in the amount of $465,000. These funds were to be used to pay a variety of operational needs—the purchase of a wheelchair accessible transportation van, insurance, drivers' pay and other costs. But you note that while the amount disbursed to your organization is $465,000, your budget for the program is only $325,000. You can search the budget of your program over and over, but cannot account for the missing $140,000.

You immediately think of the many required trainings that you have done within your institution which have taught you how to spot elder abuse, mistreatment and theft of assets. Have you discovered that your very own employer is an example of such an agency?

As you look over the grant disbursement conditions you note that there is a whistleblower provision which offers a reward to anyone who reports misuse of state funds.

Discussion Questions

1. In this case, have you discovered a misallocation of funds by your NFP employer?

2. What is the appropriate way to address this situation? Where do you go and who do you talk to?
3. Whom should you speak with first and why?
4. Do you believe that you have been given sufficient information by your employer to succeed in your new position?

"Give Me a Child You Don't Care About"

The developed world has been privileged to see the eradication of polio. But now several decades past Jonas Salk's discovery, the world has yet to eradicate it from its more remote, rural populations. Invariably included among these localities are Africa's less economically developed areas.

Irem has been hired by an international NGO to implement a program to disseminate the polio vaccine to African groups that have proven to be resistant to vaccines. Her current station is in the Democratic Republic of Congo. One week before her arrival a medical encampment in the region she was to travel to was attacked by villagers and several doctors and nurses were killed. So to say that her situation was challenging was an understatement.

She has been supplied a nurse, a traveling entourage of security personnel and a map to the northern regions where several groups, sometimes referred to as "pigmies" in the west, live.

After an arduous, days long trek to the north, she arrives in the region and through a translator begins to inquire as to the whereabouts of the Banbuti people. Locals give her some advice, but are mostly dismissive and mistrustful of her and her team. After a few weeks she is finally able to arrange a meeting of an elder Banbuti who has agreed to speak on behalf of his people.

Irem explains that she is there to give his people medicine, that this medicine will prevent his children from getting disease and that she would like him to bring the children to her so that she can administer the dose to each of them. But the chief is hesitant. For many generations, he and his people have been harmed, often killed, by outsiders. Land disputes and hunting disputes are the most frequent cause for such violence. And because violence was an underlying social condition for several generations the Banbuti people generally only interacted with non-Banbuti when they absolutely had to.

After several hours of negotiations Irem has become frustrated. The heat and the swarms of mosquitos probably did not help matters much. She was tired, she was lonely and was suffering the ever recurring symptoms of food poisoning and lack of hydration.

She finally said to the chief "Bring me a child that you do not care about. A child who you do not care whether lives or dies. I will give the child medicine and you can see whether the child lives or dies."

A discussion begins between the chief and others in the tribe. They discuss a small child that they know of, still without a name, of whom they currently have taken possession. This child was from a home of people who died following a conflict earlier in the year. The chief agrees to subject this child to inoculation. The next day he arrives with the child. It is clear that the child is terrified and believes that a serious act of violence is about to happen to her.

Irem's nurse administers the polio vaccine whereupon the chief disappears into the woods with the child.

Irem then turned to her colleagues and said "Well, I guess that's it. We will have to see what happens next."

One day of waiting turned to three. Then two weeks. She and her colleagues were becoming increasingly worried about their security in the region and had to decide what to do.

"We could go looking for them," said Elizabeth, not at all enthused by the prospect. Elizabeth was a nurse raised in the region who had made her way to the capital for her education. You have long since learned that when Elizabeth is nervous, there is probably a legitimate reason for her to be.

"I don't think it would be wise for us to stay much longer," Says Franklin, a doctor helping you in your mission. "If they were to reappear they probably would have done so already. I am guessing that they have moved to the north. If we head up there then maybe we can make contact again. But I hear that conditions are even worse up there than they are here. At some point, you just have to say 'We've done everything that we can' and call it a day."

The words of your national associates matter to you. You hired them for this kind of input. But your position makes you accountable to the head office, not to them. Nevertheless, you agree to follow their advice and depart the town. As you travel south you contemplate how you will deliver the news to your superiors that you have failed to accomplish your mission.

Discussion Questions

1. Was Irem's approach to convincing the chief morally acceptable?
2. Was Irem given a mandate from her NGO that was possible to fulfill? Or was she doomed from the start?
3. How could Irem help the Banbuti people to make autonomous decisions in a society that enacts non-individualistic decision-making?

References

Batts, M. E. (2017). *Nonprofit Financial Oversight: The concise and Complete Guide for Boards and Finance Committees*. Accountability Press in Cooperation with BMWL, Batts, Morrison, Wales & Lee.

Bragg, S. M. (2020). *Nonprofit Accounting: A practitioner's guide*. AccountingTools, Inc.

Fischer, M. (2000). *Ethical decision making in fund raising*. Wiley.

IRS. (2022, August 6). *Disciplinary Sanctions—Internal Revenue Bulletin*. Retrieved from irs.gov: https://www.irs.gov/tax-professionals/disciplinary-sanctions-internal-revenue-bulletin

Scharf, K., & Tonin, M. (2018). *Economics of Philanthropy: Donations and Fundraising*. Cambridge, UK: The M.I.T. Press.

Sargeant, A., &; Jay, E. (2014). Fundraising management: Analysis, Planning and Practice. Routledge.

U.S. Department of Treasury. (2022, August 13). *Specially Designated Nationals And Blocked Persons List (SDN) Human Readable Lists*. Retrieved from U.S. Department of Treasury: https://home.treasury.gov/policy-issues/financial-sanctions/specially-designated-nationals-and-blocked-persons-list-sdn-human-readable-lists

Intercultural and Cross-Cultural Ethics

A stereotypical feature of scholarship developed in the west is the desire for a "grand theory." (Behnke, 2001) The early sections of this very text might lead some readers to ask the plausible question "which of these moral theories is correct?" The legitimacy of such a question is bolstered by observing the unification efforts that exist in the empirical sciences. Newton's theories of motion permitted the civilization to jettison a chaotic maze of pre-modern notions, many of which conflicted with one another, on the promise of presenting a simplified understanding of the motion of objects. Much the same thing can be stated with regard to the theoretical elegance of Darwin's theory as found in his famous *Origin of the Species*. It would be a mistake to think that the desire for a "grand theory" exists solely within the empirical sciences. Theological schools of thought famously search for coherence as they articulate a "story of everything" and literary circles have from time to time done the same pursuant to the ebbs and flows of hermeneutical methods. Is it therefore possible to find a single moral theory which, when discovered and adequately refined, cuts through the complexities of cultures and histories while offering clear guidance upon current moral cases under scrutiny?

Sadly, there is not. There is no clear "winner" in the Ethics literature and it is doubtful that the enterprise of attempting to find one will be met with much success. Take, for example, Beauchamp and Childress's influential work in the Medical Ethics community. Across the United States and in much of the world their system is often used to decide who receives scarce medical treatments, whether to override a patient's autonomous choice and a potentially infinite array of other moral quandaries. As we stated in the introduction, they propose that we conceive of ethics as rooted in four sometimes competing principles: Nonmaleficence, Beneficence, Autonomy and Justice.

Now consider a case of a patient in a hospital in the United States who is a recent immigrant from a West African nation. This imaginary patient believes in the power of traditional healing practices and is skeptical of professionalized medicine. Imagine further that this patient objects to medical treatment which the physician thinks will help treat the patient. But rather than having western-style empirical evidence for the refusal of treatment (by the term "evidence" we mean evidence typically countenanced as evidence by western-trained physicians) this patient objects because of his belief in traditional healing practices.

In such a case it is a simple, perhaps flat-footed response to assert that the patient's autonomy is at odds with the requirement that the physician provides beneficent treatment. Notice, however, the oddity in this scenario. That same physician would never have informed a western, non-immigrant patient under the same treatment protocol that his or her decision to agree to treatment should be second guessed because there exists a strong intellectual tradition in west-Africa which, if subscribed to, might override physician directive. But if all patient ideological mindsets are to be placed on equal footing the physician would advise western patients accordingly. But typically, institutions resort to "cross-cultural" or "non-western" analyses only when confronted with a patient or client deemed to be a member of a nebulous "other" class. This is unsettling.

I therefore begin with the reassertion of the theories presented in the introductory chapter and offer them to the reader for what they are: time-tested theories that have proven to offer important insights into a variety of moral situations. All of them will continue to be valuable tools in cross-cultural situations. Yet as we now ask important questions regarding intercultural and cross-cultural ethics, we add to that literature by looking at a variety of sources which will also offer a different collection of insights. In no case will we find a new theory of everything. But we will find helpful tools.

The first question we must ask turns out to be not one, but several related questions: What is race? What is an ethnicity? What is a culture? A fine meditation, both bold and reasoned, has been offered by Naomi Zack in her *Thinking About Race*. (Zack, 2022) Zack points out that the concepts of race and culture are intrinsically moving targets, not fixed, static categories. Whereas "race" at one point was used in circumstances to designate a "family ancestral line" it has changed considerably over the centuries. Attempts to root race in biological terms have been not only scientifically thwarted but also morally disastrous. Much of the slave–owner discourse on race of the American eighteenth and nineteenth centuries was rooted in a biological conception of the concept. So, it would appear that whatever "race" and its many related terms such as "ethnicity" and "culture" are, they probably refer to attitudes and social structures, not physical or empirical "things."

This explains the recent interest in "critical race theory." Most scholars assume that racial language lies somewhere in the vicinity of J.L Austin's category of "performative speech." (Austin, 1962) That is, racial language is used to *do* things not to *describe* things. When a priest states "I now declare you husband and wife" or a judge strikes a gavel and declares "Guilty!" neither use words to describe facts. Rather, their speech performs an action: declaring a defendant as guilty or two persons as married. Racial language is commonly viewed along the same lines. It doesn't *describe*. It *does*. What we *do* with that language might be good or bad. It could be innocent or ignoble. One person might use racial language in order to politically manipulate members of a group, another might use it to empower them and another to minister to them. This implies that at least some, and perhaps all, of the facts about race are social facts. To delve into these profound issues just is to study the cluster of issues that constitutes the corpus of work sometimes described as "critical race theory."

One story from my international development projects illustrates this point well. Early in my career I accepted my first assignment to perform work in a developing nation. This assignment was in Sénégal where I served as a translator for a variety of western groups who were tasked with undertaking several development initiatives. It became obvious to me as I engaged in my work that tribal affiliation mattered in a way that I had underestimated. But I had no antecedent experience with "tribe" as a social category. Tribe affected who one married, who one voted for, how employees were hired, the music one liked, who bought what products and from whom, which markets were visited, what neighborhoods one lived in, the location of one's ancestral home, the language one spoke at home and a great many other social phenomena.

My Senegalese friends could identify members of various tribal groups at first sight. But I lacked the skill. Whereas they could recognize that a stranger in the market was "*woloof*" or "*sereer*" or "*djola*," I couldn't discern a difference between them. Not with any reliability, anyway. My friends therefore proposed to me that we take an afternoon in the town square during which they would instruct me as strangers wandered through on their way to conduct the day's business. It was difficult for them to comprehend that someone with so much education couldn't grasp the basics of what a *woloof* person looks like and how that differs from the high cheek-bones of the *sereer*.

"It's like trying to teach a baby to talk" they exclaimed to each other. I will never forget their laughter and amusement at my ignorance, and we had a great, albeit humorous, time together that afternoon. I never did catch on.

The point of this story is definitely not that the Senegalese have a strange way of carving up racial realities. The point is that humanity has a strange way of doing this, be it in Dakar or Detroit. Racial categories are things that are *learned*, not Kantian categories of the human understanding embedded within the minds of all persons universally. This should be no surprise to us and is the sort of thing that upon analysis is difficult to plausibly dispute. But notice the ease with which we in the developed world ignore this lesson. We assume the actual reality of the categories "white people" or "black people" or "brown people." What, other than the fact that we have been taught to believe that these categories are real, would lead us to accept that they are real? Probably not much.

Consider the 1995 presidential elections in the Ivory Coast. During that election a significant issue was the legal status of persons in the country who were recent immigrants. Some estimates put those numbers at a full 1/3 of the voting-age population. The leading politician from the Christian south of the country created a new ethnic concept called "Ivoirité" (or sometimes "Ivoiricité"). A person, according to this politician, was only truly Ivorian if their parents were born in the Ivory Coast. Unsurprisingly, his main political opponent from the Muslim north was a first generation Ivorian whose parents had immigrated. The tension caused by the creation of a new ethnic concept appealed to latent anti-immigrant tensions. And it unexpectedly entrenched animosities between groups in the country. Ultimately a civil war, and then another, were the consequences of the widespread rift in the country. (Abbascia & Poggi, 2012).

This gives us reason to think that the network within which we come to identify our choices as involving "cross-cultural" or "intercultural" features is itself a part of the problem. We must first be told that someone is "other" before we invoke these very concepts of "cross-cultural" or "intercultural" theorizing. And often times we are told of the existence of "otherness" before we have the mature capacity to question those very beliefs. The human moral universe is not so much like shipbuilders on the shore who attempt to design the best ship ever conceived as it is like current travelers on the high seas who discover that the very boat we are on is in need of repairs.

Let us now return to our moral theories. Those theories implicitly offer us a "theory of everything" as pertains to ethics. But they are competing and incommensurable. And what's more, none of them make reference to cross-cultural or intercultural issues. So while we will by no means jettisoning them, it would be helpful to find other tools which may be of use to the ethicist working in areas typified by cross-cultural or intercultural dynamics.

Fortunately there is an area of inquiry specifically tailored toward offering a theoretical apparatus within which activities oriented toward human improvement are to be conducted. We call it "Development Economics." In what follows I will offer an outline of these economic theories. But I will do so with a purpose: to show that what worries some about classical economic theories is their perceived inability to encompass the realities of intercultural and cross-cultural issues. It is my hope that understanding these theories, and what motivates them, will be of benefit to those who attempt to wrestle with the difficult dynamics of ethics in pluralistic environments.

The study of Development Economics more or less follows the same path as the re-emergence of economics pursuant to the publication of Adam Smith's *The Wealth of Nations* in 1776. (Smith, 2003) That book, unlike any predecessor, attempted to explain the processes by which nations (i.e., countries) create, manipulate and use their wealth. And while the book merits a discussion in its own right, it is important to point out that it is also a work in response to Smith's own historical environment. The western world had exited the medieval economic apparatus or lordship and nobility. One of the most significant events that the west experienced upon that exit was a variety of land reform acts. These acts caused capital to transfer out of the hands of the nobility and into private hands. Understanding this new economic world was very much a part of Smith's goal and attaining that understanding was greatly in demand during his lifetime.

We often refer to Smith's conception as a "classical" model of economics. For Smith, there was scarce difference between the concept of "growth" and "development." Noticing that labor was now a cost, he articulated a theory of pricing whereby the price to create a good was Labor + Rent + Profit. In those cases in which governments intervene with taxes or tariffs, he expanded that equation. The price of a goods in such circumstances was Labor + Rent + Profit + Regulation. Noticing that government intervention (typically through taxation and tariffs) constitutes an increase to cost he advocates for free trade agreements without government oversight or interference. Such arrangements with their correspondingly little intervention made for the most efficient markets possible in his view. What would govern the markets was the "hiding hand" (aka "invisible hand") of the marketplace, not the hand of the government. (Todaro & Smith, 2020, pp. 116–163).

This view is theoretically elegant and satisfies Ockham's Razor. But there are moral features of marketplaces and their economies that might cause a person to take exception to it. Smith views government regulation as a cost which ought to, *qua* cost, be jettisoned. But if we are justified in jettisoning costs, then cannot we also elect to pay laborers less (or not at all?) for the same reason? Slavery could be an extreme example of cost-cutting behavior.

While it would be easy at this point to enter a discussion regarding the moral problems with profit-making, these are not my aims. What I point out here is that most economies and persons who are members of them have rejected a *laissez faire* liberalism à la Smith. Because even if it were shown that stronger growth could be achieved under such models, there are human goods that we desire to maximize which never are figured into a calculation of Gross Domestic Product. The best examples of this are the wide array of NGOs and NFPs which operate so as to deliver on the many other human goods which we believe to be worthy of our collective attention. While revenue matters to them, the revenue is not (or at least should not be) their mission. Readers interested in the unique way that NFPs and NGOs can make economic, social and financial good things happen in absence of profit would be well-served by reading Karl Zinnsmeister's *What Comes Next?* as well as its successor *Almanac of American Philanthropy*. (Zinsmeister, 2016) There Zinnsmeister shows how key moments in the development of the United States occurred not on the backs of its corporate giants but within the NFPs found in its many communities.

If the work of NFPs and NGOs does not count its success on the basis of their contribution to economic growth, what economic theory would do so? And what does this have to do with intercultural ethics?

Answering these two questions is aided not by looking at the history of classical economics, but by looking at rival theories which attempt to accommodate for its known weaknesses. On a purely mathematical level, Ricardo showed that government intervention is often needed to increase growth— a fact that would not be the case if the economic world were as Smith depicted it to be. Solow later argued that not only does growth become aided by Ricardian intervention, but that this growth was not so much rooted in *things* as they are in *ideas*. Successful economies are those that create environments in which intellectual revolutions are made possible, not where financial structures are most shrewd. (Ricardo, 2004) Historically, this gave rise to an environment in which a new school of economic thought called *Neoliberalism* was made possible. Neoliberals, who are the intellectual descendants of the political right in western economies, argue that fiscally disciplined government policy is best, intervention a necessary evil to be minimized.

Whether or not political leaders in the western world actually follow the theories described above is very much an open issue. It was American Democratic President Bill Clinton who ended lifetime welfare benefits for most citizens and American Republican President Donald Trump who levied stiff tariffs on Chinese steel—neither of which policies are in any obvious way consistent with their affiliated political parties. But this much can be said: continued dissatisfaction with dominant Development Economic paradigms has caused researchers to search for more and newer models in light of the nagging suspicion that we ought to be more concerned with increasing what we value than we are with simply increasing GDP.

On a purely chronological level, the first stop was Marxist and Socialist ideologies. (Marx & Engels, 2015) History has not been kind to those nations which implemented (or tried to implement) them. While in the early 1980s roughly 1.5 billion of the earth's 4.5 billion residents resided under a communist system, today only China, Cuba, Laos and Vietnam are officially communist. This, however, does not mean that the ideological underpinnings of such systems are extinct. Far from it. If the reader thinks that speaking about "social class" is legitimate and that equality is the greatest of all public goals, then the reader shares something at the root of these ideologies. On the level of cross-cultural or intercultural ethics it is this attention to equality that reigns. Persons with different traditions or belief systems should not, we rightly believe, be marginalized just because they are different. They ought be accorded the same respect as any other. Arguably, this insight was always embodied in Kant's means-end principle found in the introduction to this book. And any religious tradition with a "golden rule" likewise finds such an emphasis.

Desiring sometimes a further elaboration upon socialist ideas, but at other times a clean break from them we encounter more recent families of theories sometimes referred to as the "post" theories. There are many such "post" theories.

"Post Colonial" theories begin with the recognition that there was something morally suspect with regard to the colonial expansions of Spain, France, England, Belgium and Germany. And what was suspected goes beyond the act of planting a flag on foreign soil. The act of colonizing foreign ethnic territory was the act of colonizing ideas, religions and ways of life. (Césaire, 2000) This caused communities to change in ways that reflected exogenous demands of the colonizers more than endogenous desires of local persons. In a classic historical study, Adam Hochschild's *King Leopold's Ghost*, Hochschild shows that Belgium's act of colonizing was constituted by an elaborate matrix of manipulations, deceptions and power-grabbing which would go on to create a great many of the neuroses of contemporary African life. (Hoschild, 1999) Those wishing to understand how the Rwandan genocide could have ever happened would do well to begin by reading the centuries of colonial history before. Post-Colonial economic theory has proven to be an exceptionally powerful tool in explaining (and offering suggestions for eradicating) the moral disasters of colonial activity. (Praykash, 1994).

"Post-Structuralist" Economic theories attempt to identify the economic structures that embody liberal and neo-liberal ideologies and modify them in ways that reflect the unique cultural needs of marginalized communities. (Rist, 2019) For example, the analysis of whether or not a dam should be built in an area is often decided via a calculation: Quantify the benefit of the dam's being constructed and subtract from that the damage caused to the displaced. We then use that tabulation as a diagnostic tool to decide what the "right" thing to do is.

But a post-structuralist would likely advocate for a different approach than the utilitarian model. They would be more interested to hear local voices represented in the discussion than those of high-level economic advisors. Because this is exactly how one would approach an issue where equality is a primary moral value. The voice of the electric company might matter, but so does the voice of a person evicted from ancestral lands.

"Post" theories value inclusion rather than exclusion. This inclusion insists upon equality of voice throughout. This can change how one deals with thorny problems in NFP and NGO operations. Let me offer two examples.

One of the most recurrent issues that vaccine programs face in underdeveloped communities in sub-Saharan Africa is the lack of community compliance. As if reading from a script, those attempting to increase compliance numbers will often discuss an education program so that facts about the vaccine might be shared. Note however the "colonial" tone of such a proposal. The assumption is that the resistant is in factual error for resisting and that a reasonable person would change their minds were different facts given to them. Because "we" have those facts and because "we" are benevolent "we" therefore offer to teach these facts to "them."

Such a proposal does not claim, as actual colonialists did, that we should take land, plant a flag and establish a new capital. But the ideological equivalence of our proposed education drive bears more resemblances to colonialism than we might be comfortable with. Educational drives might just be an intellectual equivalent to colonialism. For this reason the post-colonial economist would approach the problem by attempting to gain a better understanding of the causes of vaccine resistance, how that resistance is expressed within the power-dynamics of a community, and endeavor to discover a new way to usher in program compliance without engaging in a new form of colonial behavior. Such is the "post" theorist's approach to the economics of development. It is morally valuable for those working in multi-cultural environments to think of ways to accomplish their goals without causing destruction of cultures in the way that post-structuralists have identified.

A relevant case was related to me by a colleague who had spent a significant amount of his professional career in a rural community in northern Nigeria. That region is one of the most multi-ethnic regions on earth with only Papua

New Guinea and Indonesia being arguably more ethnically diverse. His work was sectarian: serving as a faculty member at a pastoral training school for Nigerians. And whereas a non-sectarian NGO might place a foreign worker in a locale for no more than 3–5 years, sectarian NGOs have never-ending missions and it is common for staff to serve more than three decades in their positions. This long term of service provided my colleague the opportunity to witness a long series of NGO initiatives with various rates of success. There definitely were some successes, but there were a lot more failures. Almost universally the failures were rooted in the fact that there are cultural skills that can't be learned in only three years. This includes language acquisition and a deeper appreciation of mythology. But since my colleague had spent many years learning local mythology, he had become a local expert.

One day a new NGO appeared and its representatives asked to speak with him. They had money left over from a failed rabies eradication initiative and wondered whether he had any ideas to increase community compliance. Reviewing their past initiatives revealed that they had already tried the typical approaches: education drives, informational sessions and distribution mechanisms. But all of their materials were in English (the colonial language) and no record could be found of attention to cultural decision-making practices nor to underlying cultural beliefs. So, my colleague devised a low-budget program that tackled the problem differently. He had learned over the previous decades how animal mythology played a role in pastoralists' understanding of civil life. He also knew that a large percentage of the target population could be reached by participation in a local parade during a festival. So he designed a parade float that depicted the history of several ethnic groups through the lens of the animals they cared for. At the end of the float he showed how rabies vaccination helped to strengthen their culture by protecting their animals. Data-keeping practices showed a strong uptick in rabies vaccination rates after the festival.

Stories like this go a long way toward showing that "post" theories are of great merit. When we work alongside a culture rather than in opposition to it, great things can happen. Politicized attempts to eliminate the "other," be they in Zanesville or Zambia, cause morally unjustifiable damage.

But NFP and NGO leaders need to understand that there are also known issues with the "post" theorists' approach. Take, for instance, the recent interest upon the social problem of female genital mutilation (FGM). It is almost unheard of to find a defense of the practice in the professional literature.

However, FGM is not an adjunct practice. It is an *imbedded* practice. It does not exist in an environment divorced from other social mores, beliefs and practices. It is continuous with them. So, if it is right to eradicate FGM, and I think it is, we need to be clear-headed in our understanding that probably the eradication of the practice will be consonant with the eradication of other cultural values or ways of being. That's exactly the opposite of what the post-colonial and post-structural crowd would advocate. Nevertheless, leading voices on the issue go as far as to assert that if ever there was a case to use the relative power and privilege of the west to eradicate the practice, this is the issue regarding which that heft should be brought to bear. (Nussbaum, 2016).

Another issue with "post" views is that they (often by their own admission) do not attempt to be comprehensive. Feminist development models, for example, often do not offer guidance regarding non-feminist facets of human experience. Post-colonial models have never shown how their models affect the tabulation of exchange rates. Post-structural analyses typically ignore the issue of the procedure for negotiating trade agreements. And arguably none of these theories were ever required to do so in the first place. What they offer in their own right is valuable: an increased attention upon critical facets of human experience which are too often neglected in political and academic circles.

In closing, let me turn to the specific case of religiously affiliated NFPs and NGOs. To a great extent, these entities were founded upon a well-articulated moral base that is not in need of a new theoretical textbook which articulates the features of their moral universe. The most intellectually robust of these traditions are probably those rooted in Roman Catholicism, Sunni Islam and many Jewish NFPs. This is for structural reasons more than ideological or sectarian reasons—each of these has robust pre-existing religious cultures which happen to strongly govern the many expressions of their respective faiths—including but not limited to NFP and NGO activities. Compare these to the many Protestant Christian NGOs which may not have any formal theological principle imbedded within their bylaws.

Since the religious foundations of these NFPs and NGOs are so integral to the operations and consequently moral judgments of their respective institutions, it should always be a part of employee training and evaluation to include components of those axiomatic belief sets which serve to regulate your environment. There is no one way to do this well. There is also no one way to do this poorly! But the foundation should rest upon clear communication.

An Islamic Development Bank, for example, should inquire what it is about their operations that is distinctively Islamic as opposed to merely "morally good." However it is that this question is answered, that answer must be disseminated to those who speak for your bank and interact with it. Having a clear link between your Islamic foundations and the valuable social goods achieved will do wonders for program outcomes, community participation and program compliance.

And for any sectarian NFP or NGO, it is essential to ask at what stages faith participation is a prerequisite for employment or program participation. Protestant Christian universities have sometimes implemented a litmus-test-like requirement for its faculty but only sometimes for its students. But Roman Catholic universities tend to have stringent requirements only in their Theological school. Faith-based services for homelessness frequently have no religious requirement at all for their frontline staff, but faith-based adoption services sometimes provide that service only to members of the faith. Figuring out what your policy will be is tricky business best reviewed by a lawyer, not just a theologian. And whatever those policies end up being, they should be communicated and discussed with all stakeholders, whether staff or clients or board members.

Short-Termer Headaches

Michael began his career in the International Development industry as a "short termer." He had signed up for a trip through a religious organization to an impoverished Caribbean nation back when he was in his early 20 s. Little could he have known that the short two-week experience he had on the island would turn into a career which now had lasted more than ten years. What was initially a volunteerism exercise requiring him to raise his own support turned into a payment-free stay at another NGO for three months. That put him on the radar of other local NGOs, and he now served as the country manager for a small-sized international aid organization which was somewhat strongly aligned with a religious sectarian institution back in the United States.

While the NGO had a few revenue-generating projects of their own (a plantain plantation, an arts-and-crafts boutique and a trade school), more than 80% of their revenue came from philanthropic donations. The largest single origin of those donations was a loosely knit network of churches in the United States.

He was told that managing that network would be a part of his job duties. But he could not have expected that it would become the majority of his job duties. Some weeks it was the only thing he did. His days became filled with writing newsletters, managing social network communications and making frequent trips back to the states to recruit new short-term teams.

Those short-term teams were an important source of revenue for the NGO. Each high school or college student that visited was charged approximately $3000 for the experience, about $1000 of which resulted in a per-head payment to the NGO. A team of 20 college students staying for a week added $20,000 to the NGO's bottom line.

The more Michael worked to implement the social mission of the NGO the more he disliked, even resented the short termers. Most of them could not have pointed out the country that they had flown on a map were one provided. They were loud and culturally inappropriate. They demanded food not easily available in the country. They complained about cellphone data bandwidth and lack of WiFi. And the fact that they were disproportionately obese while visiting a country riddled with malnutrition was often times a personal embarrassment for Michael.

One night Michael received a call from one of his national workers who stated that the police had come to his home and beat him up. Grabbing his keys to jump in his NGO-issued SUV he was accosted by a group of short-termers whose complaint was that there was no hot water. "I'm trying to help Maurice who was just beat up by the cops in his own home and you're telling me about the hot water!!" he bellowed. He jumped into the car and drove off into town.

It was not even 24 hours before the stateside director called Michael to get more information.

"It was terrible," Michael explained to the international director. "The police broke into Maurice's home and beat him up pretty badly. I think they harmed his wife too. I'm working with them right now."

"No," said the international director. "I meant with the volunteers. Why did you scream at them? Don't you understand that they are paying the bills?"

Discussion Questions:

1. Describe Michael's state of mind. What is he angry about?
2. Is the financial model of Michael's NGO inappropriate? To what extent does the financial model dictate the values of an NGO?
3. What realities did Michael know or not know regarding his new role as country director?
4. NGO workers often use the term "poverty tourism" to describe the attitude of short-term visitors toward the nation they are visiting. Do you find this term fitting?

"Hire a Young Woman"

You run an educational NGO in East Africa. Today, you must approve a job advertisement for a teacher position you are hoping to fill. But you are disturbed at what you read when you receive the position description from your Burundian national leader. The job description reads:

> Looking for a teacher for our new school in Bujumbura to teach secondary education courses. We are searching for a young woman at the beginning of her career to use her leadership skills to develop the school's offerings at the secondary level. Experience in reading, writing and science education strongly preferred. Interested prospects should contact…

You are troubled by this advertisement for several reasons.

Firstly, it is a principle of your NGO that where two moral systems compete (in this case, the American system and that of Burundi) you are to always default to the more stringent system. For example, if Burundian authorities require no special IRB permission to conduct a study on children but the American system does, then you must satisfy the American requirements and pass IRB review.

You fear that this principle might be at issue, as it is not illegal in Burundi to require that a prospective employee be a woman, but in the United States this would be a clear violation given the position in question.

On the other hand you know that you have an obligation to act in such a way as to fulfill the mission of your NGO. It is the charter of your educational NGO to "create woman-led initiatives in Burundi in the education sector and beyond." Teaching is a male-dominated profession in Burundi, you know that if you do not explicitly state that the position must be filled by a woman then it will almost inevitably be offered to a male teacher.

The job advertising violates one principle of your moral framework while satisfying another.

Discussion Questions:

1. Do you endorse the rule such that when two moral systems (the Burundian and the American) compete you must default to the more "stringent" one?
2. If you break with the American employment principles in this case, what prevents you from breaking with it in others?
3. Is there anything wrong with the two competing guiding principles of your NGO?

In Our Country They Would Be Married

Meredith is a nurse at a rural African hospital that is funded by a major American entity which is strongly rooted in the Christian tradition. While Meredith was brought up in that religious tradition, as she transitioned into adulthood her ties to it began to weaken. Yet while her ideological agreement may have lessened, it would be wrong to state that she harbored animosity toward it. In her eyes, she was using her medical skills in rural Africa to make the lives of her African friends healthier. And that was more than enough for her. Whether she did it within or outside a sect did not matter to her.

The clinic where she worked received funds to begin a palliative care unit—the first of its kind in the region (palliative care units are medical units used to help make the lives of persons with incurable disease states better as they inevitably succumb to their disease). She is thrilled to take part in this new initiative, having heard all too well the stories of those dying with disease in the African bush.

It only took one day of work for her to realize that she was not so much working in a palliative care unit as she was working with men suffering from untreated Acquired Immunodeficiency Syndrome (AIDS). Over the course of her first weeks in her new position she is overcome with sympathy and grief for the men (and a couple of women) who come to the hospital to help ease their symptoms.

Most contracted AIDS from visiting prostitutes, a conclusion she reaches after learning that many of them were truck drivers on a major international highway nearby. The stories of the happenings in the truck stops are legendary in the region.

One man, however, particularly captures her attention.

"Faye" as he calls himself, seems different. He appears above average educated. He speaks French like that which one would find in France rather than what one would find in French-speaking Africa. He uses words and grammatical structures that are complex when compared to his peers (once he said *"C'est la chose dont j'ai besoin"* rather than *"j'ai besoin de ça"*). He seems to evidence an understanding of the world and its politics that is not common for a rural African villager. Meredith finds in Faye a friend, not just a patient.

In one conversation Faye confides to Meredith that he is gay and that he fears that his boyfriend might be in danger of contracting the virus too. When Meredith asks whether he has told his boyfriend, Faye states that he has not. Meredith begins to plead with Faye to tell his boyfriend of his condition. But Faye is worried that if word gets out that they both have AIDS then he and

Intercultural and Cross-Cultural Ethics 141

his boyfriend risk being killed by their neighbors "well before the virus gets us."

Meredith is both sad and outraged. She is sad because her friend Faye suffers from a condition from which he will certainly die. And he will likely not ever receive the high-quality care available to those in other nations solely because he lost life's lottery and was born in the wrong place. She is outraged because Faye's fears are tragically legitimate. He is almost certainly correct that should word get out that he is gay he would face significant discrimination and violence. But she also strongly feels that if she does nothing about this situation then the number of AIDS patients in the region could grow, with more gay men contracting the virus since they do not speak freely, even among themselves. Perhaps, she reasons, if she as an unthreatening outsider were to go to Faye's boyfriend and explain to him the situation then a life could be saved.

She first goes to her boss, a missionary doctor, to ask whether she can make a trip to the village to speak with Faye's boyfriend.

"Why don't you feel the same need to go talk to the truck stop prostitutes the other patients visited?" the doctor responded. "And besides, we're in a country where homosexuality is criminalized. We can't operate outside the laws of the country we are in!"

Meredith is floored by this comment. "In any other country Faye would be married to his boyfriend!" she shouts angrily. "And in this country we can talk to the husband or wife of a patient." Meredith storms out of the meeting and hails a taxi where she travels to Faye's home to speak with his boyfriend. Upon return to the hospital, she is greeted with dismissal papers from the NGO.

Discussion Questions:

1. Should Meredith have spoken with Faye's boyfriend?
2. Does it matter that in the country in question same-sex marriage is not recognized?
3. In the United States, the status quo is that among adults, unless permitted by the patient, no communication about a patient file can be disseminated to others. But no such law exists in this country. Does that imply that Meredith may divulge information about Faye to his boyfriend?
4. Is being gay in America different than being gay in rural Africa? If so, how?
5. If you were the hospital administrator, what would you have done in this situation had you heard about it?

6. The legislative environment of many developing nations regarding sexual equality is often times very different than that which is found in Europe or the west. Should NGO workers act contrary to local law when they believe such law is immoral?
7. What moral obligations do western aid workers have toward those they serve who suffer from political persecution? And what are the perils of getting involved?

What Counts as Diversity Numbers?

Rachel was the success story that the institution wanted to emulate. She was born into an urban, chaotic home with few academic resources available to her and a family that had no ability to guide her. Rachel managed to not only make it to college but to make it all the way through the doctoral level. She graduated from a major State university with her doctorate in education and vowed that she would use her career to help others who, like her, faced so many barriers that were invisible to others.

As Rachel thought about her life, she could identify two significant challenges that she had to overcome to arrive at the place in which she currently found herself. The first was the challenge of seeing college as a requisite step to help her see the future as something she could hope for. The next was surviving the college atmosphere which only in the least significant ways bore resemblance to her high school experience.

At first, she poured her energies into her appointment within the Education Department at the small liberal arts school where she served as an Assistant Professor. She quickly earned the reputation as the flag-bearer for the program and a leader among the student community. Her open-door policy for her students was popular and she found herself offering as much life-counseling as she did academic guidance. This was immensely gratifying to Rachel.

One day while taking lunch in the cafeteria a member of the university president's advisory cabinet approached her and the two began to talk. Howard, the VP for admissions and as new to the campus as Rachel, began to ask Rachel about her experience at the university. Rachel discussed her love of her career and the meaningfulness she derived from mentoring the students. She explained that she enjoys finding the students with hidden potential and helping them unlock it.

"Have you ever thought," asked Howard, "about being a part of our team? I have been successful in creating a department of Diversity, Equity and Inclusion within the admissions department. We are trying to direct more targeted institutional efforts to increase our numbers on campus, and I think you could be an ideal person to lead this project."

Rachel was intrigued. After deliberating she agreed to take a blended position which kept one foot in the door of the Education Department while simultaneously holding an administrative position.

The first impression that Rachel had was that she was in over her head. The state and federal guidelines were complex, sometimes counter-intuitive. Often times they seemed specifically written to prevent her from doing her job. And she was not confident that she had an adequate grasp of the quickly changing legislative and jurisprudential landscape related to "diversity law." So she signed up for a series of free online conferences hosted by a variety of entities which helped to bring her up to speed.

She couldn't, she learned, use race as a consideration for admissions. At all. That path had been thrown out at the state level via legislation a generation earlier. But she learned that there were other means which had not been made illegal which would potentially serve as an equivalent to a race-based strategy. The strategies, which she scrawled out on notecards in her office were:

1. Create geographical targets—neighborhoods where minority students were likely to live.
2. Avail herself of a variety of income-based mechanisms which targeted the socioeconomic groups most likely to be ethnic minorities.
3. Create percentage quotas of socioeconomic groups which would be used in admissions decisions.
4. Hold more admissions activities in monitory-majority schools.
5. End legacy admissions on campus.

Rachel brought her list to the head of admissions so that they could discuss the issue.

"The legacy ban is out of the question." Howard said with a bit of guilt in the tone of his voice. "The kids that get in here on the basis of that program are the children of really wealthy parents that give a lot of money."

Howard could see the disappointment on the Rachel's face. He added "Look at it the way that the President would look at it. Every kid we admit under the Legacy Program is a kid whose parents have already given a large gift. Often $50,000 or more. Then on top of that they pay full tuition with no discount. Over four years, or five which is the average for that group, that translates to about $200,000 in cash payments for the university. Compare that to the Pell Grant program which your program is likely to dip into and it's not even close."

It took Rachel a moment to recover from the shock of the financial reality of the *status quo*.

"So are you saying," Rachel asked politely, "that unless my Diversity, Equity and Inclusion program yields the financial results of the legacy program that I won't get traction?"

"I'm definitely not saying that. You will never be held accountable to revenue goals," Howard said. "We have a genuine commitment to your program. But what I am saying is that money matters, and if what you come up with in the end requires us to live off of Pell Grants, then that won't be enough."

Rachel was disheartened. And Howard could see it.

"You know," Howard added diplomatically, "We could do something like what the Ivy leagues do."

Rachel's attention was instantly piqued.

"Diversity numbers are purely racial, however it is that we account for race. Some elite universities have directed significant efforts to create admissions programs in foreign nations where by US standards everyone is a racial minority. India, throughout Africa, China. Those are a few that come to mind. By targeting the children of the wealthy elite in those nations we can use their enrollment here to boost our diversity numbers. That, and they pay full fare with no discount just like the Legacy admits."

Discussion Questions:

1. What is the purpose of diversity goals within an institution?
2. What should count and what should not count when it comes to meeting diversity goals?
3. Is it wrong to use foreign nationals to boost domestic diversity outcomes?
4. What needs to be diversified in educational institutions? In your institution?
5. How should Rachel proceed?

Vaccine Resistance in Vulnerable Communities

As the Covid-19 pandemic gripped the international community, you have found yourself alternately bemused and horrified by the international reaction (or sometimes lack of reaction) to the crisis. Mostly you are struck by the fact that for so many of your fellow countrymen back at home in the comparatively safe confines of your nation are for the first time in their lives forced to confront the fragility of life on the planet.

You haven't been able to labor under the illusion of "safety" for many years now. You have been stationed in an underdeveloped nation for several years working as a director of operations. You find your job to be rewarding, albeit lonely. As those initial months slipped into years you had incrementally lost track of the news and other cultural markers that you paid so much attention to when you lived in the states. It has been some time since you could relate to the "republicans versus democrats" news that occupies 95% of the airtime in the United States. You couldn't name a popular show on a streaming service. You couldn't guess which kind of music is popular. And you couldn't care less. Living this kind of life requires the ability to adapt to a different universe of thought, ideas, powers and constraints. That's what makes it so fun.

You, just like the rest of the world, are unsure what the long-term effects of the pandemic might be. You are unsure of the lethality of the virus. You are unsure of how to treat it once infected. You have no access to testing supplies and there are certainly no hospital beds near you for those who are afflicted.

But you do notice that while locals you serve are well-aware of the pandemic, they refuse to use the word "Covid." They only refer to it as "the fever." The discussions you have with them confirm to you the reason why: most people don't believe that the pandemic is that bad and others think that it is entirely fabricated. They don't believe that news sources are telling the truth. They don't trust their government to relay accurate information, and they don't trust the medical NGOs that arrive sporadically doling out medical advice. They don't trust reporting as to the accuracy of symptoms. They don't believe public health PSAs and they don't trust the motives behind the government's rules implemented to deal with the alleged problem. They don't believe that the vaccine is safe, and they suspect that it's just another excuse to use them as lab testing subjects. As you quipped to one of your colleagues "If this was the atmosphere in the States we would call it a crisis of confidence. But here's it's called 'Monday.'".

You accept these confines within which you work. It is just a part of the job. Working in this part of the world requires a level of cultural competence which can't be taught in the states. One needs to understand the deep mistrust between the people and their authorities. Those authorities might be the police, the government, hospitals, schools or community leaders. The lack of a free press means that all information sources are mistrusted, including public health announcements. This gives rise to weekly rumors spread through social media. Indeed, the standard norms of governing knowledge back in the States had been eroded some generations ago in this nation. That the States appeared to be headed in this same direction was interesting, but not terribly surprising. People are people, whether here or in Idaho.

A new wrinkle in your operations is now before you. Some months ago you worked with the national health department to become a recipient of the COVAX program—a western-led initiative which provides Covid-19 vaccines to nations that cannot afford them. You had partnered with the Health Department in writing the proposal and it took you some cajoling to get permission to be named a vaccine provider. At the end of those negotiations the head of the Health Department said to you, not the least bit jokingly, "Let's just sell them to the Koreans. Because even if we get those vaccines we couldn't possibly get them in arms."

Your tenacity and political wrangling have paid off, and you have been informed that you are to receive several thousand doses of a Covid-19 vaccine.

This begs the question: How are you going to convince people to take the vaccine when many deny the existence of the pandemic altogether and the rest mistrust vaccines? That was a tough question to answer. The less difficult problem to resolve would be transportation from port and skilled staff to do injections. Luckily, your NGO has a truck and a driver. And you have a reliable stream of volunteer nurses that can easily do the injections.

You immediately make a phone call to the next nursing volunteer crew leader who is due to arrive in two weeks—about when you estimate that the COVAX doses will come in.

"Tell me about the team members you are sending us." You state to the team leader. "I do hope you have someone with some background in public health."

"Not really." Says the team leader. "These are nurses-in-training. None of them have their degrees yet, which I gather hasn't mattered much in the past. Anyway, I'm glad that you called, because there is something that I want to talk to you about. We have a team of twelve we are sending to you. They easily have the requisite skill to do the injections that you need them to do. But six of them are unvaccinated and knowing the six, there is little chance that they will become vaccinated before arriving at your facility. Is that a problem for you?"

Discussion Questions:

1. What ethical obligations do you have toward the population that you serve in the COVAX program?

2. How do you respond to the prospect of unvaccinated nurses serving in your NGO?
3. What moral problems exist with regard to vaccine-resistant vaccinators disseminating vaccines to the population you serve?

The At-Least-Somewhat Racist Missionary

You have accepted a position as a translator for an NGO working in a country with which you have little experience. You learned the colonial language (French) while in college and excelled at language acquisition. But nearly all of your education was Paris-centric. In fact, in all of your studies the only book you read that testified to the existence of French outside of France was Aimée Césaire's *Cahiers d'Un Retour au Pays Natal*—a work of surrealist poetry written by one of Martinique's most famous intellectuals.

But your lack of experience didn't prevent you from engrossing yourself in your new work. On a daily basis you had access to persons and situations that the rest of the world would never have the opportunity to see. On Monday it might be a prison warden in need of inmate re-entry advice, on Tuesday a dinner at the mayor's office. On Wednesday you might spend the day at your guard's home where he cared for his sick mother, and Thursday translating for a short-term building crew.

You have become a known entity in the community. Not living at the compound but instead renting an apartment in town did a lot to make you known and respected. The women of your neighborhood refer to you as "le petit chou" and the men jokingly call you "le Parisian." You've never quite figured out whether they were complimenting your French or teasing you about your accent. As your assimilation into the community deepened you found that you were frequently asked for your opinion on important issues. You even became a frequent guest at the radio station for their noontime talk show.

On that latter note, you have taken to telling a story to new arrivals about the perils of being a translator in a language that is not your first language. Your best story goes that the first time you were asked to do an interview for a radio station was after a long day of translating, and the brain-fatigue of operating in another language had long since been sent in. You couldn't dream of engaging in yet another conversation that day and just wanted the pesky interlocutor to leave you alone.

When the would-be interviewer stated that it would be on his well-known network of 9 million listeners and would take place "*en direct*" you mistakenly inferred that it would be a "direct" or "frank" discussion. So you agreed. Then you learned the moment the interview began that "en direct" meant "live." The pit in your stomach at that moment was memorable. The moral of the story for new translators you met with was "never say 'yes' just to get a conversation over with."

You have become aware of the presence of a woman in your town who hails from Iowa. You are told that she has been living there for thirty-five years and is working with the Baptist Church located just off the *hôtel de ville*. Wanting to get to know the life story of such a person, you contact her and agree to go over to her home for a dinner.

She lives in a comfortable home in the center of town. She has a car and a computer and reliable high-speed internet. Her courtyard has an orange tree and a lime tree and its walls are unusually high and well-fortified. Over dinner you meet all of her staff—locals who attend to the needs of her home such as cooking, cleaning, guarding and overseeing. You count no less than seven servants in her employ.

As dinner begins you discover that she arrived in the country fresh out of college. She has never been married and has only a few family members left in the states. As the *entrée* is brought to the table you are somewhat shocked by her brusque treatment of her staff. "Don't bring it to me on that side you idiot!" she says meanly. But you reason that you've probably said some words of your own that you regret, so why judge her? You let it pass.

As the *entrée* is taken up and the *répas* begins a tussle breaks out between her and the kitchen staff. You can't understand every word of it as she has switched from French to the local language. But the gist of the discussion so far as you can tell was a dispute over how warm the food needed to be as it arrived at the table. The tone of her voice made it clear that she wasn't happy.

"Now where were we?" she says, completely diverting her attention from her domestic servants. Not even a beat was skipped, and you try not to reveal the shock you feel at seeing her switch so effortlessly from acerbic criticism of staff to her polite attention to you. You do your best to deflect the awkward moment and the discussion continues.

You learn a lot about her work. Her church runs a training center for women in an adjoining property where they learn to sew and do crafts which are sold at market. "Some of them can learn how to do it pretty well" she says. "So long as their husbands let them do something with their lives," she adds with clear contempt in her voice. "And when their husbands beat them up and throw them out, sometimes that's the best thing for them. Because we'll take them in, give them a job and let them believe and worship as they like."

You remind yourself that you're not in Kansas anymore, but can't shake the feeling that this situation isn't quite right. Before you can collect your thoughts, she makes a pitch at you.

"So you work for that NGO, right? I'd bet I can run your women's educational program better and for a fraction of the cost of what you pay. Would you be interested in looking into that?"

You have little doubt that she could deliver on her promises. What you would have to invent she would merely have to rebrand. But you weren't the decider. You're just the translator.

"Maybe I could talk to the director…" you state.

"Gérald!" she bellows to the kitchen. "Time for the desert!" Then directing her attention back at you, turning to business in the flicker of an eye, she adds "Honey, you're going to be eaten alive out here. I've been at this for 35 years. And let me tell you, you're not going to change these people." The finger pointing back to her staff makes it clear just what people won't ever change.

Discussion Questions:

1. Is the missionary's behavior an instance of racism?
2. What dynamics does a single, white female missionary face in developing nations that she might not face in the States?
3. What experiences have led her to adopt the attitudes that she has?
4. Are you willing to pass on word of her offer to your directors?
5. When two NGOs cooperate, to what extent, if any, do they share responsibility for each other's moral tenor?

Later that Evening, in the Same Town

Your head is spinning from your meal with the missionary. You don't like to be judgmental of people, but the evening you just spent with her does not sit well with you. You therefore walk to the town center where there is a local grocery store that you frequent. The owner lets you rummage to the back of the drink refrigerator to get the coldest bottles kept at the back. As you exit the store with the mango soda in your hand you notice two things. One is that two African friends of yours are staring intently in the opposite direction. The other was what they were staring at.

Both your and their attention is drawn to a flotilla of expensive white SUVs pulling onto the main street. You've learned to tell when they are coming before you see them. Their engines are both loud and tight—totally unlike the local busses that manage against all odds to remain on the road. Just one of those SUVs could probably buy a good house for any of the people they passed on the street.

One of your African friends notices you gawking too and he states flippantly "Peace corps." He then continues to watch.

The SUVs pull up to an internet café just a few doors down from where you are standing. The doors open and out descends a procession of white women in shorts and tank tops. They scurry into the café where they will likely be communicating with their loved ones back home. (While internet cafés are almost extinct in the west, they play an important role in this town where cell connectivity is high but bandwidth low.)

You notice that you are shocked. That surprises you and you take it as an unexpected sign that you have begun to adapt to your environment. Your African friends, too, are snickering. Back home it is a normal situation to observe men and women wearing shorts and tank tops. But beginning with your training at NGO headquarters and reinforced upon hitting the field you have been admonished to think carefully about culturally appropriate dress. No one was ever to wear shorts. Ever. Only soccer players were permitted and only when they were playing. Women were not permitted to wear trousers and must instead wear dresses that covered the shoulders and which extended to the ankles. You have been repeatedly told that violations of these norms were serious. But here were the Peace Corps women showing up without shame and in violation of what you were told were the "rules."

"It's like they're naked! Makes me want to go over there!" says one of your friends to you. And you don't know how to respond. You know that the women are not *trying* to be sexually suggestive. But the look on your friends' faces makes it clear that that's exactly how they are interpreting it.

"You stay here my American friend" he says to you with excitement and bounds off to the café, "I'm going to meet my new wife." He disappears inside.

Discussion Questions:

1. Dress rules are cultural rules. Must you adopt them?
2. What are the potential consequences of not adopting local dress customs?
3. In your opinion are conservative dress customs fair to women? Does that matter to you?
4. If in your opinion is it morally acceptable to break local dressing rules, when it acceptable and when is it not?

Nurturing African Entrepreneurs

Chris operates a business and entrepreneurship incubator in a West African capital. The purpose of the NGO is to identify likely candidates for new business initiatives and to offer would-be entrepreneurs an educational experience that provides them basic knowledge pertaining to budgeting, staffing, marketing, product-placement, inventory control and other normal business operational needs.

Chris recently received a sum of seed money from a corporation that desires to spread goodwill as they attempt to expand operations in the region. The program they have funded is an entrepreneurship competition, not unlike those which air on American TV. Participants first receive the training that Chris has developed. Then staff from the CSR arm of the corporation and others elect to include travel to the capital city to act as judges in a competition during which competitors present their ideas for critique.

During this past week the CSR arm of the corporation brought in six highly qualified and successful American entrepreneurs and was also successful in attracting the interest of local television stations who subsequently aired lengthy news reports about the competition.

In the end the judges bestowed the victory upon Florence, a middle-aged mother whose idea was to create a business that sold emergency lighting from a storefront at the front of her house. Florence had learned from years of living in her neighborhood that electricity outages were common. But when an outage occurred the community collectively rushed to the nearby store to buy candles or other lighting supplies. Unsurprisingly, the price of these supplies skyrocketed at each outage, only to return to normal levels once power was restored. Florence's business involved receiving a shipment of foreign-made rechargeable flashlights which could double as cellphone battery bricks. The purchaser could therefore rely upon what on most days was their cell's power source as a means of illumination during outages.

The funds received for her victory would be used to pay for inventory and for minor alterations to the front room of her house which would now be a storefront. The amount was not inconsequential—equivalent to roughly four times the average monthly salary in the nation.

With the competition now complete and the American business personnel departed from the country, you resume your ordinary work. Two months later you decide to check in on Florence. As you walk up to her home you notice that nothing has changed. Her plans for the renovation of the front of her house indicated that there would be a small patio installed and a cashier's station established. None of this work had been completed.

You knock on the door and Florence answers. After several minutes of social politeness, you broach the issue. Why has the work not been done?

You learn over the course of a long conversation that the news of her victory spread swiftly through her neighborhood. Residents captured the video aired on television and shared it on online streaming platforms, playing and replaying it often. It was a common point of conversation in her neighborhood and Florence had become a local celebrity. But when word spread of her cash prize, her family members and others from the neighborhood pressured her to share a portion of her prize with them. Her husband's insistence that the money be shared was a decisive force.

In the end, she was left without any of the investment capital. It would not be accurate to say that her business had failed. The reality is that it never had begun.

Since funders have a right to understand how their funds were used, Chris knew that he was duty-bound to report this to the American corporation that had funded the event. When Christ made the call back to the states the staff in the CSR division were flabbergasted and outraged. The CSR staff wondered out loud how friends and family could behave so awfully toward someone they claimed to adore. They expressed sadness at the fact that a woman with such promise was deprived the ability to make a significant economic change in her life. One staff member wondered whether it was Florence's intention all along to win the funds in order to distribute them in her neighborhood. But mostly they were thoroughly unhappy with the situation and accuse Chris of running a deceptive program that misused funds.

Discussion Questions:

1. What social pressures did the organizers of the competition fail to appreciate in their design?
2. Was Florence set up to fail by the organizers?
3. Were the funds distributed misused?
4. How could events like this one be designed differently so as to avoid these problems? Can they be designed differently?
5. Is the CSR arm of the American corporation to be blamed?

The Successful West African Recycling Entrepreneur

This Case Has Been Used as a Training Tool for Burgeoning West African Entrepreneurs. For Notes on Using It with African Participants, Please Refer to the Appendix Discussion of This Case.

Ousmane established a plastics recycling business in his village two years ago. He discovered that a recycling plant would pay him 1000 CFA for every bail of plastic that he brought them. Ousmane learned that he had to be extra careful to make sure the plastic he brought was clean. Any stones or dirt in the plastic would mean the factory would reject the entire delivery. And that would mean they might not take future bails from him.

At first, he was able to deliver two bails a day to the plant. Then he realized that people from his town would like to have a job, and that this would help him to expand his business. So, he began to hire people from his town to help him. Each of his employees would receive the price of 500 CFA for each bail of plastic they gave him. Ousmane would then load the plastic onto his truck and drive it to the recycling plant.

Now he is able to deliver an average of ten bales a day to the recycling plant. He believes he can deliver much more than that in the future. But he doesn't have the right truck to be able to transport the extra bails needed for expansion (Table 1).

Here is how Ousmane budgeted his business:

People in Ousmane's village at first thought he was crazy to pick up garbage. But when they saw that he was earning money and that he had many employees, they started to admire him. He was considered a successful man with a profitable business. That's when requests from his family and friends started coming in. His brother was getting married and asked Ousmane for 40,000 CFA to help pay for the wedding. His sister asked her for 20,000

Table 1 "Ousmane's Budget"

Expenses		Weekly	Yearly
	Fuel	CFA 17,000.00	CFA 850,000.00
Revenue			
	Bails of Plastic	CFA 35,000.00	CFA 1,750,000.00
Net Revenue		CFA 18,000.00	CFA 900,000.00

CFA to help pay for her children's school uniforms. And people in his town constantly asked him for small amounts of money to meet their many needs.

Discussion Question:

1. Has Ousmame created an accurate budget for his business? Is he missing anything?
2. Should Ousmane help pay for his brother's wedding?
3. Is there any way that Ousmane can help his brother, sister and friends without harming his business?

Bibliography

Abbascia, D., & Poggi, G. (2012). *Cote D'Ivoire Election Crisis & Aftermath.* Hauppauge, NY: Nova Science Publications.

Austin, J. L. (1962). *How to Do Things with Words* (2nd ed.). Cambridge, MA: Harvard University Press.

Behnke, A. (2001, March). Grand Theory in the Age of Its Impossibility. *Cooperation and Conflict, 36*(1), 121–134.

Césaire, A. (2000). *Discourse on Colonialism.* New York, NY: Monthly Review Press.

Hoschild, A. (1999). *King Leopold's Ghost: A Story of Greed, Terror, and Heroism in Colonial Africa.* Boston, MA: Houghton Mifflin Harcourt.

Marx, K., & Engels, F. (2015). *The Communist Manifesto.* New York, NY: Penguin Classics.

Nussbaum, M. (2016). Judging Other Cultures: The Case of Genital Mutilation. In L. May & J. Delston, *Applied Ethics* (6th ed., pp. xxii–xlii). New York, NY: Routledge.

Praykash, G. (1994). Subaltern Studies as Postcolonial Criticism. *American Historical Review, 99,* 1475–1490.

Ricardo, D. (2004). *The Principles of Political Economy and Taxation.* Mineola, NY: Dover Publications.

Rist, G. (2019). *The History of Development* (4th ed.). London, UK: Zed Books.

Smith, A. (2003). *The Wealth of Nations.* New York, NY: Bantham Dell.

Todaro, M., & Smith, S. (2020). *Economic Development* (13th ed.). Harlow, UK: Pearson.

Zack, N. (2022). *Thinking About Race* (2nd ed.). Belmont, CA: Cengage.

Zinsmeister, K. (2016). *The Almanac of American Philanthropy.* Washington, DC: The Philanthropy Roundtable.

Ethics in Program Operations

How can ethics be implemented within an institution? There are many different, sometimes competing, answers to this question. In this section we will review the most common means for doing this and identify the benefits and demerits of each approach.

Ethics Committees

Governments and municipalities as well as hospitals and medical centers have institutionalized ethics committees to service the needs of wrestling with difficult moral decisions. Governments may do this as a result of a ballot initiative or at their own initiative. Hospitals tend to opt for such an approach as a part of best practices. There are benefits and demerits of this approach.

On the plus side, having an ethics committee guarantees that there exists someone whose job obligation it is to attend to difficult moral situations. Formal committees also ensure that members are properly trained or credentialed since they often times have their own criteria for membership. The existence of formal structures also communicates to staff and clients that ethics is prioritized. In Hospitals it is likely current professionals employed in-house that are selected to serve on such committees. Their insider point of view can be invaluable when making decisions over complex medical issues. Governments might do the same, but from time-to-time they empower appointed community members not currently sitting in government positions to serve in this capacity. Finally, a committee structure permits ethics decisions to move beyond "mere opinion" and into a position of authority and power. This is owing to the fact that such committees can be independent in a way that no other model discussed in this section is independent.

But there are drawbacks to this model. For starters, it is only large-budget entities that have the operational ability to reassign members of their ranks to ethics duties. For budgetary reasons the smaller NFP or NGO has practical means to implement this model. Another problem is that creating an ethics committee sends the message that ethics is the committee's problem, not the problem of the rest of the staff. This is especially true in medical situations where it is common for the ethics committee to be asked to make a tough call behind which a practicing physician hopes to take "cover." I urge all medical ethics committees to refuse the pressure to become a substitute for physician decisions. Finally, an ethics committee naively placed into an operation could cause unintentional damage, and great care must be made to ensure the autonomous operation of the HR department without the ability of the ethics committee unintentionally overriding policies of hiring, firing and evaluation (Hester, 2022).

It is also common for such committees to become a moral equivalent of a dusty main street in the nineteenth-century southwest in which grudges are settled via verbal gunslinging. So it is essential that the processes by which the committee is approached and through which it performs deliberations, ensure that confidentiality be maintained all the while assuring transparency and integrity.

The HR Department

While many NFP and NGO institutions might have no resources for a new committee, they often do have an HR department. Should the HR department be the locus of ethics decisions? As with the Ethics Committee model, there are plusses and minuses to this approach.

On the plus side, your HR department already has well-defined practices tailor-fit for your institution. Among these practices are the instantiation of process and confidentiality, both of which are bedrock prerequisites for responsible ethics discussions. Additionally, your HR department *already is* engaged in ethics discussions, probably on a daily basis. They have experience with how to handle sexual harassment allegations, job performance issues and so much more. There are well-defined legal confines within which they operate and you probably already have a means of disseminating communication paths between them and staff (Scott, 2005).

But relegating ethics to the HR department has its drawbacks. Many are the same drawbacks of formal ethics committee: ethics will be perceived as something that happens in someone else's department and it can become a mechanism for airing grudges rather than addressing injustices. But in addition it can be dangerous to locate the authority of right and wrong into the hands of the same department that decides employee policy, cuts paychecks and decides benefits. No government or hospital committee faces these dynamics. Additionally, while some HR departments view themselves as protectors of their staff, others view themselves as protectors of the institution. This can have significant consequences should that department also be given the power to decide upon right and wrong. Finally, the smallest NFPs and NGOs tend to either subcontract their HR needs to firms unwilling to take on such a role or they have no HR department at all.

Staff-Training and Grassroots Ethics

If the attention to ethics is not the affair of a new committee and if it is not to be a part of the HR department, then it must become a matter of the job-requirements and responsibilities of everyone in your institution—from your frontline worker to your board. Selecting such a method of implementation will always be decentralized, democratized and messy. But if done well it will be comprehensive, effective and add to the collegial atmosphere of your environment.

So how does an institution accomplish this?

One way to do so is to identify the worst likely events that could befall an institution and to create a training environment tailored around a discussion of "worst events." For example, an issue known to have befallen rural healthcare operations in Sub-Saharan Africa is the infiltration of pedophiles within their volunteer ranks. The staff at such an NGO are aware of this problem, and invariably have suggestions regarding how to ameliorate it. An ethics discussion with them would likely reveal a number of policies and procedures which could ensure that this tragedy does not befall the NGO. Staff know that background checks are essential (and the hosting government may require them anyway). They also will tell you that in the past they have been uncomfortable with the level of preparedness of volunteers—pointing to the need to ensure that you provide the training, not those that send them. Many other suggestions are possible. The point of this is that by bringing in both staff and leadership to the discussion, significant problems can be avoided and via sometimes clever ideas. This is an example of a grassroots ethics initiative with real-world results (Watts et al., 2021) As the reader contemplates the cases in this section, it may be helpful to analyze them with an eye toward developing such policies.

Staff in such discussions need to be given the power to raise the alarm and to have that alarm heard. In intercultural situations in which locals are involved in operations, efforts must be made to convince such staff that they will not lose their positions just because they spoke ill of a volunteer. And every effort must be made to ensure that female nationals credibly believe that they have a voice that will be heard. On this note the egoist perspective is of special value: What punishment might national staff fear risking for speaking out? And how can you create barriers to such punishments?

Many NFPs and NGOs already have robust training sessions. Adding ethics training into these sessions can be immensely helpful. Most NFPs and NGOs are in a region with a university nearby. Consider hiring a local ethicist to lead an in-house discussion during an employee training day.

An added bonus of this method of instituting ethics awareness into your institution is that it provides a unique team-building experience and a sense of collegiality. People respond to ethical dilemmas with great passion. Hearing what your staff are passionate about can be very revealing. An outcome of this is to bring awareness of ethics within your institution as well as a better understanding of one's own colleagues.

Nevertheless, I offer a word of warning. Open and free debate can easily descend into anarchy. The expertise of the discussion leader is an essential feature of successful public discussion. For further information on this I refer the reader to the discussion-leader information near the end of this book.

The Protective Guardian

You are an attorney who helps to oversee the *guardian ad lidem* program in your county. This program helps to assign independent community members to children's cases as they work their way through the courts. The most common profile of such a case is that of a child temporarily or permanently in the foster care system who must receive court oversight for certain issues ranging from school enrollment and sports participation to visitation or medical decisions. Having a community member independent from the justice system advocating for the interests of the child has proven to be an effective way to ensure that the rights of the child are consistently and impartially attended to.

Your attention today is drawn to the case of Antoine. Antoine is an 8-year-old boy who is in the permanent care of the state protective services and will in all likelihood remain there until he ages out of the system. It is not clear who his father is and his mother is in prison serving a very lengthy sentence for a federal offense.

Antoine's guardian is Maren. Maren is a 40-year-old local mom who volunteers her time to the program. She has been involved with your NFP for ten years and has by all accounts performed her duties well if not admirably. Maren not only appears before the court in proceedings regarding the care of Antoine, but also volunteers in Antoine's group home.

The following situation has developed over the past few months: Antoine has become involved in a local church which Maren also attends. His involvement includes youth activities, mid-week sports camps and sometimes Sunday morning worship services. Meanwhile, the directors of Antoine's home have advocated that Antoine be moved from his current home to a home several miles away to alleviate overcrowding in his current home.

Maren believes that this is not in Antoine's best interest. She asserts to you that Antoine is beginning to come out of his shell at the church he is currently attending. He is beginning to engage in normal play with kids his own age and is starting to respond to adults in a more age appropriate way. For the first time, Maren asserts, Antoine is making eye contact when speaking to adults. Maren insists that his involvement in the church community has been the cause of this change in Antoine.

You are aware of the guidelines within which your program operates. What is noteworthy regarding those guidelines is not so much what they include, but what they do not include. Nowhere in your programming or reporting requirements is there any mention of religion or spiritual development. But your guidelines definitely do include language regarding living conditions in group homes which presumably include staffing ratios and provisions against overcrowding. You struggle to understand how this information fits into your NFP's data collection systems, and how it fits (or doesn't fit) into state guidelines.

Discussion Questions:

1. Is it permissible for you to consider spiritual development in your program operations?
2. Do you have any problem with Maren's involvement in your program?
3. How do you respond to Maren?

4. Do children have a *right* to safe living conditions? Do they have spiritual rights?

Dealing with Noncompliance in Syracuse

You have been tasked with organizing, monitoring and evaluating a premarital counseling program funded by the state of New York whose goal is to "enable healthy marriages." The purpose of the program is to provide premarital counseling for engaged couples seeking to be married. Your task is to organize a team of counselors who will provide the counseling, to track those sessions and to receive reports. You as the program monitor then assemble the aggregate data to report back to the state.

The data points that you assemble are:

1. Census: How many prospective married couples state an interest in the counseling sessions. This is monitored via a network of pastors, judges and notaries known in your area to conduct wedding ceremonies and who have agreed to participate in your referral service.
2. Attendance data: How many appointments are booked versus how many arrive for the appointment (with a target of four sessions).
3. Marriage outcomes: The number of participating couples who become married within the 12 months following counseling.
4. Control: Compare the outcomes of participating couples with outcomes found in state-held data.

You discover unexpected results. Unsurprisingly, 30% more couples express interest in the service than actually avail themselves of it. Of somewhat greater interest is the fact that the marriage rates of participating couples are slightly lower than non-participating couples. But what strikes you most of all in the data is the fact that when couples begin counseling sessions but cease them before the required amount of sessions, marriage rates are dramatically lower than all other groups studied (50% lower than fully compliant couples).

This troubles you. You begin to wonder whether your program is harming the long-term health of the relationships you wish to further. And you wonder whether the dollars that you have been given undermine the very thing the program was intended to promote: healthy marriages.

Discussion Questions:
1. Does the data show that this is a failed program?

2. What other explanations exist, other than program failure, for the low marriage rate of those who comply with the program?
3. Is lack of compliance a sign of unhealthy relationships?

Putting Nationals in Harm's Way

You are the director of "Healing Wings," an NGO that provides air transport of personnel and supplies to various locations throughout sub-Saharan Africa. This mission is carried out through a network of pilots, mechanics, logistics personnel and ground crews. What started as a labor of love by a zealous pioneer to the industry has become a significant regional player in the transportation needs of many NGOs. On any given day your fleet could be transporting medical supplies, educational materials, ground personnel or livestock.

Your contracts are of two broad sorts: on-demand short haul and contractual retainers. The on-demand side could take any of an infinitely-many different instantiations. You've transported crates of chickens, vaccines and family members of staff under such contracts.

But retainers are typically offered to the largest of NGO's in the region and would include transporting international staff to sites for spot checks and transporting any of the many different supplies needed by them on an ongoing basis. The most common scenario under which a retainer is offered is at the bidding stage when an NGO prepares a proposal to be funded for their work. Your quote thus becomes part of their proposal to their funders.

Offering services on a retainer basis is tricky. You must be able to estimate fuel costs over the coming year. And you have a reliable assessment of when and where services are likely to be needed. This in turn requires that you retain your own ground staff in strategic locations. That staff may offload an airplane, transport its contents to the destination, or both.

The ability to offer retainers has proved to be an important element of the operations of not only your own company but also of the NGOs that use your services. The contractual demands of retainers were high, but so was the revenue.

One summer, however, there was a natural disaster followed by a civil uprising in one region you serve. Ground reports were dire. Highway banditry had increased significantly and the rule of law was declining. However, this did not change the fact that you had signed a retainer with a large US-based NGO who was currently servicing a USAID contract.

You call this NGO and describe the situation. Your pilots, all of whom were westerners, would probably be safe as they fly in and out. You weren't worried about them. It was your ground crews that you were worried about. They were nationals, not foreigners. They would have to make their trip to the airport, then back to town in the trucks loaded with valuable items. You explain that there had been kidnappings and killings on one particular route and that your trucks could likely become targets. Their goods could be lost and your staff harmed. But the staff you speak with respond by asserting that you had signed a retainer requiring your continued offering of flights as per the contract.

Discussion Questions:

1. What are the consequences for you and your employees if you violate the terms of your contract with the NGO? What are the consequences to you and your employees if you continue to operate?
2. If there is a moral failure in this situation, when and where did it occur?
3. What new ways can you think of to address the problem before you?
4. What contractual clauses could have been added to the agreement between the flight-services NGO and their customers in order to avoid this situation?

Another Feeding Program Begins

Fads exist in the NFP sector just as they do in the fashion industry. Yesterday's "social entrepreneurship" will be replaced by tomorrow's "scalable impact." In one generation one cause becomes beloved only to be replaced by a different fad in another.

One of the most consistent services offered in every age of the NFP sector, though, are food-resources initiatives. The terminology has changed, but the core mission has not. Access to nutritious, low-cost food is more pressing a need now than ever.

You work as a program director at a local food pantry. Recent demand has been nothing short of crushing. A heavy demand day when you took the job ten years ago would mean that you would see one hundred families a day. But on your most recent food distribution you saw 100 an hour.

After work one day you go out to a local bar and grill to have drinks with friends. As the evening wears on you turn to talking about what you do. You tell the group about your work, the families you serve and the depressing reality of increased demand.

The people you are socializing with are eager to hear more about your experiences, but none of them more than Beth. Beth does well with her career in banking and is interested in "giving back." She shares with you what she has recently been doing to that effect. On weekends she heads down to the park at the center of town where homeless people are known to live and sleep. She arrives with burritos to disseminate to them and proudly declares that she doesn't leave until "I give out all 200 burritos."

You are torn. You happen to take exception to her approach. You know the identities of some of the people that live down there. Some of them were banned from the food pantry for very serious security reasons. Others were transient. Quite a few suffer mental illness issues. You doubt that Beth appreciates the highly nuanced nature of this population.

As you think about Beth's investment in 200 burritos a week for the homeless, you believe that for the same financial investment quite a few more people could be fed through your food pantry—at least double.

On the one hand you are happy to see the passion and excitement in Beth's face as she describes her concern for the homeless. You share her passion. But that passion seems misdirected. In fact, it could be positively damaging. The city has had to send police to that park nearly every night for six months, sometimes for serious crimes such as assault and battery. You couldn't help but think that while there may be a marginal benefit to Beth's activity there was also damage being done.

Discussion Questions:

1. Do you raise your concerns to Beth?
2. If it is true that you could impact more people with your food pantry, should Beth stop her activities and give to your organization instead?
3. Is it wrong for people to direct inefficient labor to their favorite projects?
4. It is common for NFPs to discover inefficient or even harmful activities being performed in their community by well-intentioned people. Should your NFP address this? If not, why? If so, how?

What Could Go Wrong?

You work with college students in the United States, helping them to become more engaged with the world through civic activities. Among the 18–21-year-old population, the most popular of all international causes are Human Trafficking and Child Exploitation. You have often wondered, of all the catastrophes that occur on the planet on a regular basis, why this one has captivated the attention of so many college-age people? Malaria still kills with impunity, government corruption probably kills more than Malaria, and we still have yet to eradicate polio despite the existence of an effective vaccine.

Your work is to help young adults become more engaged with their world and to do so in a strategic, directed and impactful way. This requires increased awareness, increased action and helping the enthusiastic to articulate clear, realistic plans for their action. You also have resources, and those resources make you popular with the college-age students you serve.

In your office today is a motivated, intelligent and sincere young woman named Josephine. Josephine wants to "save kids from human trafficking" and shares with you her plan.

Josephine has learned that a "lot of trafficking" happens in the Phuket, Thailand region where western pedophiles often go on vacation to rent the sexual services of young Thai girls and boys. Josephine learned by watching a video online that those children are sold to pimps in town for a price of about $200. She describes what the lives are like of these children, what the futures of these kids look like, and how desperately they need our help.

"But this isn't just talk," says Josephine, "I've begun to act."

Josephine shares that she has raised about $15,000 from friends and family who have agreed to pay for her travel expenses to Phuket where she will use the remainder of her funds to purchase the freedom of child prostitutes sold in the tourist markets. After her enthusiastic exposé she adds, "This is where you come in. How are you willing to support me as I help to liberate these children from their enslavement?".

Discussion Questions:

1. What concerns do you have about Josephine's plans?
2. Is Josephine in danger? Does Josephine's proposed course of action pose new risk to imperiled children?
3. What advice would you give Josephine?
4. If Josephine were successful, what would happen to the kids she buys back once Josephine leaves Thailand?
5. Do the children that Josephine hopes to save face negative consequences?
6. Has Josephine thought of the political culture in the region, and what is her plan to deal with public sector complicity?

Land Title Woes in Sub-Saharan Africa

You own a nonprofit consultancy agency. Increasingly, your work has dealt with larger and larger clients. What began as a *pro bono* exercise looking over local NFP's year-end giving letters has blossomed into a strategy and market positioning service. Wanting to expand into international NGO work, you venture out in search of new clients.

One bite that you get was not from the NFP sector at all, but a consortium of international real estate developers whose most recent project incorporated a social component. This group had purchased a large parcel of land on the Gulf of Guinea which they hoped to transform into a tourist destination marketed for the local elites and intrepid European vacationers. They had good reason to think that the rise in adventure travel and off-the-beaten-path travel would make for a winning business model. It had worked elsewhere and the business model is already proven.

The principals involved in the deal, while relative newcomers to this kind of project, were experienced international business people whose previous work was in a variety of sectors of western and sometimes nonwestern economies. But while their experiences were different, their shared values were the same: they all valued financially-profitable enterprises that demonstrated social commitment.

They had seen innumerable real estate development projects done in impoverished nations which offered little to no social benefit for the citizens of that country. Or worse, they offered no benefit while exacting a high price in the form of unregulated sewage output, environmental hazards, or deteriorating security conditions in the surrounding towns. Their desire was to ensure that this did not happen to their project. They viewed themselves as persons with significant business talents which they wanted to use "doing good and doing well."

But their initiative was seeing unexpected land title issues. They had spent considerable financial resources employing trustworthy lawyers to research current title owners (who were, unsurprisingly, the families of the nation's political elite). Those same lawyers then negotiated a price and sold several thousand acres of prime gulf-front land to the development consortium.

But what they had not planned on was what happened next. While the development group was creating their own elaborate development strategy for the responsible utilization of the land, the government officials in the region who had sold the group the land then set about to sell the same land again to a variety of locals. During one spot-check the developer group showed up only to see several hundred parcels barbed-wired off from one another to stake out their new claim to the land. Months later the barbed wire turned into makeshift shacks. Then cinder-block structures.

"What the hell is going on!!!" Larry, a chief funder of the real estate initiative bellowed during a virtual meeting of investors.

What was going on was that the interest of the western real estate developers made the land more valuable. In this nation with little to no land title tradition government officials saw a new way of making money from land which was previously useless to them. For a "fee" they would sell the land again, and print a title again, to as many locals as would appear at the government building.

A *lot* of locals appeared.

"This is why we want to bring you in." You are told by the investment group during a virtual call. "We want you to give us some solutions to this problem. What do you think our response should be?"

"Well," you begin to speak, "Tell me a little more about what you have done in the past. How much time have you spent in the village near your development area? And what kind of local buy-in have you been successful in getting so far?"

The blank look on their faces was all the answer you needed.

"How about this," you add, searching for insight. "Tell me about the level of awareness of the US embassy of your efforts in the capital. I know it's far away, but the US embassy often has the ear of the government in ways that you never will."

"You mean like telling them that we are in the country on business?" Larry states. "Nope. I haven't done that."

The gravity of the situation was beginning to hit you. "Let me say this. I worked in that region for three months some time ago. While this region lacks the kinds of property protection mechanisms we enjoy in the west, there are nonetheless, shall I say, less formal mechanisms known to exist in the country. You need to know about these, because they *will* be proposed to you. Probably by the government itself. High on that list of remedies is the employment of groups of former foreign soldiers in the capital. Land disputes are frequently handled in this region by paying them a fee to shoot the locals off the land."

"WE WILL NOT KILL PEOPLE!!!" Larry yells.

"Of course not!" you respond, somewhat concerned by Larry's naïve misreading of your comment. "What I am telling you is that this is the world that you have stumbled into and that if you don't take action to address the situation in a peaceful way everyone on your land will assume that your next step will be the exact opposite of peaceful. The squatters are preparing for that, probably as we speak. Because that is how things happen there. Everyone who is on your land right now has a house back in town sitting on land with no title. That's how it works there. To us it's unusual, but to them it is normal. One day the government might roll in with bulldozers and demolish everything they own for a road. Or they might bulldoze it for reasons they never share with the locals at all. And the residents will have no recourse. During the civil war 20 years ago, the winners just walked into town and evicted the losers. Typically, by force. The people on your land right now are just the those who were on the winning side during the last war. So, your problem is at least twofold: How to show exclusive title to the land and how to bring that about peacefully? Because I can tell you there are a lot of defensive AK-47's on your land in the hands of locals as we speak. They're expecting one of two things: a payoff or a fight."

Silence fell over the room. And after a moment another of the principal investors chimed in. "What would it take to get you to go in there and start talking with them?".

"Well," you respond, "let's list the alternatives before we decide on the approach." You write them up for the group, specifically striking through the first one just to make things clearer:

1. ~~Mercenaries~~
2. Payoff the locals
3. Payoff a political elite to resolve the issue.
4. Operate within the foreign justice system. File a lawsuit against the government in the foreign court demanding title.
5. Payoff locals and file lawsuits simultaneously.
6. Identify land the locals would want and negotiate a land-swap agreement.
7. Give up. Cut your losses.
8. ??????????

Discussion Questions:

1. What are the barriers to Foreign Direct Investment in developing nations?
2. What assumptions did the investment consortium make about business in this country?
3. Why is local support important, and how does that importance change in rural Africa?
4. What coalition-building activities can you envision to help to resolve this issue?

5. What role do foreign courts play in this scenario? If forced to choose, which of the options listed would you choose and why?

Microfinance, Interest and Islam

Microfinance institutions first began as an exercise by Bangladeshi financier Muhammad Yunus. Yunus, whose work would later go on to earn a Nobel prize, correctly diagnosed that one of the facets of economic life which consistently acted against the interests of the economically disadvantaged was the lack of access to banking, whether in the form of savings accounts or loans. Typically, in the most underdeveloped nations, the amount of funds the poor could reasonably place into a bank account were far too small to cover the costs for the bank to maintain that account. And the size of loans they sought were so small that the labor needed to track repayment made the financial picture for banking institutions deeply undesirable (Yunus & Jolis, 2008).

The poor typically want to borrow money to pay for a sewing machine or an arc welder, not an SUV or a house. With no banks willing to do business with the poor, their only recourse is to borrow on the black market where the terms were unfavorable and the exploitation sometimes brutal. Yunus showed that it was possible to construct a banking model which serviced the needs of both banks and the poor. By lending to solidarity groups, for example, repayment increased significantly. Because such groups are led by village leaders or tribal elders rather than an anonymous banker in the capital city, the social pressure to repay is higher (Yunus & Jolis, 2008).

You have just come on board a well-capitalized NGO which, inspired by Yunus, implemented a microfinance program in Latin America and the Caribbean. By following his model your capitalization has blossomed from $20million USD to $60million in a short time. It's not hard to see why when you look at the numbers. Your firm charges 28% interest for each loan with a repayment rate of 97%. Your average return on equity is 20% and your portfolio risk is no more than 2.5% (defined as repayment later than 30 days).

Stated this way your firm might appear to be large. But by comparison it is not. Latin America and the Caribbean trail far behind peers in the industry in other nations, especially India and Bangladesh. In the nations you serve at best 3% of the population avail themselves of your services whereas India with its large population sees nearly 20% of its citizens avail themselves of services like yours. And every day it seems that there is a new competitor in the marketplace. You are especially concerned by the bold moves made by African telecom providers to interweave microcredit into their cell service.

You and your peers survey the nations which you think might be the best for expansion. As you compile your lists, you quickly realize the commonality among them. They are almost all robustly Islamic societies. Some like Iran pose unique problems when it comes to international banking law. But others don't.

You pick up the phone to call a friend in the industry and ask him a few questions about the other nations on your list. Your friend tells you that most microcredit services corporations elect not to offer services in the communities on your list because the banking regulators have deemed the interest rates *haram* ("forbidden" under their interpretation of Islamic law). And whether it be a back-alley loan shark or a slick western microfinance bank it all amounted to the same thing to them. Interest rates of all kinds are contrary to Islamic principles according to their regulators, and hence are forbidden.

You decide to make other calls to different contacts with experience in the nations on your list. Frustratingly, you discover that your sources contradict one another. Some say that there's no problem at all with interest rates. They charge interest all the time, so long as they lend through a specific bank run by the royal family. Others state that you have to price your earnings into the loan in a way that avoids using the word "interest." Some firms, one banker notes, add a "sliding service fee" to every loan. Others call for a "credit purchase" rather than an interest rate. And yet another banker shares with you his own idea of using the crypto market to do western banking with interest in his country in a way that can't be tracked (and therefore penalized) by banking regulators. You could charge whatever interest you wanted in such anonymous markets. The problem was the creation of solidarity groups in such an environment.

You put down the phone unenthused by what you have heard. You believe in the concept of microfinance and want to see it expanded to the poor in new countries. But your business model requires an interest rate in order to work.

Discussion Questions:

1. There is clearly not unanimity in Islamic Nations regarding the use of interest rates. To what extent does this matter to you?
2. What risks are posed to your bank if you commence activities in a nation with a hostile regulatory environment?

3. Should you avoid business in Islamic Societies where regulators deem interest immoral, and is that refusal to do business a form of religious discrimination?

Indian Nationalism and the Foreign NGO

"We have a problem," Steve says to you upon opening the morning mail. "I think that we've just been kicked out of the country."

The early 2000s saw a boom in the number of NGOs being formed in the west. Wall Street jumped on the bandwagon, funding innumerable lower-Manhattan initiatives for a variety of pet causes around the world. This was greeted by the pre-existing NGO community with a mix of envy and disdain. But whatever ill will could be found between the NGOs themselves, it couldn't possibly be matched by the ill will held by political leaders in foreign nations. Indeed, whereas NGOs has been more or less ignored by nations before that time, and sometimes even encouraged, the push of the early 2000's set in place a multi-national political revolt against, as one high-ranking politician often put it "foreign troublemakers."

One Latin American presidential candidate made this his platform, vowing to ensure that foreigners wouldn't be permitted to whip up unrest if only he were elected. This was echoed by nations in Africa and Oceana. But nowhere was the reaction against NGOs as swift and decisive as India. And Indian lawmakers set the policy norms exactly where it would hurt NGOs the most.

Initially, their regulators issued an edict which made it illegal for more than 50% of the budget of an NGO to be directed toward administrative costs. That was later changed to 20%. Then came the mandate of a cap on the percentage of funds permitted from foreign sources—a cap which was consistently lowered.

You had been aware of this changing landscape and were worried about it. But you reasoned that it was best to keep up with your work to create women's employment in rural India.

"The Ministry of Home Affairs (MHA) is telling us," Steve said, "that deposits to our State Bank of India account have been flagged as suspicious."

"Well, that's probably because they are," you say, repeating to Steve something that both you and he had admitted openly for about two years now. Back when the new rules for NGOs came into effect you and Steve made a habit of carrying as much cash as possible to India within the legal limit. And you made a lot of such trips out of the country, always stopping at the Delhi branch to make your deposits.

Those funds were vital. Both you and Steve incessantly traveled throughout India as you provided services for women in rural villages. Easily 90% of your budget was for yours and Steve's operating expenses. But that eye-popping figure never bothered you, Steve or your NGO. You had raised many thousands of women out of poverty because of your work and that work required significant staffing expenses.

"You know," you say, "We should have just done what the missionaries do. They come here, lie to the government about starting a business, and stay here for 30 years without problems."

"Right." Steve says with defeat. "Except that if I were them I wouldn't be so confident about my security in this country either."

Steve was right. There were already stories circulating about the businesses of foreign missionaries being audited by the Home Affairs office. And it was rumored that quite a few of them had already been removed from the country.

Yet words on the paper in Steve's hand could not have been clearer. The two of you had been notified that your visas had been revoked and that you were required to leave the country within 72 hours of receipt.

Discussion Questions:
1. Is the work of the NGO in this case legal or illegal?
2. Does an NGO have a right to work in a nation where it is not wanted?
3. What errors on the part of the NGO community contributed to the new policy from Delhi?
4. Is there a distinction between missionaries lying to foreign governments and non-sectarian NGOs' lying to foreign governments?
5. India is the world's largest democracy, and the anti-NGO position resulted from fair elections. Does this matter when it comes to how to evaluate this case?

Lying to the Police

Henriette, a local resident, is the house mom at a "school" for abandoned children in Sub-Saharan Africa. She and her funders call it a school more out of political convenience than as an accurate descriptor. The average child in their school is a former *talibé*, although from time-to-time children stay at the school for other reasons such as exiting prostitution or slavery.

The problems that the *talibé* face are significant. These children, always boys, are from impoverished homes in rural areas. The options for their parents are few. There exists no child welfare policy, no safety net for kids in most sub-Saharan African nations. When a family has children that they can no longer afford to feed and clothe, they may elect to surrender that child to a local or regional religious leader. Parents are told that by surrendering the child to the custody of this religious leader then the leader will provide the child with food, lodging and education until they arrive at an age sufficient to take care of themselves. All that will be asked of the parents is that they lend permission for their child to help the religious leader with various tasks at the religious compound. Such a request is not out of the ordinary. These same children would be asked to contribute in tangible ways were they to remain with their parents, too (Bernard, 2019).

But the reality of this agreement often differs from the initial promise. Often such children leave the financial peril of their own homes only to be forced into a life of mendacity at the orders of the religious leader. Stories are common which show that the kids are banished from the religious compound until they have raised a certain amount of cash via street-begging. Community members have learned to identify them on the basis of their attire which are typically potato sacks or grains sacks. They travel in packs and they usually do not have shoes or socks. It is not uncommon to observe fleas, ticks and headlice on them. None speak the colonial language, suggesting that they have never received the promised education.

Years earlier Henriette started her "school" as a means of providing somewhere for these children to go. And it had to be called a "school." Because if it wasn't then she would not have a good enough reason to offer authorities as to why so many children were staying with her. Besides, she and the other community members and occasional visiting volunteer would teach the kids literacy and reading skills which was more than what they received where they had come from.

Henriette is a religious minority in her nation. Much of what she does for the children she attributes to her faith. But this proves tricky as the religious leaders from whose custody the children arrived are public leaders of the nation's majority faith. So as long as Henriette engages in her activity of housing, feeding and teaching the students she places herself in a situation of significant social peril.

Late one night there is a knock on the door of her home. Henriette summons the house guard and together they open the door. Appearing before them is the local religious leader who begins to angrily interrogate them. The religious leader asserts that he has heard that Henriette is hiding his kids in her house. He angrily accuses her of stealing them. Appearing from behind him is an older woman. She begins to speak, stating that she had given her son to this religious leader so that her son can have an education and make something of his life. She names her son and Henriette instantly knows which of the children in her home happens to be her son.

"Tell me now" says the woman. "Is Moussa there? Do you have him?"

Henriette is now in a difficult position. Henriette believes that the children are being abused by the leader and that their condition is in every way equivalent to slavery. She does not believe that the money earned from begging goes to help the kids but instead helps to pay for the religious leaders' lifestyle. She believes that the woman with the religious leader has been manipulated to side with him.

Henriette could decide to lie to the religious leader and to the child's mother. But if she did that then she would be on record as lying to this man and word would quickly spread throughout the community that she had done so. Already a religious minority, her situation in the community would worsen.

But Henriette believes that it is not ever acceptable to lie. She roots this belief in her religious faith. She believes that what she says is ultimately accountable to God, no matter who it is said to and no matter the motivation. But Henriette has difficulty accepting the position that she should tell the truth. Telling the truth to the pair in the doorway dooms all of the children in her home to a return to slavery since they will inevitably discover that not one but twenty children are living with her. And if she tells the truth she believes she would be playing into an unjust social system that she had spent so much time combatting in her community—she would in effect be admitting that the religious leader has the right to do as he pleases at will with the children.

But Henriette must decide quickly what to do. She must answer now.

Discussion Questions:

1. Is it wrong for Henriette to lie? Is it wrong for her to tell the truth?
2. However it is that you answer the questions above, what are the potential consequences for the mother, the religious leader, for the kids and for Henriette?
3. Has Henriette taken unwise risks with her initiative to shelter kids? Is the concept of an "unwise risk" a concept we (westerners) foist upon her?
4. How can an NGO help someone like Henriette?
5. If an NGO funds persons like Henriette, what obligations does that NGO have for her security?

Closing the Orphanage

Miriam had been raised in a politically unstable nation where she managed against all odds to attain a professional, salary-earning job. That job had taken her around the world and back again. In her home nation at best 5% of all workers managed such a feat. But she had a salary, benefits, a career and a way out. Everyone she knew wanted to have what she had.

But as Miriam's life progressed so did her religious faith. She began to perceive the world less and less as a place of business, economies and nations and more and more as a spiritual location. This change of perspective proved especially potent when the military rebellion came. Shortly after the beginning of that insurrection her faith and her moral conscience instilled upon her the conviction that she had to do something for her people. She was especially grieved by the presence of the homeless children on the street. These kids had obviously done nothing to warrant their fate. But their sufferings and their exploitation were ever before her, viewing large groups of them take shelter each night in the alley below her apartment balcony. It was a disgusting and despair-inducing sight. As one year of this turned into five she then saw those kids become criminals and victimizers themselves.

Then one night she heard what she felt to be a solemn conviction. It was late in the evening and she had knelt down in her living room to pray for the kids outside. And in that moment, she heard a command, as if from a voice. The voice said one word. "Go."

It could not have been simpler and yet more difficult. She had to go. She did not understand why. But she firmly believed that she had to.

She gathered up a bag of some belongings, looked back at her apartment in the capital city, then turned and walked. She took with her some water, a little cash and her passport. She did not bring a suitcase, a phone or anything else. And as she walked away from her comfortable apartment building, she motioned to the homeless children to follow her. They did.

Miriam did not speak much about what she saw on her walk, although she let some stories slip now and again. She once shared how she ate insects as her main form of food for months. She mentioned once being victimized herself while on the road, but offered no details. And then there was the matter of her "husband" whose existence she acknowledged but no one had ever seen. Other than these terse vignettes, Miriam never spoke about herself. She never offered a rational justification for her actions. Her autobiography was a mystery. But her values were transparent.

Now Miriam was the "maman" of an orphanage on the coast. She was able to unite local churches to subsidize the food and rent for her operations and managed a home of 40 children: 20 girls and 20 boys. Visitors were common. Most were the church members that supported the orphanage, but increasingly they were westerners on short trips. And what all visitors found was a place of happiness and peace. Yes, these kids and their maman had nothing. But they were *happy*. They learned within the walls of that orphanage how to be safe, how to respond appropriately to adults and how to have a daily routine to run their lives. The kids received medical care from a local missionary hospital and dental care from a retired dentist down the road. All of them were required to go to school, no exceptions. Every one of them graduated high school. Some of them even passed the *bac* exam which guaranteed them college.

About ten years into her work Miriam found a colleague. Jacques was a former Assemblies of God missionary who had decided to leave the ministry and pursue more direct community efforts. In Miriam he found an ideologically like-minded friend. Together they worked to advance the cause of the orphanage. Miriam was able to focus on the orphanage more directly while Jacques, being from the west, was able to bring in more westerners to the cause, often via short-term trips after which some of them would become donors. Jacques himself would later divert his French government pension checks to the orphanage.

It was hard work in every way. The kids would never know the kinds of sacrifices that Miriam and Jacques would together endure just to keep the kids stable. Nor would the churches that supported them. But the sacrifices were significant, including to the detriment of their health and their financial livelihoods. The orphanage stayed afloat but was in constant peril.

Then one day Jacques became ill. At first he said it was just "a little bit of a cold." But the cold turned to yellowing skin and eyes. His doctor ordered him to return to his European nation, judging that it was too risky to be seriously ill like this in Africa. But Jacques wouldn't do that. He was committed to the kids. And to Miriam. Jacques slept on the concrete floor of the kitchen while he was on-site, giving Miriam the shed on the side of the property.

That was about the time that another military insurrection developed. The highways closed, the stores closed, the churches closed, the Western Union offices closed and all of the funds for the orphanage dried up. As the gunshots could be heard outside the walls, Miriam and Jacques gathered with the children in the courtyard. One eight-year-old boy looked up at the two. "Maman and Papou, what are we going to do?".

The situation was dire. There was no food. There was no money. There was no electricity. No transportation. Miriam looked at the steel double door that opened out into the street. It was barred shut. There was one thing that she and Jacques *could* do. One last act. They could open those doors to the murderous mélée on the street outside and announce to the kids what Miriam had once heard herself. "Go."

Discussion Questions:

1. Miriam is a real person. So is Jacques. Does your NGO have any Miriams or Jacques?
2. What are the institutional perils of operations like Miriam's and Jacques' orphanage?
3. What kinds of structures do initiatives like this need in order to be more stable?
4. Would it be immoral for Miriam and Jacques to order the orphans out?
5. If your NGO or NFP were to collapse, who would pay the price for that failure? What are you doing now to protect them?

Professorial Malfeasance Abroad?

You have arrived at a remote, culturally significant village with a goal. You have been funded by a granting institution in the USA to study baseline macroeconomic conditions of this tourism-dependent region. That funding proposal was rooted in the hypothesis that economic conditions would be significantly different in those locations that offered services to foreign tourists when compared with those that don't. This being a UNESCO World Heritage town provided you the opportunity to gain an insider perspective on the lived experiences of residents and the ways in which their economic livelihood was linked to the historical facilities.

After a long first day of enjoying the tourist amenities, you invite the manager of the UNESCO site to dinner so that you can negotiate means to deploy your research project. What you hear in that conversation is shocking and disturbing.

At first you discuss the many ongoing projects that he and his team are working on. You are impressed with the high degree of professionalism and skill exhibited by him and his staff. They are experts in the ancient culture whose ruins are housed in the town. He and his staff speak several different modern languages and can also read and write the ancient languages represented in the site. They are intelligent, hard-working, educated and enthusiastic.

They also collectively manage several international teams or researchers, investigators and scholars. But as they discuss their various initiatives with international development agencies and the universities they work with you sense that the tone of the conversation has changed. As the director discusses one such initiative you notice that he is glancing at his colleagues as if to ensure that they agree with his depiction of their activities.

"Is everything going well with their studies?" you ask.

Elias, the director of the site, demurs for a moment. "There have been problems," he says sheepishly.

"What kind of problems?" you ask, regretting that you were so pointed in your questioning.

"Well," Elias responds, "We aren't really sure what they are doing. We question many of their findings, and we can't get much information out of them. They come, do something, and then leave."

Over the course of the dinner and the dessert that follows you acquire a more comprehensive picture of Elias's qualms with some of the foreign researchers. The problem seems to stem from the activities of an internationally renowned university in the United States that has had a relationship with the administration in the national capital for the past century, albeit in spurts. The grievances that Elias lists are shocking.

The relationship did not begin well, nearly a century ago. The anthropologist from that university announced to the world that they "discovered" the site. They spent several years there and at the end purchased the land for the equivalent of $50 USD. Later on that same land was confiscated by the government in an effort to re-claim national patrimony. But the university managed to continue its relationship. Over several phases of operations, the largest being since the late 1990s and extending to the present, this university self-funded a great many separate initiatives to perform studies at the site.

But while many promises were made to Elias and his staff, it always ended up being a financial burden. The university made their agreements with the politicians in the capital city, not with Elias and his team. That meant that when money exchanged hands from the university to his nation, Elias never received any of it and never acquired any of the equipment specifically listed as being included in the project.

"One country brought in a fleet of excavators, dump trucks and pickup trucks. They never ended up here, I can tell you that!" Elias said in exasperation.

Another troubling feature of the researchers' behavior is that they were known to have caused significant damage to several sites. One site that had stood for approximately 1500 years had recently caved in after this university dug a tunnel through it. Other tunnels that had dug were beginning to show signs of collapse. The destruction to these historical treasures was incalculable to Elias and his team and they feared for the jobs in town that would be lost if the historical site became unsafe for human visitors.

"What did they say in their final report of their activities?" you ask Elias.

"What final report? They never report anything, never compile anything and never speak with us. We are just given orders from the capital to house them and let them do whatever they want. The only way I ever learn what they did is when they publish something in a journal that no one reads. And we're pretty sure that a lot of what they say is wrong anyway. Last time they were here I later found out by reading academic journals that they claimed to have found the tomb of the third king. But we did our own investigation which seems to show that they were completely wrong about that."

You explain to Elias that the university in question is likely working with grant money to fund their operations. Invariably, that grant money includes a stipend for the chief investigator, an institutional cost rate and certain stipulations. Invariably one stipulation is that a final report is rendered. The university and the professors are *obligated* to report on what they do.

"Well, all I can tell you is that they have done a lot of damage, they never deliver what they promise, and they leave without saying a word to us. If it were up to me I'd ban them from the country permanently. We can't afford to fund their damage anymore."

After the discussion you do your own digging. You search for the identities of the researchers Elias had complained about and endeavor to find their funding mechanisms. You believe that the researchers are faculty members at an elite American university whose international reputation is excellent. You believe this because faculty publications and university press releases correlate with the timeline Elias mentioned. You believe that the university faculty had acquired their funding from another equally well-known and internationally prestigious foundation. Because you have worked under similar conditions, you believe it likely that their financial arrangements follow a more or less standard template. That template includes a 30% "cut" for the university from grant monies, a significant stipend for the faculty researcher and other costs associated with the project. These "other" costs often include travel, equipment and M&IE. You know that many such faculty members acquire more annual income from grants than they do from their contractual salary. It is not unusual for such faculty members to manage three to four high dollar value grants at any one time.

The thought then crosses your mind that you might have an obligation to do something about this. You had reason to believe that there was financially motivated unethical behavior being done by universities in your own country. You were able to personally verify the cultural damage referred to by Elias.

You had acquired a hypothesis as to the financial structure of agreements that motivated the cultural "crime." But unlike Elias you have resources and protections.

If Elias blows the whistle, he and his team would risk being banished from their government positions. Their federal government seems to have benefitted financially from the many agreements they held with the American university, and the likelihood that the government would stop those agreements was low. Almost certainly, they would just replace Elias and his team with others that would be more compliant.

You conclude that Elias and his team are powerless to do anything about the situation.

But you are not powerless. You could raise this issue with the university and the foundation in question. However, you are at a significant political disadvantage if you do. You are not currently employed by an elite university. The reputation and wealth of your institution, while definitely not bad, is nothing compared to the university who is alleged to have originated research malfeasance.

You also have several current proposals pending before the foundation that funded the projects that Elias and his team complained about. Would raise this issue with the foundation threaten the success of those proposals? Foundations like to advertise their relationships with prestigious universities as a way to bolster their own public image. To approach the foundation with a complaint might not be greeted by the foundation with enthusiasm, potentially threatening the funding of your own research.

You therefore think for a moment about doing nothing. But the sense of guilt is overwhelming. You find it outrageous that a research university would damage a UNESCO site. You find it outrageous that the expert foreign staff would be treated so poorly by American researchers. And you have disdain for the fact that what made all of this happen was something as stupid as money.

Discussion Questions:

1. Do you have an obligation to do something about this situation?
2. What responsibility do you have to vet the accusations that Elias and his team have articulated?
3. To what extent should you be concerned with repercussions to yourself?
4. How could future initiatives be structured so as to avoid this situation?
5. In what ways might your response to this situation pose harm to Elias and his team?

References

Bernard, G. (2019). *Talibé: enfant des rues Roman.* Paris, FR: L'Harmattan.
Hester, D. M. (2022). *Guidance for Healthcare Ethics Committees* (2nd ed.). New York, NY: Cambridge University Press.
Scott, E. D. (2005). The Ethics of Human Resources Management. In J. W. Budd & J. G. Scoville, *The Ethics of Human Resources and Industrial Relations (LERA Research Volume)* (pp. 173–201). Champaign, IL: Labor and Employment Relations Association.
Watts, L. L., Medeiros, K., McIntosh, T., & Mulhearn, T. (2021). *Ethics Training for Managers: Best Practices and Techniques.* Abingdon, UK: Routledge.
Yunus, M., & Jolis, A. (2008). *Banker to the Poor: Micro-Lending and the Battle Against World Poverty.* Philadelphia, PA: PublicAffairs.

Digital, Online and Cyber Ethics

The rise of digital, online or "cyber" instruments to societies will certainly be a facet of our era that Historians discuss for centuries to come. No person yet has adequately comprehended the implications that this will have on all facets of human experience. But already we, who find ourselves in the midst of this revolution, sense that there is more than just a technological facet to these changes. There are serious moral implications to them as well.

For starters, the ways in which information is possessed and safeguarded has changed. It was once enough to keep the accounting books inside the company safe so as to protect the integrity of the accounting process and to safeguard the personal information of employees. Suffice to say, those days have long since passed. But when we combine this with the fact that NFPs and NGOs service core human needs pertaining to issues with the utmost need for confidentiality and privacy, we quickly realize that these are not issues that a company can safely resolve. What was once merely a financial crisis can easily become both a financial crisis and a federal offense.

NFPs and NGOs must be in the habit of viewing network security as an endeavor which when poorly done becomes a business-ending event. The IT administrator needs to be a part of the executive team, not the resident of a closet next to the server. That, and NFPs and NGOs must budget routine external audits of this IT infrastructure. Someone must watch the watchers.

The NFP and the NGO must understand that the persons who seek their services are typically discovering the existence of the NFP or NGO from digital sources. And if they are discovering information about an NFP from digital sources then they are also discovering misinformation from the same sources. The proverbial book has not yet been written in this issue and only now are we beginning to see the potential consequences of the existence of misinformation. The rise of "deep fakes" is a particular concern, and NFPs and NGOs are accustomed to thinking that this is a problem for national politicians or celebrities. It is not. We are currently no more than one generation away from deep fake apps which offer pranksters and the disgruntled ways of disseminating embarrassing and false information about an NFP. Plans must be undertaken now before a spurious video appears of a fake sexual escapade between the CEO and a client.

We are currently unclear as to the extent to which the veracity of misinformation is presumed by those who watch them in the west. One school of thought asserts that those who fall for misinformation are those who want to fall for it. This coheres with our well-understood appreciation of confirmation bias (the tendency of persons to pay attention to confirming evidence rather than disconfirming evidence). Another school of thought asserts that such fakes are convincing the unconvinced. (Bialy, 2017).

But in the non-western world misinformation is especially pernicious. One stop-gap the developed world has consistently relied upon to ensure an environment of accurate information is an independent press. Despite constant accusations of bias within media sources, the situation in the developed world bears little resemblance to that of developing nations. Many such nations have *never* had independent information sources. One consequence of this is that when information is shared through the press, residents assume that it is government-inspired manipulation. When misinformation is introduced into the midst of this void there is therefore no independent source to verify it. Since such cultures tend to still use the axioms or oral transmission but in digital form, false information spreads more quickly than at any time in the past. (Vasu, et al., 2017).

The intrinsically democratic nature of the spread of information is a blessing and a curse. It is a blessing because citizens are able to give voice to their thoughts in ways that were impossible in the past. It is a curse because it can be used to quickly enflame simmering rivalries and tensions which in the past would have taken travel, time and resources to do. In the past, foreign nations invested considerable resources to spread disinformation abroad through their intelligence agencies. Today such efforts are considerably less onerous. (Livingston, 2011) The CIA does not have to penetrate a foreign worker's union with an on-the-ground plant when they can accomplish the same ends via social media.

The policy environment regarding online resources is highly variable across the world. Many western European nations have laws which require that "cookies" be consented to. But these laws have not adapted to the reality that there are a great many ways that online activity can be tracked without using cookies and that future versions of HTML will likely not even use that technological device. Some nations have enshrined the right to internet access in their constitution (Norway) but thereby deprive themselves of the right to advocate, as happened recently, that Russia be cut off from the internet after their military action against Ukraine. Policy-making on the international level is made all the more difficult in light of the fact that most of the elements of online life are dependent upon the private intellectual property of American businesses.

One thing, however, will remain consistent. Ethics will not change. Assessing the consequences of actions, thinking about personal virtues and discussing the impact of our behavior upon gender dynamics will continue to be important. The moral insights from the first chapter of this book survived, in some cases, every recorded stage of human history. They will remain the same throughout the cyber revolution too.

Archiving a Nation's Text Messages

Word frequency analysis is a powerful tool. It has been used to better understand messaging in political campaigns, study the nature of literary works and much more. It can also help to understand what issues people most care about.

You work as a network administrator for a telecom giant in West Africa. You have just been approached by a European NGO that works with an internationally-known provider of medical services to persons in rural areas around the globe. This NGO's mission is to provide insights into the health outcomes of rural localities and predict where disease outbreaks will occur. With their word frequency analysis tools, they use text messaging as inputs, conduct the analysis and use the results to predict where disease states are outbreaking in the nation.

They show you a previous case study. In this case they were able to receive permission from a telecom company in a neighboring nation where flare-ups have been known to occur of a variety of diseases. These flare-ups have probably happened in that country since before recorded history. In generations past this caused the government to institute a brutal protocol when dangerous diseases emerged in rural areas. When a village saw a break-out of such a disease, the military was sent into quarantine the village. No one was permitted out, and no one—including medical personnel—was permitted in. When the disease "burns out" the blockade was lifted.

The situation has changed, though, given the new rise in mass transport and better roads and transportation hubs. And with new international airports a sick or infected person can easily transmit that disease to the far reaches of the globe within a few hours—possibly during incubation.

This NGO explains to you that by acquiring real-time access to messaging they were able to accurately predict the early outbreak in a rural village before that outbreak became a regional, national or international problem. Medical personnel arrived before the military did and the subsequent treatment prevented the spread.

The NGO worker then explains that these same health issues exist in your country. You nod in agreement, knowing all too well that villages in rural areas have been wiped out from endemic diseases.

They continue to their pitch. They propose to you that they be granted access to real-time data from your network—the largest in the country. Using that data is crucial to understand where word frequencies are spiking in certain terms (like "vomiting" or "rash"). Having access to all the data of the nation permits the researchers to rule out other areas of the country, effectively using them as a control group.

However, this troubles you. You know from your academic training back in the states that this request is illegal in the US. But in your country there are no laws at all which safeguard digital privacy. You end the meeting with a promise to get back to the NGO with an answer, and then assemble your team.

You explain to your team that this NGO has delivered results in the past and explain the case of the neighboring country.

Your marketing director immediately expresses concerns. She states that if word got out that your company was saving and archiving all the text messages in the nation that this would constitute a potential business disaster. People *will* assume that the government will get the messages too. And they will use those messages for political reprisal, not healthcare outcomes.

Your VP for network infrastructure quickly agrees. He adds that the government is constantly at the door asking the company to spy on its customers on their behalf. You have been able to deflect many of the requests because you never archive data and hence have little interest to share with them. If the company reversed this protocol, then the company would be deprived an answer to the government's persistent requests. What would they have to say to the government when they want to spy on the political opposition? Or people suspected of being gay?

Another colleague, though, points out that she grew up in one of those rural villages. She has heard what it is like to suffer through "the plague." She shares a story of having to find a way to smuggle in food and water to one town when she was a child, then being ostracized by her own family upon return. She points out that while for we who live in the capital city it is a big deal to have our messages read, that's a small price to pay for the benefit of saving the lives of people in those rural towns. Those rural villagers already have so little, and it is a small thing to ask that we give up privacy in order to help them.

Discussion Questions:

1. What are the positive benefits of agreeing to share the information? What are the negative effects?
2. Is the NGO's request unethical?
3. Is there a right to data privacy? Are there ever circumstances when those rights can be violated?
4. Does a private company have the right to refuse access to potentially life-saving technology?

Where There Are no Government-Issued IDs

It is a common procedure at the pharmacy to be required to present identification to pick up prescriptions, at least prescriptions on a certain schedule list. But the need to verify identity extends well beyond managing addictive substances effectively. The root word for "pharmacy" is the Greek word *pharmakon* which means both "poison" and "cure." Since ancient times, we have recognized that the same medicines that save lives can also end them when administered incorrectly. Identification verification is an important method to ensure that patients do not harm themselves through drug interactions or overdoses.

Melanie is a medical researcher working in rural Central America on drug availability issues. Specifically, she researches whether and how persons identify needed drugs, whether and how they acquire them and what their final medical outcomes are. This is tricky, as the medical infrastructure of the nation that she works in is as informal as the employment sector. The sick who manage to get drugs for their illness often do so by arriving at a pharmacy and pointing. In many cases no doctor is consulted.

In a focus group of pharmacists, Melanie discusses the situation. Every pharmacist nods their head in agreement that this is a serious issue—a true threat to public health. But the answers needed to rectify this situation are elusive.

Melanie asks, "Could we all agree to request that a customer show ID? That way we can track, at a minimum, what other medications they are already taking."

Skepticism is immediately apparent in the room. Most people in the region don't have IDs. The government charges too much for them (some pharmacists wonder whether the reason why is to suppress the voting rights of residents of the region who are known to vote for the opposition party. If they don't have IDs, then they can't vote).

"There are other ways that we can address the problem. We could, for example, use a fingerprint ID scanner. They're cheap. I'd bet I can get a grant to fund one for each of your pharmacies."

The pharmacists in the focus group worry about this too. But their worry is different. Many of the people in the region are manual laborers. Their hands are leathery and calloused. Most do not even have detectable fingerprints.

"But they all have eyes." You add. "What would you think about using a rental scanner to verify identity? They have dropped dramatically in price. While slightly more expensive, I'd bet that I could get a grant to pay for them. They typically come with software that can be coded to your systems currently in place. So instead of having 90% cash transactions with no ID verification you would have 90% cash transactions with everyone having their IDs verified."

This drew remarks from the focus group of approval. Many shared stories of customers denied large doses of dangerous medications at one pharmacy counter only to go to the next pharmacy to get the extra amount that they thought they needed. They all agreed to participate in a test-run of the program, if Melania was able to acquire funding.

So Melanie set herself to writing the grant that would be used to acquire the technology. She designed the program, identified the products to be bought and submitted the grant to the American foundation.

Assume that you are the grant reviewer at the American foundation as you respond to the following questions:

Discussion Question:

1. Has Melanie taken care to address the needs of online data security?
2. What are the possible implications of collecting the data that Melanie wants to collect?

3. Are there any flaws in her approach?
4. Would you fund this pilot project?

Political Disinformation, Community Outreach and Vaccine Drives

Your community health foundation is one of the largest resources for healthcare in your region of Appalachia. As the CEO it is your responsibility to manage the programmatic needs of the foundation, the corpus of which originated from the sale of a public hospital.

One of your primary objectives at the moment is to arrange a Covid-19 vaccine drive. Judged by demand, previous phases of the drive have been highly successful. You experienced a very strong demand for the vaccine when rationing prioritized those over the age of 65. In the region where you work you saw the number of vaccinated increase in that demographic from 0 to 75% in just five months. This was faster than anyone had planned on.

This incredible demand exerted strong pressure on your NFP and its staff. Much of your work related to addressing rollout logistics that you had never envisaged when you began. Unforeseen issues included vaccination centers with the insufficient waiting-room area given physical distancing guidelines and unexpectedly-high budgetary needs on your paper-products budget line. But the political will at the state and federal level combined with your fortitude in the local trenches enabled you to deliver results that made for incredible gains in vaccination rates.

But now the age-limits have been redrawn and anyone over the age of 18 is permitted to receive the vaccine. At first you saw demand much like the demand in the 65 and over population. You expected this to continue until you made your way through the much-larger population of 18–64. But inexplicably, demand appears to have, as your staff informed you, "dropped off a cliff."

In your weekly planning session you make this the top issue of discussion. Why has demand decreased so suddenly?

"For starters," your head of vaccine rollout states, "Our state didn't do what the state next door did. They strongly linked the rollout to local pharmacists with whom the patients already have a relationship. So the people telling them to get vaccinated were the people they have trusted for years. We aren't doing that here. In our state we are running independent clinics where no patient knows any staff and in a location they have never been to before."

Your CFO, Mark, then says "I can't help but think that this has something to do with it."

Mark turns his laptop around to display to the planning group a well-known online information source known to be strongly associated with a radical political orientation. The message communicated was unequivocal. It was robustly anti-vaccine, conspiratorial and deeply ideological.

"Our clients," Mark states, "are being told lockdowns don't work, masks are useless, the vaccine doesn't prevent illness or the spread of the virus, that the vaccine has caused deaths that have been covered-up, and that the entire Covid response is a gigantic power-play by federal politicians. Heck, I am waiting for a story about the Illuminati to appear next."

In your opinion, it is highly likely that the population you serve is listening to this information source. But you have no opinion regarding how to respond to it. One problem is that as you sit in your executive's chair you have no long-term data about the vaccine or its effectiveness—so analogies to other well-regarded vaccines are not fitting. But nevertheless, you and everyone else in the industry have strong confidence that the CDC exercised due caution when approving of the vaccine.

Turning to your director of PR and Development you ask "What do you think?"

"Well," Deobrah responds with some resignation, "I think that there's truth to the point that Mark made. People are listening to those messages. But a real and present peril that we face is making it look like we are taking a political side. If we do something that makes our clients think that we favor a political party, then our credibility in the community will be diminished. And I might point out that some of the largest donors to our organization are also people who read from those same sources."

"Then let us start at the most basic level. I believe that we can all agree that the vaccine is a good thing, right?" You survey the room and see nodding agreement. "So then the question that we must answer is 'How do we make the drive more successful given that Covid politicization acts against us?' Once we answer that question, we can begin to tackle the problem."

Discussion Questions:

1. Many moral disagreements are rooted in disagreements over the facts. Poll those around you with a simple question such as "Do available vaccines prevent contracting or spreading Covid-19?" If you found factual disagreements among respondents, what do those disagreements mean?
2. What are the motives of those who spread misinformation?
3. To what extent does a healthcare-oriented NFP have an obligation to combat misinformation?
4. Must clients have true medical beliefs in order to receive your services?

5. How can an NFP work in a politicized environment and not take sides? Is this possible?

Election Season and Viral Online Videos

You work in the US offices of an NGO with operations throughout Latin America. Not only must you be apprised of all programmatic issues of your NGO, but you must also ensure that you are up-to-date on the major news and political stories of the nations in which you work. This is no small task, as your operations stretch throughout 15 different countries in Latin America and the Caribbean. But it is an important task. Political shifts must be predicted if at all possible. Because those shifts can cause a new priority set for activities within a country. They can also cause the US embassy to advise different regional strategy. Since US federal dollars are a key part of your funding, you must keep a careful eye on this.

You are proud of the fact that key managers of your operations are not US citizens but carefully-recruited nationals whose years of experience and expert insights into their own cultures have consistently proven to be a powerful asset for your NGO. You have come to know many of them personally and value both your professional and personal relationships with them.

In one country in which you have significant operations it is election season. No less than 10 political parties have put forward their candidates. It is never easy to classify them. On the one hand there is a candidate from an old, well-respected national party who has been successful in having their candidate elected in three of the past five elections. The reputation of that party is that of a pro-establishment center-right ideology. But other candidates, both on the far left and far right, are drawing an unusual amount of attention.

You notice that Juan, your institution's head of mission for the region, has been sharing with you an unusual number of political images and videos through a mobile-based messaging application. This is not unusual behavior in and of itself. He has been in the habit for years of sharing with you messages of relevance that he picks up from social media, and many have been worth knowing about. In the past these included public response to NGO operations, comments on social issues which you address through your NGO and an occasional cat video.

But you notice that he is uncharacteristically animated in his discussion with you regarding the political messages he is sharing. Many are messages specifically detailing the corruption of one particular candidate in the election. Others are presenting strange and disturbing conspiracy theories—tales of secret international thought police and hidden agendas of nations. One such message that you find preposterous depicts two people in a newsroom. One appears to be a reporter and the other appears to be an interviewee. They are speaking English with Spanish subtitles at the bottom of the screen. The topic of the conversation is the US partitioning part of his country into separate spheres of influence with one region allotted to ethnic minorities and the other to the political ruling class. You notice that the "expert" being interviewed is speaking English with a Slavic accent.

Juan probably could not pick up on that latter fact. He speaks great English, but with an unmistakable accent. It is unlikely that he would know how to identify a Slavic accent.

You have known Juan for many years and have a high opinion of his work. He is dependable, driven and ethical. He has never given you cause to think that he is anything but excellent at his work. But you believe that Juan is being manipulated by online misinformation. For whose benefit, you cannot say.

On the one hand you can just let it go. Let Juan continue to share with you these vignettes and leave it be. But on the other hand, Juan is empowered to speak for you in the nation in which you operate. You worry about what someone, whether Juan or someone else, might say if asked the "right" question by a reporter. Revealing that your director of operations is susceptible to misinformation could cause significant problems for your operation.

Discussion Questions:

1. What reliable, non-partisan, independent sources of information exist in Latin American or Caribbean countries?
2. If independent information sources are few or nonexistent, then how do persons in such countries acquire information?
3. What damage is Juan capable of causing for your institution? And how can you be certain that other directors wouldn't cause the same?
4. If you decide to confront Juan, are you engaging in political activities in a foreign nation?

Revealing the Location of Vulnerable Women

You are the head of operations for an NGO in a Latin American nation that operates safe houses for women who need temporary shelter. Some of the women are fleeing domestic violence. Others seek your services in order to have an environment free from addictive substances. Others have escaped the sex trade.

Your programs are excellent. You do more than offer a safe bed and a warm meal. You take great care to identify the impediments to the success of your clients and have a strong track record of providing a successful launching pad for a healthier future for the women that you serve. While they reside with you the women receive counseling, mentorship and job skills. They leave in a better position than when they arrived.

Every year several hundred women avail themselves of your assistance and as word-of-mouth spreads awareness of your existence, demand is increasing.

Your most reliable supporters are the women you once served. With regularity they appear at your facility to offer words of encouragement, a hand with daily chores, or assistance in the kitchen. These "alums" have turned into a powerful force for the mentorship of those currently seeking your services and a strong network of empowered women has naturally developed as a result of your services. Such alums are one of your two most reliable funding sources, as they routinely send in funds to give back to the organization that once helped them.

Another source of revenue for your operations are short-term teams. These teams arrive from American churches that wish to offer their parishioners a rewarding international experience. Generally speaking, they are welcome visitors whose addition to the programming of your NGO has proven to be helpful for your staff and for the women they serve.

But something happened today that worries you. A man appeared at the gate of your facilities looking for someone inside. He named the woman he was looking for by first and last name and described her physical appearance. You recognize that this is a woman who has recently come to your facility to escape the sex trade in the capital city.

"I don't know anyone by that name," you say to the man.

He takes out a cellphone and says "Then what is this?" He shows you a picture of the woman, clearly taken at the very gate you are standing in front of.

The discussion grows heated and the strange man becomes threatening. He makes it clear that he has friends and that these friends lost money too. But as the commotion grew louder, some of the large, burly men that work in the safe house appear at the door to see what the trouble is. This causes the stranger to back off and eventually depart.

You close the gate and lock it.

How could this have happened? How could this man have gotten a picture that shows that the woman was there? Is the NGO being spied on?

You discretely ask for a gathering of the American team. And you calmly ask them "Are any of you sharing the photographs that you are taking? Like a blog, or online, or through social media?".

Everyone nods their heads in agreement. They all are. You quickly learn that pictures are being posted to many different social media platforms, most of which are publicly available. They're also available on church websites back in the states.

That is how it likely happened. The man at the gate found the location because your guests revealed it online.

Discussion Questions:

1. What are the potential consequences of this breach? Take time to list as many as you can.
2. Some of the consequences that you listed in response to the first question demand action on the part of the NGO. How does the NGO respond to each?
3. What can be done to prevent this circumstance from happening in the future?
4. What are the liabilities that NGOs face when they invite short-term teams to their foreign facilities?

Child Porn, Revenge Porn and Non-Fungible Tokens

You work as a lobbyist on behalf of a national not-for-profit that advocates for the rights of persons who have faced sexual exploitation of a variety of kinds. Based in Washington DC, it is your job to raise awareness before lawmakers and their staff regarding the legislative and policy needs of those you serve.

Much of your work consists in education—specifically, the education of legislators and their staff as they contemplate, negotiate, write and implement legislation pertaining to your activities. This is a common field of work, and much of what becomes the policy of the nation or law of the land began with the work of those like you and others.

You have been concerned for many years with the dissemination of illegal pornography such as child porn. You are also concerned with other kinds of pornography which, while not illegal, strikes you as immoral. Revenge porn—the posting of pornographic content as an act of revenge—is of particular concern for you.

Previous methods of eradicating these kinds of pornography have not been successful. A root problem is that the images never go away. Even when websites are seized or shutdown, when servers are discovered and pulled offline, the images invariably circulate in other areas of the internet. This is probably because copies are saved and shared by others who then upload and disseminate them elsewhere.

Another method of eliminating this type of pornographic content has met with marginal success—pressuring credit card companies to not provide payment gateway services for certain websites which are known to disseminate the images or videos. This approach has successfully limited the number of sites willing to host the content, but has not been effective at eliminating it.

A final underlying problem is the inconsistent legal environment regarding online activity. Arguably, the developed world is not in a substantively better position than any other nation as it, like any other country, struggles with concepts of privacy, access and democratized knowledge. This combined with the widely different criminal law of many nations has made for difficult international prosecutions.

You have recently become aware of the concept of a "Non Fungible Token." And you are wondering whether a policy proposal might work which avails itself of this new technology.

"Fungibility" is a financial term which refers to the indistinguishability of one unit of asset from another. For example, if a person has three dollars in their pocket, each one of those three is financially indistinguishable. Fungibility is therefore linked to liquidity: the ability to exchange an asset (such as cash) for different assets (such as a car or a candy bar). This is why NGOs much prefer cash donations in a time of crisis rather than receive donations of food and water. It is difficult and expensive to move crates of water to remote locations suffering from tragedy, but transferring the cash to the location is easier, faster and less wasteful of resources.

A token is "non-Fungible" just in case it *is* possible to identify one unit from another. When our bank account has, say, $1000 in it, and we know that we need to transfer $1 to a friend, it does not matter to us *which* of the dollars is transferred. Any one of those thousand dollars will do. Because every one of the 1000 different dollars is indistinguishable. However, a non-fungible asset assigns a blockchain identifier to the token effectively making it possible to specifically identify the token. It can be tracked via blockchain.

You are considering working on the following proposal to lobby to lawmakers: Propose that victims of the kinds of pornography you advocate against be given property rights to the images or videos by declaring each to be a Non-Fungible Token (NFT), the possession of which is held by the victim. You take your idea to your executive team to seek their advice.

"I believe that if we can get legislative support for declaring these images to be the property that can be verified, we will have another tool to fight our cause. If we can make these images and videos into NFT's, then the dissemination of the images will constitute a new kind of criminal behavior—theft. Whereas the international law regarding online activities is chaotic and spotty at best, the international norms regarding theft are far better defined. This is why software piracy is easier to prosecute than privacy rights violations. What I want from you are your thoughts. Is this a good idea? Are there any unforeseen problems with it? Any blind alleys I need to be aware of?"

Kareem, your legal counsel, is the first to speak up.

"An intriguing suggestion," he says. "This has already been used in art theft cases. Artists creating digital content have for years complained that it is often stolen online and sold by a variety of retailers without consent or compensation. They've begun to convert everything they do to an NFT before they release it. Violations of which are then prosecuted just like cases of theft."

"But..." you say, knowing that there is always a "but."

"But a problem that they have also encountered is that when the thief files their own NFT for the stolen art, it becomes paradoxically harder for the artist to prosecute the case."

"That's it?" you state, "We can solve that pretty easily. We advocate that a legal means be provided which permits victims to claim ownership."

"Not exactly," Kareem says. "The problem is that an artist has commits no crime when they create art. But we're talking child pornography here. And revenge porn. At least one of those two is a crime. Maybe both. Your proposal seems to make possession of a criminal instrument fall into the hands of the victim. That's troubling."

"But who owns the rights to their own bodies, Kareem!" you respond. "These victims suffer many different wrongs by these kinds of acts, just one of which is that without their consent their very person is used to exploit themselves. Certainly, it cannot be either illegal or immoral to use one's self."

"I hear you," says Jackie, your policy aid. "But we need to think about all of the cases out there, not just some of them. We know that a lot of child pornography happens in families—a husband, a cousin, an uncle, a parent is often the one that creates it. US law won't tolerate a situation in which a child is assigned ownership of pornography. It would be the guardian assigned ownership. Would we want the US government to assign intellectual property rights to the very guardian who, in some cases, committed the crime?"

There is silence for a moment while the group considered the problem. Then Jackie continued.

"There is also the issue of re-traumatizing the victim. At some point they would have to be subjected to the images or videos again. Because they would have to state that the images are in fact images of themselves."

"I hear your point. But I cannot shake the suspicion that this technological invention might help our fight." You say. "So hear me out on this. At the root of the moral wrong caused by these kinds of images and videos isn't just that the material is objectionable. Although it obviously is. The moral violation suffered by those we serve consists in a repeated, non-consensual violation of their own person. The images are the instrument used to commit that violation. To give NFT's to the victims is to permit them to take back possession of themselves."

"Something else for you to consider." Kareem interjects. "Revenge porn was often, *at the time of recording*, fully consensual. We could argue all day long about whether it is rational to offer consent to create such videos in the first place. But this does not change the fact that at the time of recording many were agreed to by those depicted in the recording. So if it was consensual, that seems to imply that both parties should have joint-ownership of the NFT, not just one. One of those parties will be fine with posting it online, and the other not."

"That's a great point," you reply. "But that just implies that we need to be careful about how we articulate the policy. What I am asking this team to do is to explore whether we can use the notion of an NFT to fight our battle. Is there a way to use this technological instrument to fight child porn and revenge porn? In the final analysis, maybe we discover that it won't work. Or maybe we discover that it causes more problems than it solves. But that doesn't mean that we shouldn't consider it. So I repeat my question: Can we use NFTs as an instrument to fight our battle?"

Discussion questions:

1. Policymakers often cite two facets of policy-making: feasibility and desirability. Is this proposal feasible? Is it desirable?
2. There is widespread agreement that both child pornography and revenge pornography are immoral. But there is not agreement as to why they are immoral. Why are these immoral? And are these two immoral for the same reasons?
3. What are the moral issues involved in assigning ownership to victims of the instrument of their own victimization?

Bibliography

Bialy, B. (2017, Summer). Social Media—From Social Exchange to Battlefield. *The Cyber Defense Review, 2*(2), 69–90.

Livingston, S. (2011). *Africa's Evolving Infosystems: A Pathway to Security and Stability.* Washington, DC: Africa Center for Strategic Studies.

Vasu, N., Ang, B., Teo, T. -A., Jayakumar, S., Faizal, M., & Ahuja, J. (2017). *Fake News: National Security in a Post-Truth Era.* Singapore: Rajaratnam School of International Studies.

Appendix I: Discussion-Leader Tips

Several cultural forces act against the person who leads ethics discussions. It is not uncommon for participants in such discussions to confuse the difference between rage and reason, volume and cogency, confidence with certainty. But discussion leaders can also take solace with the fact that this has always been the case. Review the dialogues of the ancient Greek philosopher Plato and you too will hear the account of a thinker attempting against all odds to have a reasonable discussion with his peers.

Over the course of my decades of teaching Ethics I have adopted a set of guidelines which I articulate here as tips to other professionals who are attempting to do the same. In no particular order they are as follows:

1. **Authority Silences Speech**. Often times the person leading the discussion is an authority figure—a professor, a boss, a religious leader, etc. Authority can exert unintentionally powerful coercive forces upon the participants. Some may want to tell the discussion leader what they think that leader wants to hear. Others will disengage fearing reprisal. Discussion leaders need to strategize how they will wield their authority and they must find ways to show participants that they are free to speak their minds. Antecedent office political partisanship or proselytizing almost certainly undermines the ability to provide free discussion. Absent meeting this essential requirement to ensure intellectual freedom, it is not possible to have meaningful ethics discussions.
2. **Lack-of-Authority Causes Chaos**. A mistake made by those who correctly fear the silencing-effect of authority is to create an environment

which (falsely) conveys the message that there is neither authority nor structure. This is likewise a mistake and can lead to an environment in which hurtful words are exchanged or shouting matches commenced. The result will be the same as that in which participants fear their authority: Discussing ethics will be impossible. The compromise position to this is civility—an attribute conveyed to participants more by modeling than by teaching.

3. **There will be Tangents**. When people speak from their values, the discussion can go just about anywhere. A discussion about the ethics of commissioning fundraising might devolve into how one's grandmother raised them or what it was like in another's community as a child. This is part of the process. Human interaction is inefficient, time consuming and necessary.

4. **Be Mindful of Time**. Holding ethics discussions can be intense, sometimes passionate. That takes a toll on participants, especially introverts. Never let ethics discussions drag-on without brakes or pauses.

5. **Let Participants Have Time**. The leader of a discussion has almost always thought much more about the topic than those participating in the discussion. Resist the temptation to correct reasoning errors or verbal mistakes on every occasion in which they occur. The learning process requires processing, and processing takes time.

6. **Avoid taking sides**. Since you the discussion leader have probably experienced the dynamics of the cases in this book, you correspondingly know with greater clarity just how disastrous the wrong call in a tough case can be. Resist the temptation to immediately correct "wrong" answers. Ethics debates must be safe spaces to make bad calls. And swatting down comments you disagree with can be chilling.

7. **Make the Limits Known in Advance**. Racist, hateful or violent speech exists. The discussion leader must never permit such speech to be a part of a free discussion, and this requirement must be articulated in advance.

8. **Redefine "Expertise."** The expert in ethics is not the one who knows what to do every time. Rather, the expert is the one who knows best how to *think* every time. So resist finishing a discussion by telling the participants what the "right" answer was. Instead, demonstrate that the process they engaged in as they debated the topic was an integral part of obtaining the goal.

Appendix II: Structuring an Ethics Discussion

I will assume in this appendix that the participants of a discussion have used this text and are ready to discuss the cases in it. Therefore, the first part of the structure of such a discussion is a homework assignment: read the book.

But this settles very few of the requirements for a solid discussion regarding ethics cases. Such "discussions" may take place in written form, in verbal form or both. The discussions might be evaluated or not. They could be led by either professionals or amateurs or those who lie somewhere between.

Therefore, the next question which the leader must tackle is *how* the discussion will take place. I will begin by noting several different models, none of which are *ipso facto* correct or incorrect. Correspondingly, each has several benefits and several drawbacks.

1. **Prior Written Responses**: Participants arrive at the discussion with prior written responses to the case in question and present those responses to the group. Presumably, the group then discusses or criticizes that response.
2. **Posterior Written Responses**: Such an approach assumes that some sort of discussion takes place antecedent to the writing process. In an academic setting, this would likely include a classroom setting discussion followed by the requirement to write a formal response. This model helps to provide the writer more "priming intuitions" since a discussion will take place before writing is required. Those discussions will reveal facets of the case that individual participants might not have noticed on their own. The subsequent written response often benefits from this. However, this

approach requires more organizational efforts (including time) from the discussion leader or instructor.

3. **Assigned Positions**: It can be fun—and challenging—to create a discussion prefaced upon the notion that participants have been told to defend a position on the case (whether they agree with that position or not). This relieves participants from the pressure of defending *their* point of view and turns attention on the quality of arguments for a particular viewpoint. A drawback of this approach is that it can sometimes come off as contrived and great care must be taken to identify in advance which positions ought to be assigned.
4. **Participant-Led Discussion**: Assign a discussion participant the duty to lead a discussion on a case. This method relieves you from the burden of playing the expert and often promotes freer discussions. But it also places the discussion under the leadership of someone who is less experienced. If using this approach, it is helpful to begin by modeling your own discussion leadership first before handing the discussion over to participants.
5. **Leader-Guided Discussion**: The instructor/boss/chair acts as discussion leader of a case, presumably facilitating the free expression of thought. This is the most common model used in higher education environments.
6. **Outsider Discussion Leader**: This is a common method in training sessions. The benefit is that the participants feel no coercion from the authority of the discussion leader. But the downside is that institutional leaders must arrange the session. Professors who are inclined to invite guests to campus should consider having a guest lead a discussion on a case relevant to their expertise.
7. **Organized Debates**: It may helpful to arrange debates between two contrived "opposing" sides. In higher education, "ethics bowls" are a common format for this. But the same can be accomplished in a classroom or an employee seminar. Two sides are given the same case and separately think of their solution. They may or may not be assigned "pro" and "con" positions. They then present their positions before a moderator (which may include responding to the opposing side). This is a fun, interactive activity. But the less outgoing are sometimes marginalized.
8. **Threaded Discussions**: This is a popular online modality for discussions of a variety of sorts, not just ethics discussions. Several classroom management software suites have such a capacity together with built-in evaluative tools. The corresponding benefits and demerits pertain more to the benefits and demerits of online learning than they do to ethics specifically. The

exception to this is that many online evaluation mechanisms are great at counting the *amount* of contribution, but struggle to assess its *quality*.

9. **Research Papers**: In scenarios in which ethics is a core part of job obligations or educational outcomes, it is common to assign a final research paper as a requirement. There are several journals and publishing houses dedicated solely to the publications of these sorts of writings. Included in such research papers will be examples of how others reasoned about similar situations, details of relevant professional guidelines, how proposed courses of action cohere (or don't cohere) with moral theories, and the author's own position. From an academic standpoint this is probably the "gold standard." Graduate-level ethics classes will commonly consist of a semester-long series of readings and lectures followed by one and only one submitted assignment—a final research paper. But this approach demands considerable expertise from the discussion leader/professor and significant time dedicated toward evaluation (Table 1).

Table 1 Teaching modalities

Modality	Advantages	Disadvantages
Prior Written Responses	• Permits participants infinite time to collect their thoughts • Yields higher-quality responses	• Less interactive • Evaluation can be burdensome
Posterior Written Responses	• Discussions prime student intuitions • Written material reflects more than just student response, but also input from others	• Requires more time, since both classroom and homework are included
Assigned Positions	• Focuses on reasons for positions rather than the person doing the reasoning • Less threatening to the participant	• Sometimes participants are uncomfortable defending a position they disagree with
Participant-Guided Discussion	• Removes potentially coercive effect of your authority • Makes learners responsible for discussion	• Discussions led by those without experience

(continued)

Table 1 (continued)

Modality	Advantages	Disadvantages
Leader-Guided Discussion	• Makes for high-quality discussions • Skilled moderators make for efficient and targeted talks	• Leader authority sometimes limits free speech
Outside discussion leader	• Exposes participants to experts they otherwise would not have access to • Multiplicity of viewpoints on the part of discussion leaders	• Outside experts have interests beyond education • Organizationally burdensome
Organized Debates	• Offers structure • Depersonalizes debate	• Loud voices can dominate • Requires an antecedent organizational plan
Threaded Discussion	• *De rigeur* in online educational spaces • Easily amenable to quantifiable evaluation (ex: number of occasions upon which a person commented)	• Suffers from the demerits common to all online learning environments • Not conducive to qualitative evaluation
Research paper	• The "gold standard" approach • Ideal for environments in which the study of ethics is the goal, not just a module • Consonant with best practices in academic ethics	• Extremely burdensome upon both instructor and student • Requires significant research, drafting and reflection • Extremely burdensome for the professor or discussion leader

Appendix III: Evaluating Ethics Argumentation

A training seminar or work institute almost certainly would have no need of an evaluative structure pertaining to the quality of Ethical reasoning exhibited by participants. In fact, creating an ethics evaluative structure in the workplace or boardroom would likely cause more harm than good. It is enough to host meaningful discussions in such environments, hoping that the result will be a greater appreciation for moral issues and an understanding of how one's peers reason regarding them. At most, such environments should record participation in an employee file, not the quality of their thought or nature of the positions they defend.

But in academic environments the opposite is often the case. Often times such environments include ethics material as a component of graded exercises. This can be vexing for professionals who have operated in a facts-based or quantitative environment. Whereas in a mathematics classroom there is comparatively little room for debate regarding whether a derivative has been calculated accurately, there will always be room for reasonable debate regarding the moral status of a wide variety of human action and institutional behavior. This is why responsible educators in ethics never grade on the basis of the side that was taken in a debate, but only grade on the basis of the quality of the defense of a position.

What, then are the best practices for evaluating ethical reasoning? The first point to be made is that it is not a given that the instructor must do so. For example, some instructors have seen fit to include ethics discussions as a smaller component within a much larger educational structure. In such

Table 2 Facts vs judgments

Issues of fact	Evaluative judgments
What is the categorical imperative?	Is the categorical imperative a plausible moral rule?
Egoists often presuppose that people both do and should behave self-interestedly	Is the egoist right to assume that ethics is a matter of pure self-interest?
Foreign cultures tend to have different attitudes toward what counts as government corruption	Must westerners follow western norms of corruption avoidance when working in cultures that do not share those same standards?
Feminist Ethicists insist that understanding women's issues requires understanding social structures	Is it wrong to open the door for a woman?
An objection often posed to the utilitarian is that they cannot accommodate for the notion of "human rights"	Is the objection that the utilitarian cannot accommodate for the notion of human rights a fair objection?
The virtue theorist thinks that rightness and wrongness are not the property of actions	Do we care more about what people do, or about what they are like?

circumstances it may be enough to record participation (perhaps via a presentation or discussion) and leave it at that. This is definitely within the best practices of ethics education, and the gains in collegiality and engagement can be quite significant. But this method is almost certainly inadequate for educational atmospheres in which the education of ethics is a curricular goal.

For such ethics-intensive environments it is often helpful to differentiate between what on the one hand the facts happen to be and what, on the other hand, is subject to reasonable debate. Consider the following chart which differentiates between related "fact-based" issue and their corresponding evaluative issues (Table 2).

A list like this shows that there are a great many features of the study of ethics that are fact-based. For example, it is a fact that the categorical imperative asserts that we should act in such a way that we could consistently will the maxim presupposed by our action to be a moral law. But it is not a fact that the categorical imperative states that all persons behave self-interestedly. It would be common (often via essay-writing) to pose fact-based questions to students as one method to diagnose retention of material. When doing so, it is essential to ensure that questions are posed which clearly point the student in the right direction. Vague or imprecise writing prompts can cause the prepared student to take wrong turns through no fault of their own.

Appendix III: Evaluating Ethics Argumentation

Table 3 Good and bad writing prompts

Poor writing prompts	Better writing prompts
What is Kantianism?	Immanuel Kant articulated both the categorical imperative and the means-end principle. In an essay, explain both of these principles and illustrate how they might be used
Are egoists bad people?	The egoist often endorses both the thesis of psychological egoism and ethical egoism. What are these two theses and how does the Egoist think that they explain what people do and why they do it?
Would the virtue theorist defend stealing printer paper from their employer?	In an essay, use virtue ethics to defend the position that persons should not steal printer paper from their employer. Be sure to use reasons that a virtue theorist would use, rather than reasons one would expect to be used by other theorists
Is a man's opening the door for a woman an example of gender oppression?	In an essay, present a feminist argument whose conclusion is that a man's opening the door for a woman is an instance of gender oppression

Here, then, is a chart of potential writing prompts. On the left are poor or ill-advised prompts, and on the right are better suggestions (Table 3).

The poor writing prompts on the left are poor for a collection of reasons. The first line offers a poor prompt because it leaves the student guessing as to what should be included in their response. Although such "prompts" are quite common at the graduate level, they can be frustrating and unfair at other levels. Students of good will and who have prepared are left wondering what the instructor is demanding with regards to such a prompt. This is why the better version of the question builds-in to the prompt an account of what needs to be addressed in order to create an acceptable written answer.

The second prompt is likewise poor because it is both vague and imprecise all the while requiring the respondent to defend their own personal opinion. Offering such a writing prompt invites a situation in which respondents write a collection of very few assertions, all of which are variations of "yes" or "no." The better prompt on the right provides the structure that you the evaluator expect of a written response.

The poor prompt on the third line is not an *utterly* poor one. Such questions are definitely the topic of discussion in the professional literature. But I advise that at the undergraduate level or with less-than-fully versed students who have labored to understand the underpinnings of each of these theories that the instructor shy away from requiring that the student take definitive positions regarding what any particular theory *should* defend. Admittedly, this admonition probably changes in a classroom environment in which the exclusive topic of study is a moral theory. In such a classroom, the "poor" question would be fair-play.

The final line of the grid is a more extreme version of the same trouble. But here the prompt on the left does not ask what the feminist ethics position is, but rather what the opinion of the essay-writer is about the feminist position. Especially (though not exclusively) with regards to the feminist position this is to be avoided. It is common for those not familiar with feminist ethics to have strong emotional reactions to the material. This creates a situation in which essay-writers feel invited to vent. But venting is neither substantive nor academically robust. This is why a better way to asses a student's understanding of feminist ethics is for them to recount the way that Marilyn Frye discusses the door-opening ritual rather than to declare their own opinions regarding her presentation. Whether a student agrees or disagrees with Marilyn Frye is a different matter.

But while a large amount of the study of ethics can be assessed via fact-based assignments, not all of it can be. And much of it shouldn't be. Notice that the cases in this book have a very wide-array of possible "solutions" to them. In almost none of them is there just one or two courses of action available to those who found themselves in the listed situations. There are many. And aside from the fact that the text bids the reader to choose a solution, there is also the issue of how an instructor diagnoses whether the solution they chose is a good one or not. How can the instructor evaluate a student's decision to come down on a "side" in a given case?

There are several things that ethicists look for in a plausible solution. And those things bear strong resemblance to other fields of inquiry far beyond ethics. Let's take an analogy from literary studies.

If I were to be asked to write an essay regarding what "*Tom Sawyer* is really about" then probably my answer had better to do with much more than just the plot of *Tom Sawyer*. Probably, a good account of what the book is *really* about will include a discussion of the politics of north vs south, the issue of slavery, and the differing psychic universes that occupy the minds of insouciant youth at the frontier of both worlds and the psychic world of escaped slaves. A *good* reading of Tom Sawyer is more than just about the facts of the plot.

So also is a good ethics position typified by more than a simplistic account of what is happening in a case. The more comprehensive, the more attentive to the dynamics imbedded within a case the better. Here are some common features of good ethics analyses and bad ethics analyses (Table 4).

It may be of help to call the reader's attention to the fourth line of the table above in which the term "pseudo argumentative fallacy" is used. A pseudo argumentative fallacy is a form of false-reasoning that violates the norms of good reasoning in identifiable ways. The need for educated persons to identify these is so great that it is common for philosophy departments in universities to offer general education courses in Logic or Critical Thinking whose primary goal is to learn and detect these defects of reasoning. Edwin Hurley, whose *A Concise Introduction to Logic* is one of the leading texts in the field has gathered together a definitive collection of both pseudo argumentative arguments as well as other related errors in reasoning (Hurley, 2012, pp. 125–193). His list follows, although I am editing out those more germane to his text's goal of introducing first order predicate logic. Where the name of the fallacy is Latin, I offer a translation (Table 5).

Table 4 Good and bad analyses

Features of good analyses of ethical situations	Features of bad analyses of ethical situations
Conforms to well-accepted writing norms Written in grammatically correct language, with few stylistic and word-choice errors	Violates well-accepted writing norms Contains grammar errors, especially those that make meaning uncertain. Word choice is imprecise or vague
Comprehensive A good response to an ethics case is one that takes into account all of the facts, not just some of them and not just those facts that are most convenient	Incomprehensive Only some persons/consequences/situations involved in the case are included, ignoring other morally important features of the case
Reason-Based Good ethics analyses use reasons to motivate the plausibility of the position adopted. The writer does not merely state what should be done but also why the selected course of action is best	Opinion-Based The analysis asserts (and probably re-asserts) a position but offers little or no reasons for the reader/listener to think that this position is right or the best

(continued)

Table 4 (continued)

Features of good analyses of ethical situations	Features of bad analyses of ethical situations
Avoids pseudo-argumentative fallacies No rhetorical or sub-rational devices are used to persuade	Commits pseudo-argumentative fallacies The writer/speaker commits any of a great variety of pseudo-argumentative fallacies including, but not limited to *argumetnun ad populum*, appeal to authority, the genetic fallacy, etc
Builds a case Case-building involves collating many different perspectives into a comprehensive whole. This might include citing relevant moral theories, identifying morally relevant facts and offering reasons to endorse a position in light of these	Repeats a position Poor responses begin with the conclusion and make little or no attempt to case-build
Admits weakness Real-world ethics cases are rarely cut-and-dry. A good ethics analysis admits difficulties with the position adopted and acknowledges differing lines of reasoning. The best ethics literature then responds to these lines of reasoning	Denies or ignores weakness Poor analyses deny the existence of alternative ways of approaching cases and/or make no effort to respond to points of view that are critical to one's preferred means of "solving" a case
Demonstrates insight Good ethics analyses attempt to peel back the outer shell of a case and understand the deeper issues that the case presents	Remains shallow A poor ethics analysis always sticks to shallow and easily apparent features of a case

Table 5 Informal fallacies

Informal fallacies	Example
Argumentum ad Baculum (lit "appeal to the stick") AKA **"Appeal to force"** Threaten harm to those who don't accept your position. This harm may or may not be physical	If you don't agree with me then I'll tell your brother what you did last weekend!
Argumentum ad Misericordiam AKA **Appeal to Pity** Asserting that pity for a person/situation constitutes a reason to morally judge the situation in a particular way	Said to a Prosecutor: "I know I said that these were business related expenses, but if you declare me guilty then I'd be ruined!"

(continued)

Table 5 (continued)

Informal fallacies	Example
Argumentum ad Populum **Appeal to the People** Uses a person's desire to be loved, admired, respected, accepted, (etc.) as a reason to accept a moral position	"If you agree with me, then all of those people are going to think that you are the greatest person ever" "If you don't agree with me, then those people are going to hate you"
Argumentun Ad Hominem (lit "Against the Man") Arguing that because a position is defended by someone who is or should be disliked that therefore the position is incorrect	"So-and-So says that we need a border wall. But that's what all immigrant-hating republicans say" "So-and-so says that we should adopt this policy. But she's a leftist radical communist that hates America. So we should reject her proposal"
Accident Applying a principle or a rule to a case it was not designed to apply to	"Freedom of Speech is a guaranteed right. So if Mike wanted to yell 'fire' in a crowded theater then who are we to judge?"
Straw Man Attacking a weak version of an opponent's argument rather than the best version of an opponent's argument	Representative Colostrum has argued that we should fund free community college for all residents of the United States. But that's a position that progressives would defend. And progressives are communists. Communism destroyed countries. Therefore, we must reject Representative Colostrum's position
Ignoratio Elenchi **Missing the Point** The reasons offered to support a conclusion are different from or not related to the conclusion that is defended	There is a troubling rise in incidents of hate-speech among current students. So it is with a heavy heart that I must place all current students on academic suspension
Red Herring The arguer diverts attention from the main issue and directs that attention to a different (but often related) one	Joe Biden wants to pass the Green New Deal. But didn't you know that his own son was on the board of a Ukrainian oil and gas company? Joe Biden is wrong
Argumentum ad Ignoratium **Appeal to Ignorance** The assertion that the lack of proof constitutes a form of evidence	"No one has ever proven that God doesn't exist. So God must exist" "No one has ever proven that God exists. So God doesn't exist"
Hasty Generalization Assuming that a commonality among a small group is a universally obtained regularity	"Every guy in this bar is a pig. So all men are pigs"

(continued)

Table 5 (continued)

Informal fallacies	Example
False Cause Linking reasons with the conclusion via an imaginary cause	"Every time I wore these socks, we won the soccer match. So I had better wear them today"
Slippery Slope The conclusion of an argument is alleged to be supported by the belief that a series of cascading and linked events will lead to an undesirable end	"If we permit gay marriage then who's to say that in the future you won't be able to marry your dog or your underage child? So we should oppose gay marriage"
Weak Analogy An argument by analogy is used, but relies upon an analogy not strong enough to support the conclusion	"Electricity is like flowing water. Amperage is like the width of the river and volts are like the speed of the river. So if we make a wire very wide it will always have greater voltage"
Begging the Question Allegedly supporting the conclusion of an argument while in reality missing key premises to support that conclusion	"Murder is wrong. Therefore warfare is wrong"
Complex Question Presenting a person with two positions to defend, often in an impossible-to-satisfy combination	"Have you stopped cheating on your taxes?" "What's it like to not care about the unborn?"
False Dichotomy Presenting two (or more) options when in reality there are more options (or other options)	"You're a Republican? So do you hate women or do you hate immigrants most?"
Equivocation Motivating an argument on the basis of the accidental fact that one word can have two meanings	"America runs on gas. Joe Biden runs the country. Therefore Joe Biden runs on gas"

Appendix IV: Assessing Written Case Analyses

On the basis of the preceding appendices, we can now see the difference between case analyses that are high-quality responses to a case and those that are not. The difference between the two will never consist in the conclusion that is argued for but in the reasoning that leads to it. Correspondingly, the point of these examples is not to show the reader *what the right answer is*, but rather *what counts as a good defense of a position*.

In this example, we will use "Meltdown in Monrovia" on page 71 of this text. I demonstrate one "bad" response and two "good" responses.

Example 1: A Poor Response to the Case (Advocating That the Country Director Do Nothing)

Christine, as a woman, can do whatever it is that she wants to with her life. In this case, Christine's local manager (Laura) has told the country director that Christine has been out with various political figures at social events. The country director seems to wonder whether it is appropriate for Christine to be doing that.

But it is obviously fine for Christine to do with her time whatever it is that she wants to do. First of all, there is no information in the case to the effect that Christine is breaking the law. We have no information which would make us think that she is buying or using illicit drugs. All that we are told is that she is "drinking the night away." And while that might not be the choice that

I would make with my life, it is inappropriate of me to judge another person for making that choice. Alcohol is legal in Liberia.

I also point out that no one is getting hurt in this situation. Christine has not forced anyone to go out with her. The people she is (alleged to be) hanging out with are other professionals in the country—employees of local consulates. Given that there probably aren't a lot of other people to hang out with after work it makes sense that she would seek-out other professionals in the area. Those might be the only people in the region that she has similarities with.

There seems to be the implication that Christine might be doing more than just drinking with diplomats. The country director might be worried that Christine is sleeping with them. But that isn't anything that the director should be concerned with. The director would never raise such an issue were it the case that Christine were sleeping with politicians in New York City. The assertion that it would suddenly become an issue just because she finds herself in Liberia smacks of racism—it's okay to sleep with white people but not with black people.

Finally, the case clearly states that Christine is not violating any workplace obligation. Her direct supervisor states that she is getting all of the work done. And we have no reason to think that any of the core job obligations are being poorly attended to. She is performing her job duties, and all concerns in this case are in regards to off-the-clock issues. Those should not be issues with which the country director is concerned.

Therefore, Laura should do nothing.

Example 2: A Good Response to the Case (Advocating That the Country Director Do Nothing)

In this essay I will defend the position that no investigation of Christine's off-the-clock behavior should commence.

In this case we are told of a conversation held by the country director and the local program operator (Laura) relating to the job performance and personal choices of Christine (a frontline program staff member).

The facts are that Laura has been compiling reports of the initiative to the south and has come across the personnel file of Christine. The country director is concerned about a change in behavior which includes a transformation from an introverted, diligent worker into an extroverted partier. Those notes include the fact that she is a known guest at foreign diplomatic outposts and is known to attend social events with those dignitaries. Those notes state that she "drinks the night away" at those events. Also of note is the fact that the personnel file states that Christine is performing her job duties as expected.

The central issue of this case is in regards to whether or not it is the case that the country director should conduct further investigation regarding Christine's behavior. I argue that the country director should not.

In taking such a position, it might be tempting to adopt an egoist's perspective: To assert that Christine has an unqualified right to do as she pleases. One might alternatively adopt a utilitarian defense—assert that Christine and those she consorts with are doing what the most want to do and that, furthermore, because there is no evidence that anyone is harmed that therefore there is no moral concern.

But both of these lines of reasoning would be in error.

The egoist defense fails because it presents us the wrong sorts of considerations for a case like this. At issue is whether a director has cause to engage in further investigation, not whether a person has moral justification to behave in a particular way. Availing ourselves of an egoistic defense forces Christine to make a defense of her behavior where no such defense is obligated (i.e. "She has a right to do as she pleases").

Likewise, a utilitarian defense to the effect that Christine (and her friends) are doing as they please and no one is getting hurt is also beside the point. It may very well be true that Christine and her friends are maximizing their own utility and that there is no undesirable consequence for this maximization being paid by any other person or group of persons who may be directly or indirectly affected by the action. But this does not constitute the reason why the country director should not intervene.

The director should not intervene, including engaging in further investigations, for reasons often discussed by feminist ethical theorists. Such theorists assert that actions (or in this case, proposed actions) are commonly engendered in surprising ways. So not only are Christine's actions of consorting with foreign diplomats engendered, but so also is the director's contemplation regarding whether or not to intervene. And the director is thinking of engaging in investigations because Christine is a woman.

A helpful tool to begin thinking about this case from a feminist perspective would be to imagine how one might respond were genders differently distributed. If Christine were a male known to go to the consulates for late night parties would there have been concerned raised? Here I confess that I must be somewhat speculative. But I do nevertheless fear that in a scenario with different genders involved that there would be lessened pressure to conduct a further investigation.

Investigations are being contemplated in this case not because Christine's behavior is suspect, but because her gender raises additional suspicion. But this is unjust. It is wrong to engage in personnel-related fact-finding solely because of the gender of the person being investigated. Investigations and personnel file additions should not be conducted or modified contingent upon the gender of the person in question.

Finally, I must add that none of what I have stated takes any position regarding whether or not Christine is right or wrong, wise or unwise regarding her decisions. For all I (or any other reader) know there may be saints or there may be scoundrels participating with her in her revelry. Her decision to spend time at the soirées may be wise or it may be foolish. But the position that I do defend is that the deliberations regarding whether or not to investigate should not be concluded contingent upon the gender of the employee in question. It should not be the case that women incur upon them an additional scrutiny solely because they are women.

Correspondingly, the country director ought not engage in any additional fact-finding.

Example 3: A Good Response to the Case (Advocating That the Country Director Do Something)

In this essay I will defend the view that the country director has an obligation to conduct further investigations into Christine's behavior.

In this case we are told of a conversation held by an unnamed country director and a local program manager (Laura) regarding the job performance and personal choices of Christine (a frontline program staff member).

The facts are that the country director has been compiling reports of the initiative to the south and has come across the personnel file of Christine. The director is concerned about a change in behavior which includes a transformation from an introverted, diligent worker into an extroverted partier. Those notes include the fact that she is a known guest at foreign diplomatic outposts and is known to attend social events with those dignitaries. Those notes state that she "drinks the night away" at those events. Also of note is the fact that the personnel file states that Christine is performing her job duties as expected.

The central issue of this case is in regards to whether or not it is the case that the director should conduct further investigation regarding Christine's behavior. I argue that the director should.

But as I endorse this position I should be quick to point out that some lines of reasoning might indicate otherwise. An egoist perspective, for example, might argue that Christine is merely doing what she most wants to do, leaving the rest of us to endure the tacit assertion that we have no such right to question her decision. But this line of reasoning could likewise be inflicted upon others who reasonably ask questions of concern regarding those around them. When persons of good faith perceive that others around them are engaging in dangerous choices, it is never unreasonable to express—and act on—concern. This latter position is bolstered by the fact that the evidence in the file shows that there has been a behavioral change in Christine recently. Behavioral change could constitute evidence that there are further and deeper issues in play.

Appendix IV: Assessing Written Case Analyses

A more powerful argument to the effect that we ought not to engage in further investigations stems from a feminist perspective. That perspective would likely note that one only considers additional scrutiny of Christine because (presumably) Christine is a woman. Were Christine a man perhaps fewer culturally prompted warning bells would sound. Hence the decision (or contemplation) to investigate further is the symptom of gender attitudes held by the director, not the result of any decision that Christine has made.

Perhaps. But these reasonings are somewhat speculative and hard to substantiate. I concur with those who, from a feminist perspective, argue that additional scrutiny because the subject is a woman is immoral. But I also assert that there are more gender perspectives in this case than just the director's and Christine's.

Consider the case of the Ghanan diplomats that Laura mentioned to the director. We are provided facts to the effect that they are men, that they host parties where alcohol is served, that the parties last deep into the night and that Christine is a consistent attendee at these parties. Furthermore, we are given the information that this streak of extroversion is new to Christine from which I infer a noteworthy behavioral change.

We are offered no information as to the profiles of the Ghanan diplomats other than their gender. But it is morally important for us to ask questions about the gender attitudes, or likely gender attitudes, of them. Stated succinctly, is it likely or unlikely that such diplomats understand and respect the respect for women advocated by the feminist ethics perspective? The most defensible answer to this question is chilling: we do not know.

And it is this fact—the fact that we do not know the intentions of these men—that constitutes the most significant moral feature of this situation. Given that the country director does not know their names, much less than their intentions, it is morally incumbent upon her to conduct further investigations. And this fact is further bolstered by the fact that the case states that the extroversion streak in Christine is new. Sudden changes in behavior can be powerful signs of something good and right, but also bad and harmful.

This reasoning is supported by several moral theories. The utilitarian would reason that provided that the investigation is conducted with decorum, it will either cause no harm or will prevent significant harm. And I concede that the hedge "conducted with decorum" is essential in this analysis.

Using the medical ethics fourfold system provides intriguing insights. On the one hand it is tempting to state that the principle of autonomy bids us to let Christine live as she wishes. But the change in behavior on the part of Christine gives us reason to wonder whether her behavior is fully autonomous in the first place. And when we reflect upon the principles of nonmaleficence and beneficence, the case for intervention becomes stronger. Given that there is a sudden behavioral change, the requirement to ensure that she flourish (beneficence) and not be harmed (nonmaleficence) becomes stronger. Once again, this points to the need to intervene.

Finally, let us return to the feminist position. Has this defense unintentionally engaged in the violation of reasonable prohibitions to not place women in a double-bind situation? No, it has not. Because my admonition to investigate further is not rooted in her gender, but upon the behavioral change she has exhibited together with the potential for harm that might befall a person with imperiled autonomy. If she is actually "melting down" then it would be right to initiate action which might prevent further harm.

Reflections on the Three Preceding Analyses

The first analysis of the case suffers from several demerits. Let's begin by looking at the first paragraph, which reads:

> *Christine, as a woman, can do whatever it is that she wants to with her life. In this case, Christine's local manager (Laura) has told the country director that Christine has been out with various political figures at social events. The country director seems to wonder whether it is appropriate for Christine to be doing that.*

Ignoring the issues of "familiar vernacular" such as ending the last sentence with "…doing that" there are other problems with this paragraph. The first sentence is at once unclear, but (on a reasonable reading) preposterous. Let us assume that Christine is indeed a woman (a plausible assumption of the case). This first sentence embodies within it a number of assertions which would be difficult to defend. The writer tells us that "as a woman" Christine "can" do "whatever it is that she wants" to do. The first problem of note is that the writer is not being clear regarding what the underlying assertion is. Here are some hypotheses.

1. As a woman Christine is morally permitted to do as she pleases, but as other things (perhaps, as a human being?) she is not.
2. The fact that Christine is a woman means that Christine is morally permitted to do whatever she likes.

It is unclear which of these two the first sentence is endorsing. There are probably other interpretations. But whichever it is, the claim is almost certainly false. Christine is not morally permitted, no matter her gender, to engage in a cargo theft ring at the port. She is not permitted to engage in murder-for-amusement just because she is a woman. She is not permitted to cause harm to innocent persons without powerful justificatory reason.

Another problem with the first sentence, and with the entire approach throughout, is that this response conceives of the central moral issue as being in regards to whether Christine has done anything wrong. One senses that the writer thinks that Christine is being "judged." But nowhere in the case is this asserted. And it would be a bizarre moral world in which we only have the responsibilities to act when people make morally wrong choices.

The second paragraph reads:

> But it is obviously fine for Christine to do with her time whatever it is that she wants to do. First of all, there is no information in the case to the effect that Christine is breaking the law. We have no information which would make us think that she is buying or using illicit drugs. All that we are told is that she is "drinking the night away." And while that might not be the choice that I would make with my life, it is inappropriate of me to judge another person for making that choice. Alcohol is legal in Liberia.

Here the writer is trying to make the argument that because Christine failed to violate laws that her behavior therefore presents no significant moral (or other) issue to the country director. But this is likewise a poor argument. As discussed in the opening chapters of the text, it is a serious error to confuse ethics with the law.

> I also point out that no one is getting hurt in this situation. Christine has not forced anyone to go out with her. The people she is (alleged to be) hanging out with are other professionals in the country—employees of local consulates. Given that there probably aren't a lot of other people to hang out with after work it makes sense that she would seek-out other professionals in the area. Those might be the only people in the region that she has similarities with.

This paragraph continues along the theme according to which the central moral issue is in regards to whether or not Christine is behaving immorally. But note that the case never tells us that this question is *the* moral issue at stake. But bracketing off this point, also notice that for the first time we do see moral reasoning. The author states that "no one is getting hurt" which appeals to utilitarian intuitions. But this case would be made stronger by making reference to the utilitarian theory directly. This, however, was not done.

> There seems to be the implication that Christine might be doing more than just drinking with diplomats. The country director might be worried that Christine is sleeping with them. But that isn't anything that the director should be concerned with. The director would never raise such an issue were it the case that Christine were sleeping with politicians in New York City. The assertion that it

> would suddenly become an issue just because she finds herself in Liberia smacks of racism—it's OK to sleep with white people but not with black people.

Here the writer would benefit from a more clear and precise writing style. Take for example the sentence which reads "But that isn't anything that the director should be concerned with." This is an example of a lack of clarity. The issue this case presents is not in regards to the director's "concern." The issue is in regards to whether (or how) the director should respond. That there is a concern is evident, and it seems pointless to chastise persons for what the happened to be concerned with. Rather, we are interested in whether the director has a responsibility to investigate further.

The point that this same concern wouldn't arise were the situation occurring in the states is a delightfully provocative one, and probably constitutes the finest point made in this essay.

> Finally, the case clearly states that Christine is not violating any workplace obligation. Her direct supervisor states that she is getting all of the work done. And we have no reason to think that any of the core job obligations are being poorly attended to. She is performing her job duties, and all concerns in this case are in regards to off-the-clock issues. Those should not be issues with which Laura is concerned.

But this paragraph then proceeds to undermine what would otherwise have been an interesting line of exploration. Embedded within it is an unsubstantiated presupposition which, when articulated, proves to be dangerously close to self-refuting: No intervention is ever warranted so long as a person is doing their job well. This unspoken assertion would not survive serious scrutiny.

The demerits of this first response are made clearer by looking at the following two alternate responses. Those two, while defending different conclusions, are well-reasoned attempts to diagnose the locus of the moral problem and offer a concrete suggestion regarding what to *do*. Each evidences a comprehensive knowledge of moral reasoning, each discloses and responds to alternate points of view. And each uses a case-building method to arrive at a conclusion. That the second case argues that we ought not intervene but the third that we should is hardly of consequence. Rather, it illustrates the very real phenomena that persons of good will differ sometimes.

Appendix V: Discussion Guides to Each Case

In this appendix, I present the discussion leader with tips regarding how to lead discussions on each case. The underlying thrust of this section is not so much to proscribe an educational approach as it is to offer optional tools for the discussion leader. As such, and above all else, the discussion leader should feel free to address each case as they see fit.

While all of the cases are capable of sparking conversations in their own right, from time-to-time issues emerge that merit background reading and research. Therefore, the discussion leader will see that within these notes are a variety of references to background information which the leader may or may not elect to use.

Covid-19 Vaccine Policy in a Medium-Sized NFP

This case places the student in the midst of the Covid-19 pandemic and bids the participant to decide which policy ought to be endorsed given the lack of perfect information. The discussion leader must understand that the purpose of the case Is *not* to come up with a solution given all of the information that we know *now*. Rather, this case tests the student's ability to make decisions under conditions of ignorance, stress and conflict.

This case lists several morally significant points. They are:

1. At the time in which the case occurs, the FDA has not approved the vaccine. It is still only an "emergency use" medical intervention. Consequently, it would be immoral, and quite likely illegal, to require anyone to use the vaccine (with the possible exception of medical personnel and military personnel). This has since changed (The Food and Drug Administration, 2022).
2. The hyper-politicized environment in which the pandemic is discussed.
3. The wide variety of attitudes regarding the Covid-19 threat of staff members who will be impacted by the policy decision.
4. A leadership committee which must decide on a pressing issue without full information. This feature, more than any virus-specific data-points, is the one which will have much more enduring consequences. Leadership teams are frequently in a position of having to make policy decisions with less-than-perfect information. While this case pertains to Covid-19 response, every NGO and NFP will encounter other policy judgment calls which take place under similar conditions of ignorance.
5. Every option available to the leadership team has both good and bad consequences. No response will be perfect.

It is equally important to be aware that several issues that could be raised by discussion participants are likely red herrings. These include, but are definitely not limited to:

1. Whether those unconcerned by the virus are "science-deniers."
2. Whether Trump/Biden responded appropriately.
3. Whether or not people's views on the Covid-19 pandemic are good faith positions or not.

Each of these, and probably many others in addition, are red herrings since even if they were discussed and definitively adjudicated, they likely would not help the leadership team to decide what their policy judgment ought to be. Even if, for example, those who oppose the vaccine are "science-deniers" we are still left with the question regarding which policy to implement in an environment in which employees hold sincere false beliefs while simultaneously there being no FDA-approved vaccine.

Another likely facet of the discussion of this case is the well-known phenomena of enflamed passions. Discussion leaders should expect fireworks should they elect to discuss this case. And fireworks, just like classroom silence, can be good or bad. Extra effort must be taken to strike a balance between letting participants process the case, and ensuring that the loudest voices do not squelch opposing voices.

The discussion questions listed at the end of the case are as follows:

1. How can NFP leadership avoid the politicization of their own Covid-19 vaccine policy?
2. What are the effects of the politicization of healthcare policy?
3. Perform a cost–benefit-analysis. What are the pros and cons of demanding a carte blanche vaccine mandate policy in your NFP? And how would that be enforced?
4. To what extent do the reasons of your staff for not being vaccinated matter?
5. Do you believe that the Covid-19 pandemic is the last time your NFP or NGO will face decisions like this? Why or why not?

The discussion leader will see that each is articulated to address the issues mentioned above. The final question is intended to be provocative while calling attention to the broader issue that while this case specifically invokes the pandemic, the issues involved in the case are much broader than that.

Several moral theories are of direct relevance to the resolution of this case. They are:

1. Utilitarianism: Which course of action produces the best consequences? This is specifically implied by question number 3.
2. The Principle of Autonomy (from medical ethics): Question 4 probes the relevance of this principle. Even if false, should staff be permitted to "live" consistent with their beliefs? And likewise, that same principle requires us to think of the best interests of the children in the homes who will be directly affected by the leadership team's judgment call.
3. Egoism: NFP leadership teams often implement policies which benefit the institution primarily. Is this the way that this case should be decided?

Finally, if a reference to law and policy is of use to your discussion, it may be of interest for your discussants to consult OSHA and CDC policy guidelines. The CDC has created an employer reference page (The Center for Disease Control and Prevention, 2022). And OSHA has written a free-to-use template which helps businesses create their own policies (Occupational Health and Safety Administration, 2022).

The Helpful Board Member

This case presents a scenario common in NFP operations—the unique moral requirements that institutions have when offering services to children.

This case presents a scenario in which a board member has access to children while bypassing background check protocols. However, it is written in such a way as to lead discussants to merely detect this problem—this is not stated directly. Therefore, the discussion should be structured in such a way as to ensure that participants understand the seriousness of this point. Any NFP whose work includes services to children ought to have a background check policy in addition to policies relating to behavior in the presence of children.

Also note that this case does *not* intimate that there is improper activity occurring. Rather, the board member is making a good faith and kindhearted effort to help deliver on institutional goals. But the board member has unknowingly violated important legal and moral guidelines in so doing.

Another key discussion-point of this case is in regards to *how* this situation is rectified. Here context matters. The person who has committed an unbeknownst violation is not an unknown outsider or a person whose intentions are unclear. They are a key supporter of the mission of the NFP.

In such circumstances a private conversation can easily be had which dispatches with the issue in a single conversation. Such a background check can be scheduled in an afternoon.

Another issue that merits discussion is the etiology of the situation in the first place. Either the board member was never made aware or has somehow forgotten institutional protocol. On this note it would be helpful for the board to be made aware of this gaffe and quite likely the board member in question in this case is the ideal candidate to offer the protocol refresher.

Finally, the motives of the board member may or may not be of concern. It would be wholly welcome to embrace the leadership of a board member who derives satisfaction through the delivery of the mission of the NFP. But a board member who retreats to the mission of the NFP in an effort to assuage private emotional problems is of concern. It would be worth reviewing the Kantian means-end principle to reveal the reason why.

When Democracy and Mission Collide

In this case we confront the issue of the benefits and demerits of democratic governance boards. In it we find that the pure democratic model used by the community development association made the association highly amenable to a hostile takeover by privateers and politicians. Also, of moral pertinence is the behavior of the mayor who appears to have been complicit in the takeover.

It is clear that the events which transpired in the case were not welcomed by those who started the organization. It is clear that the community members were blindsided by the events. But it is not clear what ought to have been done, if anything, to prevent the situation.

If there was a moral wrong committed in this situation, it is worth exploring what that wrong was and who committed it. Likely, the wrong involved the manipulation of rules in unanticipated ways by persons with agendas that differed from those who created the rules. Hence, those who bear scrutiny in this case are:

1. The community organizers: Were they remiss, or perhaps naive, in the articulation of their NFP's bylaws? If so, what should they (or could they) have done differently?
2. The Mayor: What did the mayor know and when did the mayor know it? Was the mayor in collusion with the development company without making the community NFP aware? Is the behavior of the mayor improper?
3. The Development Company: To what extent is the developer responsible for this situation?

To a significant extent, some issues implied by the above cannot be resolved since we are not given information regarding the extent of collusion between the developers and the mayor. But it is reasonable to assume that some form of collusive activity existed.

It may be of help to look at the fourfold Medical Ethics system (Nonmaleficence, beneficence, autonomy and justice) and better understand how each party in this situation would conceive of the satisfaction of the demands of this list.

1. The Community NFP: Members probably believe that they have been harmed (nonmaleficence) unfairly (justice) by a collusive, agenda-driven process (autonomy).
2. The Mayor: The mayor is not just the mayor of this neighborhood but of all the city. New development brings in tax dollars for everyone and creates relationships that could be of political benefit. Arguably, the Mayor is impinging upon the autonomy of the NFP, potentially causing some harm (nonmaleficence) to their plans, but for the purpose of acquiring

a social good (beneficence) that extends within and beyond the community. High-density housing accrues more tax dollars than other forms of development, for example.
3. The Developer: The developer exists to develop. It is not unfair to assume the primary form of beneficence with which they are concerned is benefit to themselves and their customers.

Finally, virtue ethics provides an explanation as to why we are concerned about this case even when no law was violated and even when all NFP bylaws were followed. This is because we demand more of persons than just that the rules are followed. We expect them to behave consonant with certain moral virtues. The mayor seems to have acted inconsistently with any such virtue. A conversation regarding which moral virtues the mayor failed to embody might be helpful.

The Employee with Family on the Board

This case would be especially valuable for boards to discuss.

In this case we are presented with a common situation in NFPs, especially small NFPs. A board member has a direct line of communication with operations staff and this line of communication is being exploited contrary to chain-of-command protocol for the purpose of furthering a defeated board agenda item.

Two persons confront difficult moral situations in this regard:

1. The Board Member: is the board member engaging in inappropriate behavior?
2. The NFP Director: How can the director effectively navigate this tricky situation?

It would be helpful to analyze the behavior of the board member using an egoistic theory. Framed this way, explaining the board member's behavior is straightforward: The board member's interest is in pursuing their own agenda, and endeavors to use available means to do so.

But other moral theories are likewise helpful. Clearly the board member's actions fail both Kantian principles.

1. Categorical Imperative: No governance structures would exist in a world in which governance structures are always bypassed.

2. Means-End Principle: The board member using the NFP to forward his own agenda and is using his son in the same way.

A thorough utilitarian analysis will also be of aid. If successful in muscling through his own agenda, the board member satisfies their own interests. But that same act undermines the interests of the NFP to deliver effective, mission-driven services. This *prima facie* appears to sacrifice greater utility for the sake of maximizing individual utility, and hence is immoral.

Social Enterprise vs. Social Service

A cluster of related questions are posed by this case. They are:

1. Is it dishonest to market an NFP as an NFP for a former military when not all persons served by it are former military?
2. Are NFPs always the best way to create social good?

Of relevance to question one is that NFPs, *qua* NFPs, are chartered under a mission. But a for-profit entity need not have any mission statement at all. So an NFP whose stated mission is to serve former members of the military engages in mission drift even when they effectively deliver services outside that charter. In a situation like the one posed in the case two options are available: modify the mission or exclude non-military. Neither option is without negative side-effects.

A "third" way is to cease being an NFP and to re-launch as a for-profit entity.

A good strategy to lead discussions on this case is to lead discussants through the undesirable consequences of either course of action under NFP status. After doing so, it may be helpful to then introduce the possibility of conversation to for-profit status as a way to resolve the issue. It may be that upon analysis this alternative is rejected. But taking this alternative seriously can help discussion participants to seriously inquire as to whether NFPs are always the best way to maximize the social good.

The Board member's Pet Project

This case presents the discussant with the often-repeated phenomena in NFPs and NGOs of programs that appear to have outlived their initial purpose. To that end, if discussants are current professionals in the NFP sector it might be helpful to begin the discussion by listing the annual events or programs that their NFP or NGO is best known for, and to lead a discussion regarding whether the event/program continues to be justifiably offered.

In a case like this it is also worthwhile to discuss which features of a program justify the program's existence: writing out a list might be helpful.

Thinking about the utilitarian perspective is of use. NFPs have an obligation to deliver on their mission. And the utilitarian perspective requires that if an NFP administers a program that harms the delivery of the best possible results, then that program should be cut. On utilitarian grounds, given the way the case is presented, this appears to be a program that should be cut (or modified, or minimized, etc.).

Inexperienced discussants might miss the important detail that the program is a favorite program of an influential and generous board member—a board member with whom we have no reason to question her commitment or professionalism. It is often the case that a board member advocates for a program that NFP leaders would not wish to continue. Therefore, referencing the above utilitarian analysis, included in that analysis are the possible consequences of offending or sidelining the board member in question.

Discussion participants may express unease with what feels like a moral compromise embedded within the case—especially if the position is defended which states that the program is to be retained on pain of estranging a wealthy donor. This sentiment beautifully expresses the different moral perspectives of consequentialism and deontology. The consequentialist is inclined to tolerate a situation in which the ends justify the means, and the deontologist is not.

Regime Change and the Perils of Being a Hero

This case presents a situation in which grants funds have been misallocated—funds given to the NFP to administer an afterschool educational program were diverted to build a football stadium. This case is written in such a way as to ask the reader, as a good faith administrator of a grant-funded program, how they would proceed to respond given the discovery of diversion of funds.

With regards to cases like this which involve obvious—and shocking—moral lapses, it is especially important to gain clarity regarding the exact nature of the moral wrong. It is easy for discussants to side-track into related-but-imprecise complaints. For example, it may be the case that athletics constitute an outsized voice in educational NFPs, and cases like this give us evidence to that end. But the allegedly outsized voice of athletics existed both before and after this scenario took place. It was a background condition, not the locus of the moral wrong.

Quite probably, the locus of wrongdoing in this case is an instance of institutional deception: the NFP accepted funds for one program with the promise of delivering a program, then violated that promise and used the funds for something else. As such, the case presents a case of deception.

Additionally, the case also presents the tricky issue of what to do as a program administrator who was not him or herself responsible for the deception.

Clearly, lying for the purpose of acquiring money is not a morally defensible policy for an NFP. This is easily demonstrated by using any of the moral theories presented in this book. It may be of help to point out that this kind of lying fails even on egoist grounds: Once an NFP becomes known for deceptive fundraising practices, this significantly harms the future fundraising activities of the NFP. Foundations of the size that gave this gift have ongoing relationships with other foundations and will communicate their experience with peers in the philanthropic community. That word gets out beyond the professional philanthropic community (as is evidenced by the fact that this case is in this book!).

Even on egoist grounds, this NFP has acted immorally.

The harder issue is in regards to how the good faith employee ought to respond. Is continued employment tantamount to tacit approval of the misdeed? Since no *person* was directly harmed it is unlikely that the Human Resources office would be an appropriate or effective place to register a complaint. And a decision like this would likely have been discussed with the advancement/development department in advance of the diversion, not posterior to it. So it is not clear that a discussion with that department would have any effect.

In this actual case, the employee who wrote the grant felt that his NFP had undertook a course of action which posed significant harm to his own reputation. This caused him to question whether continued employment was possible and the employee departed the NFP out of a desire to rescue his reputation.

The Possessive Major Gifts Officer

In this case we are asked to appraise the behavior of Marjorie who is portrayed as acting possessively regarding her relationships in the fundraising department. Inexperienced discussion participants may be unaware of the pressures that exist in fundraising departments which can cause dynamics like that which we find in this case to instantiate. Some background may be of help.

Fundraising is often divided into several discrete endeavors: Grant-writing, events, wills and bequests, and major gifts. In reality, the lines between these are often blurred. And from time-to-time other categories are added.

Major gifts are typically gifts solicited from individual persons, not foundations or philanthropic organizations (although, again, there are exceptions). This is significant, since the vast plurality of philanthropic dollars allocated every year to NFPs is from individuals, not foundations or grants-making entities. The NFP's investment in "major gifts" operations is wholly justified and consonant with the best practices of the NFP fundraising sector. Nearly every successful NFP invests in this activity.

Furthermore, while the *Association of Fundraising Professionals* (AFP) deems it unethical to place fundraising quotas on fundraising professionals (Association of Fundraising Professionals, 2022), the reality is that fundraising is a high-pressure endeavor whose dynamics much resemble the for-profit sector's "sales" department. Just as a salesperson does not last long without making substantial sales, so also fundraisers do not retain their positions without accruing philanthropic dollars. And, again, while the code of ethical standards articulated by the AFP asserts that tying compensation to fundraising totals is unethical, it almost always is the case that the fundraiser bringing in the most dollars also has the largest salary. It is not unheard of for the fundraiser to have a higher salary than the CEO.

Marjorie is an employee who has placed herself into this high-pressure environment and has performed well. As the case states, her tactics have led to the increased revenue of the NFP. But two problems are noted in the case. They are:

1. Marjorie does not permit NFP staff to interact with donors.
2. No funds are being "set aside" from gifts. Every dollar donated is a dollar spent.

We therefore are confronted with a "balancing" problem not unlike that which the medical ethics system was built for. Marjorie views herself as acting for the maximal beneficence of the NFP, but the CEO fears that her methods might be unduly impinging upon the requirement to be non-maleficently (due to #2 above). Moreover, there is a clear question as to whether the methods implemented by Marjorie are fully-just. Is it wrong for her to occupy prime office space for her efforts? After all, her argument is that by depriving street-level access from clients and staff (a violation of the principle of Justice) is being done for the purpose of increasing the NFP financial bottom-line (the principle of Beneficence).

Finally, it is important for current and future NFP leaders to think about the potential harm that a situation like this can create for a chain of command. When a fundraiser wrestles institutional control of revenue away from a CEO this can create a chaotic situation in which rational decision-making can be imperiled.

When Personal Problems Threaten the Mission

In this case the discussion participant is asked to play the role of a board member as they uncover information to the effect that family issues have caused work-performance issues on the part of their CEO.

Board members must understand that they operate under the mandate to protect the interests of the NFP/NGO, not the NFP's/NGO's CEO. This is especially important to recall in such a case as when the appointed CEO is beloved by the board.

Nevertheless, board members also must ensure that CEO's are treated fairly, including in those cases in which personal problems arise in the private lives of their appointed leaders.

It is important for discussion participants to attend to not only the issue of whether or not Alan should be fired or placed on leave. They also need to consider how any course of action affects the operation and morale of the NFP. Aggressive moves from a board which directly impact operations can be viewed as threatening to those who work for the NFP ("If they can fire Alan, then am I next?") Therefore, the issue of *what* to do is just as important as *how* to do it.

Meltdown in Monrovia

The discussion leader should refer to Appendix IV for a detailed set of writing samples regarding this case, all of which reveal important facets of the pertinent discussion.

Broadly speaking, there are two moral issues that emerge in this case:

1. Whether there should be further investigation of Christine, a young female worker at the NGO.
2. Whether Christine's female gender plays a role in motivating the question as to whether we should investigate.

The first question is easily analyzed using any of the variety of moral theories presented in this book. For example:

1. Kant: Investigation does not fail the means-end test since Christine is not being used for a further end. And such investigations pass the categorical imperative since we can easily justify asking probing questions of an employee we fear may be in trouble.
2. Utilitarianism: A strong argument can be made to the effect that asking further questions (aka, investigating) is justified since it could prevent significant harm, albeit at the potential expense of causing minimal harm (perhaps embarrassment on the part of Christine).
3. Egoism: Further investigation into the issue is justified since is hurts the NGO should it be the case that she is in an imperiled situation.

But the feminist perspective is of great importance in this case. Are we only considering asking further questions of Christine's behavior because Christine is a woman? Would the same issues arise were it a young male NGO employee?

A feminist ethicist would be suspicious of a course of action if it was undertaken consonant with unarticulated-but-unjust background gender assumptions. For example, the often-unconfessed presupposition that "women need to be protected" is just such an assumption. Investigations because a situation is dangerous is one matter, but investigating just because the subject is a woman appears straightforwardly immoral. When such a line of thinking is implemented as policy, whether *de jure* or *de facto,* women can face a situation of increased scrutiny and oversight solely because of their gender.

Cutting Vital Services

This case presents a scenario that is not unique to one sector, but an emerging trend in many different NFP service sectors: Declining state reimbursement rates. Many NFPs were created under a state reimbursement rate scheme which has changed since the NFP originated. Rarely is it the case that such schemes have become *more* generous. Typically, rates have fallen with some states reimbursing less in absolute dollars today than they did three decades ago!

This phenomenon has caused a cash crunch at many NFPs, including the one discussed in this case.

The discussion participant is asked to troubleshoot a variety of courses of action:

1. Eliminate a vital program
2. Retain the program
3. Fundraise for the imperiled program

Each of these three presents undesirable consequences. It is essential to lead discussion participants through each option and arrive at a clear-eyed picture of the opportunities and obstacles they propose.

Eliminating a program sacrifices the welfare of some persons for the benefit of the others. Specifically, money-losing programs are eliminated so as to bolster the institutional bottom-line. It may be of use to your discussion participants to point out that many for-profit institutions that increasingly compete with the NFP sphere are created under the acknowledgment of exactly this situation. They identify all and only those programs which have reimbursement rates which permit profitability and design a corporation which services only those needs, leaving the NFP sector to service the needs of the unprofitable ones.

The third option above will likely appear enticing to those who have not done fundraising before. But it is perilous and could cause unintended consequences. Fundraising is an ideal tool for one-time needs and capital improvements. It is a poor fix for a budgetary shortfall. Since it has been discovered in this case that the budget is imperiled by this program, requesting that the fundraising department fill the gap is to ask that they fill the gap *forever*. This places pressure on the fundraising arm of the institution and incentivizes fundraisers to behave as if they have dollar quotas. A potential "fix" to this situation might be to prioritize fundraising an endowment which will be used in part to fund the money-losing program.

Often times, selling assets is posed as a "quick fix" in situations like this one. But it would be poor practice to sell an asset solely for the purpose of addressing a budget shortfall. NFPs that do this typically fail to address the budgetary problem, thereby *delaying* the onset of the problem rather than *solving* the problem. And since the asset has been sold, when the problem re-emerges it will re-emerge with fewer available tools to respond with.

Changing Staff's Job Descriptions

Many facets of this case are related to the unique and changing landscape of the faith-based NGO. The most discussed of all facets of this sphere is the impending decline of dollars donated from individuals. The discussion leader would do well to review some of the empirical data on this issue. Barna

Research Group has compiled rigorous social scientific studies on faith-based NFPs and NGOs that could be of help (Barna Research Group, 2022).

Additionally, on the presupposition that a discussion of this case is led within a faith-based context, it will be helpful to read-up on the many instances of "Business as Mission" (BAM) literature. There is no one leading source and no one leading NFP or NGO. Rather, "BAM" is an ideological movement increasingly of interest to the faith-based NGO.

When discussing this case in faith-based organizations it can be helpful to understand both *whether* and *why* there are prohibitions against soliciting federal dollars. Many faith-based NGOs (though definitely not all) would be ideal recipients of such funds should they demonstrate the willingness to create the reporting in a structure requisite for such revenue streams. Often times the prohibitions against accepting such funds are fear-based, not evidence-based. This is made clearer by observing that such prohibitions follow cultural lines—it is typically the American Protestant (evangelical) organization expressing such misgivings. It is not, for example, the American federal government who has created congressional records detailing the practice's constitutionality (Subsommittee on the Constitution of the Committee on the Judiciary, 2001). In the United Kingdom the "Faith New Deal Pilot Fund" operates in much the same way (Kruger, 2020).

Regarding whether it is morally appropriate to re-assign job expectations to current staff, it can be provocative to ask whether the NGO in question would be justifiably accused of lying to its staff in so doing. Posed in such a way, the question as to whether the re-assignment of job duties is immoral is self-answering. But it also leads to a further observation: the NGO in question is not entertaining the possibility because they believe it is the best way to deliver on the mission. They are posing the possibility because they fear that their current model is destined to financial collapse.

This is why the final question in the discussion question section directly asks whether NFPs should exist forever. If the NGO is encountering mission-ending financial dynamics, could it be that this is a reason to think that the NGO should no longer exist?

Child Sponsorship in the Afterschool Program

Several independent NGOs run child-sponsorship initiatives. A typical structure is one in which a donor or prospective donor is given the contact information of a child. Then a pen-pal type relationship ensues in which the donor continues to write messages (and give dollars) while the linked client abroad reciprocates with messages in response.

There is considerable literature on the subject, including internet news articles critical of the practice (Nolan, 2022). Yet NGOs that engage in the practice have defenses of their own, and fairness requires considering their own perspective. See, for example, Compassion International's treatment of the issue (Compassion International, 2022).

Since child sponsorship is a well-tested and powerful fundraising mechanism, it is unlikely that it will cease in the near future.

Almost certainly, the central moral issue of the ethics of child sponsorship relates to the Kantian Means-End principle. Are sponsored children being *used* as a tool to accrue donation dollars? A strong and uncomplicated argument can be made to the effect that they are. This then poses a secondary line of discussion: even if they are being *used*, is it wrong to do so? That is, given that there is a sense in which children are being used as a means, are they being used as a *mere means*?

Finally, it would be wrong to think that this fundraising tool will forever be relegated to the international NGO scene. Sponsorship initiatives have been proposed in a wide variety of other environments including disabilities services, afterschool programs, post-incarceration NFPs and others.

Accepting Crypto Donations

This case relates as much to an institutional policy as it does to institutional finance and management. Should an NFP accept crypto donations, and under what conditions ought they do so (or not do so)?

Whereas in the past there was just one crypto currency (bitcoin), today there are a great many. So many that books can (and are) written to detail their nuances. This fact is important since the typical NFP does not have the resources to track such digital instruments.

Therefore the discussion should be centered around policy-related issues at least as much around financial-related issues. For example, a common policy of NFPs is that whenever receiving a non-cash donation of financial value (stocks, for example) that the donation be sold within a certain time period and converted to cash. This time period rarely extends beyond a month, with a great many NFPs specifying that the gift is converted to cash "immediately."

Discussion of the policy issue can help to resolve the ethics issue in this case. Since it appears to be good policy to not "hold" financial instruments it would be inappropriate to accept a gift like this one.

Furthermore, it will be a helpful discussion for current and future NFP leaders to identify warning signs that are seen in this case. The incidence of being offered crypto donations will increase, not decrease.

The White Savior in the Dark Continent

The central moral issue of this case is in regards to whether a photograph used by an NGO imbeds improper racial attitudes and if so, how to respond.

Discussion leaders should be aware that the issue of whether NGOs avail themselves of racial stereotypes and attitudes has been long discussed—including by NFPs and NGOs themselves. That is to say that this is not a taboo subject not discussed within the industry. It is a common and ever-present source of debate.

Specific to this case is the notion of the "dark continent," a racially charged term that was coined by British explorers when discussing endeavors in Africa. This term has gone on to be harshly criticized as constituting the equipoise of racial ignorance and gall, effectively implying that it is "white man's" responsibility to bring light to the "dark man's" world. But the adoption of this attitude was not solely by the British, with novelist Victor Hugo echoing the sentiments before the Marseille Worker's Union (Barbou, 1882) and other currently existing NGOs sometimes being accused of doing the same.

It will be difficult to discuss whether the image that prompted this case is an instance of "white saviorism" since that image is not reproduced here and we have made no effort to acquire its rights. But a more general discussion of embedded racial attitudes would be helpful.

Consider assigning students the task of assessing the imagery on the websites of their favorite NFPs and NGOs with an eye toward diagnosing the racial nature of the images contained therein. The results of this exercise can be quite revealing, effectively offering the opportunity to do for the study of race what once was the purview of academics who studied how advertising embedded (and profited from) gender stereotypes in the past.

A helpful discussion will be in regards to *how* to use imagery at an NFP or NGO which is not exploitative. Clearly, the simple act of depicting persons who are members of certain racial groups cannot *ipso facto* be immoral. But what does a responsible depiction of races and racial interaction consist of?

A further moral issue is in regards to how an NGO or NFP is to grapple with the likely incidence of its supporters offering their support *because of* their own embedded racial stereotypes. A litmus-like test for supporters is likely both impossible and undesirable.

Internship or Exploitation?

NGOs and NFPs have always housed interns and probably always will. But some NFPs and NGOs use their internship program as a significant revenue mechanism to fund their mission. Such cases include a situation in which the intern pays for the opportunity in excess of the costs of the experience (with the NFP/NGO taking a profit from the transaction).

This case asks whether such a practice is morally acceptable.

The Kantian "Means-End Principle" is of direct relevance here. It is important to recall the language of that principle from chapter one: "Treat all persons as ends and not as *mere* means." The word "mere" matters. It points to the fact that while some arrangements might involve "using" both parties for a common goal, that such a circumstance is not intrinsically immoral. A shop owner uses a customer for revenue, and the customer uses the shop to buy a bottle of soda. This is not immoral.

Rather, we confront a violation of the means-end principle when we find a situation in which one party's interests are sacrificed in order to further the interests of the other.

The question is, then, whether or not the interests of the would-be interns are sacrificed for the purpose of furthering the interests of the NGO. There is a strong argument to the effect that they are. If the students believe that their self-funded participation will likely lead to a career but the internship provider does not, then it appears that the internship provider is sacrificing the interests of the interns for the purpose of serving its own interests—the desire to fund their operations.

This case presents an elegant way to illuminate the difference between the moral universe of the egoist and that of the Kantian. The above seems to show that the Kantian disputes the moral permissibility of this practice. But an egoist analysis could be used to defend a very different position: That if it is in the interest of the NGO to run this program and if others approach the NGO to participate, then it does not matter whether participants get out of the experience what they had desired to. This "ends justify the means" reasoning will probably not sit well with NGO leadership. And if it does not, then it is worth asking what the motivations are of the NGO that offers such programs, if not egoistic self-interested.

Yet it cannot be the case that consequently *all* internships are exploitative. So a deeper question to explore in discussion is in regards to how such programs can be changed (or messaged) so as to provide would-be interns with a better understanding of the experience.

Graft at the Top

This case posits an instance of known graft, and asks the discussant how they would respond to it. The first question in the list of discussion questions at the end of the cases is of special importance: Which persons, and in what order, are to be consulted. Answering this question is at least as much an issue of strategy as it is ethics.

It is helpful to lead readers through well-known approaches to dealing with such a situation. The first stop has already been completed: an outside auditor has discovered the graft. The role of NGO leadership is now to implement a wise strategy for responding to it. Likely, the first step will be to bring the issue to the attention of board members and the HR department.

A key question for the NGO/NFP leader to contemplate is in regards to how publicly the issue ought to be addressed. Many times NFPs and NGOs would rather quietly dispatch moral lapses without a greater awareness of those outside being made aware. This makes sense given that NGOs and NFPs are fundamentally *moral* entities whose reputation can be damaged by awareness being spread widely. Yet if scandal spreads bad press, so does the discovery of a coverup!

Another problem with dealing with the situation quietly is that restitution will likely never be made since such restitution tends to be court-ordered and subject to public record. It is not unheard of for an NFP or NGO to incur a large financial loss in order to avoid bad publicity. Boards—who have legal requirements to oversee the finances of NFPs and NGOs—face special pressure to do exactly this.

This points to the deeper issue in this case: how it is that this environment of graft was created in the first place. Here we have the beginnings of an explanation. The person committing the graft was a well-regarded business leader who was brought-on to the institution in order to implement business practices at the institution. But all appearances are that his behavior was never completely professional (the drinking, the big-spending, etc.). Probably, he (correctly) felt emboldened *because of* the board's approval of his work in the institution.

Misallocation of Resources or Unreasonable Donor?

This case presents the following moral questions:

1. Is the donor's request reasonable/appropriate?
2. Is the development officer's response reasonable/appropriate?
3. Is the response of the university president reasonable/appropriate?

Embedded within each of these questions is the thorny issue of what a donor is giving to when they give to a cause and what level of post-gift intervention is appropriate. Relatedly, also at issue is how the university in question-related information to the donor regarding the use of funds prior to the gift origination. The details provided in this case are silent regarding these latter questions, but arguably those very questions present to the reader the crux of the moral issue. Accordingly, it would be wise to direct discussion toward them.

It would be helpful to therefore direct discussion to policy issues embedded within this case. Such policy issues include:

- Whether giving a gift entails control over all aspects of the gift's use within an institution.
- Whether accepting a gift entails ceding control to the donor.
- Under what conditions a gift should be accepted and should not be accepted.
- What kind of documentation should be issued subsequent (and prior to) a gift origination.
- The institutional consequences of each of the above.

It may be helpful to direct discussion participants to the "donor bill of rights" which serves as a framework for morally appropriate gift-giving (Association of Fundraising Professionals, 2022). This bill of rights does not detail specific practices, but rather identifies the best practices related to donor interaction and expectations.

The justification for the university's using the building for other purposes at off-times are utilitarian. And such practices are clearly within the best practices of space utilization at a university. It would be rare to find a university that does *not* act so as to maximize its classroom space. It is therefore suspicious that the donor would have been unaware that this is a best practice when the donor approached the university to give in an operational area in which such a best practice is known to exist. This fact lends credence to the position that the donor was being used by the university as a means to an end.

Lean or Starving? On the Tyranny of Low Administrative Cost Rates

This case pertains to the institutional implications of internal budgetary practices—specifically, the oft-repeated phenomena of an NFP with a low administrative cost rate.

Those participating in the discussion may need an introduction to the concept of an "administrative cost rate." Such a cost rate is the proverbial "electric bill" cost that institutions frequently budget as they deliver on their mission. This cost rate typically pays for a great many essential features of an institution's daily (and annual) operations ranging from maintenance and repairs to janitorial and custodial services and even the HR office. However, many NFPs do not budget such a fixed rate and those that survive on grant dollars are often told by funders that administrative costs lie outside the scope of grant-funded initiatives. They would not win grants if the grant proposal included a provision for such funds.

Additionally, some metrics that measure "effectiveness" of NFPs and NGOs gage that metric solely on the basis of how many "pennies" out of every dollar go directly to services. The closer that number is to 100 the more "effective" the NFP/NGO is rated. But this alleged effectiveness entails that electricity/maintenance/etc. is left unfunded.

This case poses the question as to whether this situation is acceptable and how to address it. And this case presents an informal discussion of the most common ways NFPs undertake to respond to this problem. These methods are:

1. Recurrent grant initiatives that overlap with each other.
2. Fundraising for emergencies as they arise, or otherwise using fundraising to meet administrative needs.
3. Creating a surreptitious savings account which bypasses board or funder scrutiny.
4. Shifting administrative staff off of the operating budget and requiring that they raise their own support.

Each of these approaches contains within them various elements of alleged (or real) deception or dishonesty—or institutional damage. This is why the final question is posed: is there anything wrong with a Board's decision to run an NFP in a way viewed by staff as sub-optimal?

That Time When Your NFP Became His PR Crisis Response Plan

It is tempting to view this case as being resolvable solely as a matter of crude utilitarian analysis: "calculate" the consequences of accepting the gift and compare to the consequences of not accepting the gift. Such a calculation will reveal that by accepting the gift many vulnerable women will be helped, and that by declining the gift they will not be helped.

But the discussion leader must ensure that more than just a naïve utilitarianism is implemented. Consider other perspectives, including a more nuanced utilitarianism:

1. Virtue Ethics: The act of taking the gift demonstrates the moral character of the institution that receives it. What virtues (or vices) are expressed by taking the gift?
2. Feminist Ethics: What is being communicated to the clients you serve by accepting this gift? By accepting the gift, would your NFP be associated with the power structure that brought about the need for the services that you offer?
3. Utilitarianism: What are the negative consequences to the NFP after the gift is received in terms of public perception, client perception and future fundraising?
4. Egoism: Differentiate between short-term and long-term reward. It is clear that the short-term reward will be large. Is this offset by any long-term reputational damage this may cause the institution?
5. Kant: By taking the gift are you agreeing to be used as a means to an end?

A Successful Event

This case provides the opportunity to discuss the appropriate use of special events in the operation of an NFP or NGO. Notoriously, such activities are staffing-intensive, expenses-intensive but often not linked to significant revenue. In fact, many NFPs run their special events with the goal of breaking even, not earning a profit.

It is important for participants to appreciate why this issue matters. If you are leading this discussion with persons who have ever done small-time fundraising you may wish to have them share their recollections and perspectives regarding the "fundraisers" that they have engaged in. Often times these fundraisers were labor-intensive but revenue-scarce. Examples of common fundraisers are selling coupon books, selling proverbial lemonade on a street corner, and the likes.

The situation in which NFPs find themselves often times resembles these inefficient initiatives more than they ought to. It may be helpful to use your discussion time to create an imaginary event for an imaginary NFP/NGO and to inquire with the students what the costs are that go into the event. Ensure that discussion participants discuss more than just "day of" costs, but also the significant administrative costs that occur beforehand or afterward. No one list of such items will ever be exhaustive, probably because there is no one kind of event. But here is a list of common event-costs that participants in events often overlook:

1. Venue contracts: An employee must search for a venue, solicit contracts and decide which one to take. And that employee will want to be paid.
2. Insurance: Some events involve activities requiring an insurance policy
3. PR and Marketing of event: This includes mailers, mailing lists, and so on. Each of these (and other) requires staff to execute.
4. Programming: Someone must decide how the event is programmed, even writing scripts. This is a skilled trade and requires payment of a professional.
5. Transportation: Some events require transportation of a variety of means, ranging everywhere from private airplanes and chauffeurs to mileage accrued in employee vehicles.
6. Merchandising: If there is more revenue accrued from an event than just a ticket, then a merchandising scheme must be created. If using an auction, most states require that the auction be performed by a licensed *external* auctioneer.
7. Thank-You Letters: Participants must be thanked, and it is common for this to be done via mail, not electronically.
8. Guest-Lists: Especially if the NFP/NGO desires to attract new stakeholders, it must be someone's job duties to prospect for new attendees. This, too, is a skilled trade and requires the input of an expert.

A final question which many NFPs and NGOs often ask themselves is whether it is a problem to lose money on an event. This is not an easy question to answer other than to point out that it can be important for an institution to face the reality that many events are revenue neutral or revenue losses.

Missing Money at the Group Home

This case illustrates how the failure to create or implement policy can be a significant contributor to institutional problems. Discussion participants who have worked in NFPs of the sort described in the case will likely immediately see that the root cause of the moral predicament was a failure that pre-dated the scenario in question. But those without institutional experience may need to be led to this conclusion.

A key outcome of the discussion of this case is systemic: What should the practices be which relate to safekeeping financial assets of clients? There is not one such system, but all of the most effective ones involve the participation of TWO staff members on every occasion in which group banking occurs. Furthermore, the presence of two staff members must be attested to by each of the members. Absent such a protocol articulated via policy (which is subsequently *followed*) it is not possible to resolve a case like this.

In cases like this it is often the NFP that incurs the financial loss. On other occasions it is the group home banker who personally incurs the loss. Neither of these is a desirable outcome, and even if compensated for an alleged lost sum of funds, it will not be possible to know where/whether a deception occurred.

All of this is preventable given the articulation and implementation of a policy.

Bribery or Just Doing Business?

This case raises the issue of whether participating in a known practice is an instance of corruption and, additionally, whether such participation is wrong.

Several known-issues are present in this case.

Firstly, this issue is a ubiquitous presence for every NGO worker who has ever served in a developing nation. Each such worker can share many stories relating to the behavior of border guards, hotel security, roadside checkpoints, and traffic monitors. If this story is being presented in a group with such experiences, it can be helpful for those who have encountered public corruption to share their stories.

Secondly, there is the background definition of corruption as routinely used by both the United States government and other western nations: *Corruption involves a financial arrangement in which a public official uses their position for private gain.* Correspondingly, most western government apparatuses have a carte blanche prohibition against participation in such practices. So raised in a setting involving discussion participants who are official representatives of a government, there is one invariable policy-driven conclusion: it is wrong to pay the border guard. But the discussion leader must know that this conclusion, when drawn by official representatives of a government, is at least as much a matter of policy as it is a matter of ethics. The two are different.

But it would be a mistake to conclude that the way that government entities reason about this case is idiosyncratic solely to governments. Many

NGOs adopt policy language that ties its decision-making to that of government information sources. For example, many NGOs and NFPs will institute a policy regarding travel given state department threat rankings. An NGO might (and often does) say that they will travel only to those states ranked threat level three or lower, or that any travel beyond threat level three requires supplementary justification. Likewise, NGOs and NFPs that receive federal compensation will sometimes be required to abide by Federal Government guidelines regarding corruption. Such language is present in more than just USAID and the State Department, and may extend to any relationship held by an NFP/NGO and other branches of western governments (taxing authorities, business and industrial affairs, etc.).

Nevertheless, many NFPs and NGOs have no such ties to the federal government and thus have made no explicit or implicit promise to abide by any such guidance. A discussion regarding whether this is wise or unwise would be a highly-informative issue to address during the discussion of this case. Many protestant faith-based NGOs (though not all) will have instituted strict policies rooted in an understanding of the "separation of church and state" which entail that they *will not* ever adopt policies or strategies solely because a government has articulated them. These entities do not view the issue of corruption to be a policy issue at all. For them it is solely a moral issue.

Turning to the case itself, we see the virtues and the vices of utilitarian analyses. On the flat-footed depiction offered in the case, whether or not to pay the bribe is solely a function of whether or not the consequences are good subsequently to paying it. Arguably, paying the bribe "makes things better." The bribe-payer avoids serious security consequences. And note that depicting it this way makes this reasoning appear more egoistic than utilitarian.

But there could be long-term consequences to paying such bribes. It is a known truism that once one begins to pay bribes, the bribes will never cease. And often they increase over time. So a utilitarian analysis should include a discussion of this potentiality.

Finally, the issue is raised in this case as to whether or not the definition of bribery noted above is adequate. In the case the person paying the bribe asserts that there is a similarity between paying the $20 and paying for the US federal government's global entry program. That analogy is weak at best since no *person* is being paid the global entry fee, but government personnel *is* being paid the bribe. But nevertheless, it can be useful to discuss why this transactional difference makes a moral difference. After all, employees of a great many state and federal agencies in western democracies serve short terms of government service in order to have insider knowledge only to subsequently jump ship and work for a private company in the same sector, effectively merchandising their government knowledge for private gain. It is worth exploring whether such common practices are likewise instances of corruption.

Coalition Building or Finder's Fee?

It is a well-known, well-articulated guideline of fundraising that both commission and finders fees are unethical. But while this assertion is often times asserted, it is almost never defended. This creates a situation of ambiguity for the NFP (For further reading on this issue, see Hanson (2022) for a detailed discussion) (Hanson, 2022).

This can entail seemingly inconsistent moral situations: While it would be immoral to compensate a fundraising professional $10,000 for services via commission, compensating them for the same work/results through a contract in the amount of $10,000,000 is not. However, it should simultaneously be noted that no law exists in this regard. The use of finder's fees or commission structures is not an illegal act.

In this case we are posed with several related issues: Is this an instance of a finder's fee? If it is, then is there anything wrong with this situation? Finally, even if upon analysis, if there is nothing immoral about it, does that imply that the NFP would be wise to do it?

A helpful discussion of this case might begin by discussing cases in which commission or finder's fees are clearly immoral. There are many such cases and it is easy to identify them, whether imaginarily or as a matter of the experience of the discussion leader and/or participants. It is then helpful to show what those instances of obviously immoral practices have in common. Those commonalities tend to be:

1. The NFP/Fundraiser has strong financial incentive to increase donations *for the sake of the commission, not the mission.*
2. Solicitations are made of persons who are probably not ideal donors.
3. The above appear to be clear violations of the Kantian means-end principle.

Given this, it is appropriate to ask whether the case in question is an instance which shares these obviously immoral commonalities. This case is used in the book because it is *not* clear that it does. In fact, the bank is "charging" less than other NFPs in the industry charge to manage monies. Financial efficiency is increased through these methods, not decreased.

This therefore raises the question regarding whether or not, even if not immoral, the NFP should initiate the plan as described in the case. As a matter of common practice, most NFPs would not. Whether or not the financial arrangement is immoral, they refrain so as to avoid the appearance of immorality. That is, the position often adopted is a PR and marketing position, not an ethics-based position.

Is this an acceptable way to reason about moral issues?

Inheriting an Albatross

This case pertains to due diligence in NFP mergers.

On the for-profit side (say, in an investment house) it is standard practice to staff a due diligence department that is empowered to stop deals before consummated. But it is unheard of to have such in-house skills at an NFP. This means that doing due diligence on potential mergers is an activity that current staff and board would have to undertake themselves.

It is clear in this case that due diligence had not been sufficiently performed. The consequences were disastrous. The discussion of the case, therefore, should be in regards to what sorts of due diligence should be practiced. It would be helpful to have your discussion participants to think about the kinds of details that must be investigated under these circumstances. Invariably, the list of items that the group arrives at is quite large. And this drives toward a "resolution" to the case: NFPs considering mergers should only do so if they simultaneously hire the temporary services of a person whose skill lies in mergers and acquisitions.

The School for Civil War Orphans

Cast as a case of "mission drift," we would be led to inquire as to whether the inclusion of non-civil war orphans in the life of the school constitutes "drift." But also embedded within this case is the interplay between fundraising strategy and donor-driven NGOs within an African context.

It is obviously not immoral to provide schooling for a child whose parents died from the disease. It is also obviously not immoral to raise funds for civil war orphan services. But is it immoral to raise funds for one goal and use those funds for a slightly (or very) different one? Furthermore, does the very western practice of creating target areas of service translate appropriately to the African perspective?

Let us begin with this latter point. The discussion leader may wish to consult David Maranz's *African Friends and Money Matters* which constitutes a veritable masterclass in sub-Saharan African perspectives regarding the identification and use of resources (Maranz, 2001). This text and many others like it will reveal that many sub-Saharan Africans feel that it is a moral imperative to use resources for urgent needs regardless of whether the resources were earmarked for such needs (e.g., using funds earmarked for diesel engine repair to fund the surgery of the NGO national secretary). It is not uncommon for budgets for one area to be diverted to another just in case the most recent need was in that other area. Hence, what the African NGO leader was being asked to do (to not permit the orphan to attend school) was inconsistent with local moral customs.

Regarding the will of the visiting donors, we see a classic conflict between utilitarian and Kantian impulses. From a Kantian perspective, we see that it would be dishonest to accept funds for one thing, but to use it for another. Such deception clearly fails the categorical imperative. But from the utilitarian perspective one can create even better consequences by offering services to one child whose profile lies outside the profile that was used to raise the funds. The Kantian balks at accepting the orphan into the school, but the utilitarian might positively require it.

One way to avoid an ideological standoff is to discuss the ways in which revenue strategies (in this case, fundraising) can cause unintentional harm in those places where the programs are delivered. Program officers should have known that this would become an issue—the need for orphan services is well-known in sub-Saharan Africa.

The Best President We Could Ever Dream of

This case pertains to that of a leader who stayed too long in their position.

Discussion participants should first understand that NFP presidents report to the board, not to those who work for the NFP. Hence, if there is a problem posed in this case, it is a problem for the board. That is, while it is tempting (and probably justified) to criticize the behavior of the president, such a discussion will never uncover the root of the problem: How it is that a president became empowered to behave in the unusual way that this president did.

Here the institutional experience of the discussion leader is of great importance. Discussion participants may need to understand why "staying too long" in leadership is unwise. They need to understand that presidents who are beloved by boards may remain as long as that love lasts, and sometimes regardless of their performance.

The Post-Mortem "Take"

The case described is not unusual, and NFPs employing major gifts officers must articulate in advance what the guidelines for their professional behavior should be. In fact, it would be wise procedure to make such expectations explicit before a hire takes place.

The actions of the fundraiser clearly violate professional guidelines (Association of Fundraising Professionals, 2022). But a discussion of the case must include a discussion of why this situation is morally unacceptable. Here (and probably in other cases) it is helpful to imagine the possible consequences of this situation. Those include:

1. The impact of its becoming common knowledge that this inheritance structure took place.
2. The capability of isolated fundraisers to "go rogue."
3. The impact upon future fundraising.
4. Damage to the reputation of the NFP.
5. Accountability of fundraising professionals.

These issues and others lie at the core of this case.

Missing Money?

The key to understanding this case is to analyze the math embedded within the following paragraph:

> You see that the state of Rhode Island has given your organization a grant in the amount of $465,000. These funds were to be used to pay a variety of operational needs—the purchase of a wheelchair accessible transportation van, insurance, drivers' pay and other costs. But you note that while the amount disbursed to your organization is $465,000, your budget for the program is only $325,000. You can search the budget of your program over and over, but cannot account for the missing $140,000.

Note that the difference between the amounts received and the budget allocated to the program director constitutes a difference of exactly

30%. A 30% institutional cost rate is common in NFPs (especially universities), and if the NFP is following this standard procedure, it would be wholly consistent for the NFP to receive a different amount than what was given to this program director to utilize.

That is, it is not likely that money is "missing." It is likely, rather, that the inexperience of the program director leads them to believe that it is. The central moral issue of the case therefore is in regards to the training and preparation of program officers, not the ethics of finances.

"Give Me a Child You Don't Care About"

This case poses the question as to whether the methods implemented by the health care professional were morally acceptable. Yet it is troubling because the medical professional implemented a method which she knew would be effective given the tribal structure of the culture described. Yet this same method strikes the reader as morally troubling. Discussion readers may wish to consult an excellent historical ethnography written by Tshilemalea Mukenge (Mukenge, 2002).

Those involved in healthcare in developing nations are often required to follow the same moral rules in those nations that are followed in developed nations. Hence it would be useful to use the Medical Ethics fourfold analysis system in this case.

1. Nonmaleficence
2. Beneficence
3. Autonomy
4. Justice

As we consider whether the method used by the NGO professional was morally appropriate, it is consequently helpful to review this fourfold system.

Nonmaleficence: we know that the vaccine will not harm the child. However, we must appraise all harm, not just some. Does the healthcare professional perpetuate harm by manipulating the low-status of the child for the purpose of increased healthcare outcomes? Will this child become further stigmatized among the Bambuti by being the only one to receive the vaccine?

Beneficence: We know that the child is benefited by the vaccine. But the healthcare worker appears motivated for her own beneficence, not that of the tribe.

Autonomy: By definition, children are non-autonomous persons. But in western nations we routinely invoke the principle that parents or custodians are the autonomous agents. Does it matter in this case that custodians are making a sub-optimal decision for the child?

Justice: Are the Bambuti people being treated fairly? Is the healthcare worker herself being given a mission she can fairly expect to accomplish?

Short-Termer Headaches

Discussion participants must understand that in many NGOs there is a social distinction, not unlike a pecking-order, between "short termers" and "long termers." Short termers are typically those who volunteer to assist the activities of an NGO. They often are present for no more than 2 weeks, although stays of up to 3 months are not unusual. "Long Termers" are those whose work is ongoing. Often they remain in their positions for 3–5 years although "lifers" are not unheard of.

Discussion participants also need to know that there is a degree of animosity on the part of long-termers vis-à-vis short-termers (despite the fact that most long-termers began their careers as short-term volunteers). Those reasons are mentioned in this case.

Furthermore, the small, independent NGO often depends upon revenue from short-term visitors. It is not unusual, for example, for a small NGO to first invest in a "team hotel" before investing equivalent funds in services.

If those participating in discussions of this case are long-term employees of an NGO, it would be helpful to have them share their experiences housing short-term visitors. The stories they share can be helpful for others to hear. Conversely, if this case is discussed with short-term volunteers, it may prove to be helpful for them to understand the circumstances into which they are entering and how their experiences differ from that of those who do the long-term work to make foreign sites functional.

Two issues present themselves in this case:

1. How long-term NGO workers reconcile the need for and existence of short-term workers.
2. Whether the pressure to accommodate the needs of short-term visitors is morally suspect.

Since many smaller NGOs are faith based, a discussion of this case may require a sensibility to the dynamics that influence this segment of the NGO industry. Such NGOs are almost never influenced by the social sciences or development policy. In fact, most such NGOs have no person on their staff with any proclivity in these areas of knowledge. Rather, such NGOs are rooted in the protestant evangelical missionary tradition. This historical fact goes a long way toward explaining their behavior, their sometimes self-justificatory positioning, and their motivations for doing their work.

"Hire a Young Woman"

In many developing nations, including in Sub-Saharan Africa where this case takes place, employment practices are normalized which would be illegal in western democracies. In this case, an age/gender requirement is listed for employment at an educational NGO. Discussants should understand that such a requirement is common in job-listings in many nations and would by no means constitute a legal violation. Nevertheless, discussants should likewise understand that NGOs are often under the mandate to follow western legal norms while operating abroad.

These two competing normative systems can often cause friction in the NGO. And there is probably no better moral system available for "balancing" the requirements of competing moral principles than that of the medical ethics community. Again, recall that this system revolves around four principles. They are:

1. Beneficence
2. Nonmaleficence
3. Autonomy
4. Justice

However the discussants elect to reconcile these competing normative systems, it would be valuable to grapple with the implication upon issues not raised in this case. For example, one of the most well-funded areas of development work pertains to "women's issues." Programs are commonly offered in developing nations whose design would be deemed prejudicial for a government to do so in developed nations. Does the means by which discussion participants balance these competing systems affect the moral status of such programs?

In Our Country They Would Be Married

This case is exceptionally complex. Recognizing the complexity requires an understanding of this issue *within an African context*, not from an outside western context.

It may be helpful for the discussion leader to refer discussants to state department security rankings for nations. Such ranking systems now include information for LGBTQ travelers. I refer the reader, for example, to the entry for Sénégal under the "Local Laws and Special Circumstances" section (U.S. Deaprtment of State Bureau of Consular Affairs, 2022). But a great many other nations likewise have similar inclusions. These threat rankings reveal that non-binary sexual orientations are both criminalized and persecuted.

Understanding Faye's reticence to speak even to his boyfriend about his diagnosis requires understanding the psychic world of a person whose sexual identity is criminalized and whose government would condone life-ending violence against him. That is, before we (potentially) criticize Faye's decision to not tell his partner of his condition, it is essential to understand that power-dynamics which he perceives (correctly) to encircle him.

This matters greatly since the action Meredith undertakes directly violates Faye's method for navigating the power-structures of his society. Faye's method is nondisclosure while Meredith endorses the principle of disclosure.

So as discussion participants deliberate about the moral status of Meredith's actions, it is important to ask whether it is appropriate for Meredith to override a patient's autonomous choice in these circumstances, *given the power-dynamics that the patient perceives to influence his choices.*

Additionally, there is the issue of whether or not the NGO is to be blamed for dismissing Meredith. In this case the NGO is linked to a faith-based entity which the reader would be right to assume takes a principled position against same-sex relationships. But in addition to this the NGO is only present in the country at the permission of the country's government, and that government likewise takes a principled position against same-sex relationships. Therefore, the NGO views Meredith's actions as a threat both to ground operations' relationships with their leadership, and ground operations' relationship with the government of the nation.

This raises a troubling question: The issue of LGBTQ relationships will not be the only issue upon which there is friction between the values of those in an NGO and those of their board or country's government in which they work. At what point does an NGO "cave" to the political demands of each in order to continue offering services to those who would otherwise be left without them?

A thorough discussion of the four medical ethics principles would be most illuminating.

What Counts as Diversity Numbers?

The discussion of affirmative action requires both moral and legal acuity. And the legal environment is radically changing with experts from a variety of ideological viewpoints predicting the end of affirmative action as a legally condoned national policy in the United States. For a fair assessment of the recent case law I refer the reader to Schuck's (2002) assessment of the legal state of the issue (Schuck, 2002).

Adding to the difficulty of assessing this issue is that there is not *one* environment in which affirmative action is implemented. Standards articulated in South Africa would be illegal everywhere in the United States. And within the United States, each of the 50 states articulates differing standards.

Barring a thorough legal analysis of each jurisdiction, the discussion leader should not feel compelled to express a comprehensive knowledge of affirmative action law. This would be a significant expenditure of time and would never address the moral issue.

One commonality among all western democracies is that Affirmative Action comes in legal and illegal forms. Typically, racial quotas are illegal everywhere, but programs which happen to target persons of a certain racial group are not.

This could come as news to discussion participants, at least some of whom assume that affirmative action by definition requires racial quotas. It does not, and there are a variety of means by which the same end can be pursued without quotas. The most common ones are provided in this case.

This case, therefore, poses the following questions:

1. What is the purpose of Affirmative Action and is that purpose morally desirable?
2. Is goal of Affirmative Action served by the methods often used to achieve it?
3. Are there methods which are legitimate and those which are illegitimate?

This case additionally raises the morally dubious issue of counting minority-race foreign elites as members of a racial minority group. Discussing this issue may be an effective means of inquiring whether Affirmative Action programs should be transformed into economic class initiatives.

Vaccine Resistance in Vulnerable Communities

While this case pertains to the issue of whether or not to permit vaccine resistant nurses-in-training to aid in vaccine distribution in an NGO, another significant issue presented in the case—an issue which experienced professionals will immediately recognize—is the disassociation of long-term NGO staff from the ebbs and flows of partisan news cycles in their country or origin. This point is not to be underestimated and contributes to understanding the frustration that such an NGO worker perceives in the case as presented. In this case a life-saving therapy is (potentially) being distributed by those who are so privileged as to be able to elect to refuse it.

On the one hand, the NGO staff could refuse the nurses-in-training until such a time as they become vaccinated. But this would likely mean that the most resistant would not volunteer rather than submit to vaccination. This therefore invites a utilitarian pro-and-con cost–benefit calculation.

On the other hand the NGO could accept the volunteers, an option which has several implications. One is that unvaccinated nurses-in-training might themselves be introducing the virus into the community—a community already without basic health services. Another is that the NGO would be employing the work of NGO volunteers with ideological objections to the very service they were being asked to deliver (and as unbelievable as this situation sounds, this is both real and not unheard of!).

On this latter point, virtue theory is of great help. A virtuous person is the one that embodies certain traits of character and behavior. A frustrating aspect of this case is that a beneficial therapy is being delivered by those who have not themselves adopted the corresponding behavior which one would expect of such persons. This situation will cause rational persons—such as the patients who receive vaccines—to be rational in mistrusting the healthcare system delivered by the NGO.

While a potentially explosive topic, it is worth exploring in the discussion group the issue of the politicization of medicine during the Covid-19 pandemic. There is a difference between principled objections to therapies (e.g., well-discussed Jehovah's Wittness cases) and objections for political reasons.

The At-least-Somewhat Racist Missionary

Discussion participants who have significant field experience will recognize several aspects of this case, as they recur with some frequency: the mental fatigue of the translator, the sense of wonder at discovering a new social world, and the single female foreign worker with decades of service. These are known phenomena which occur. In fact, many development workers refer to the single female long-term worker as a "development widow."

It is probably too easy to treat this case as one in which we are asked to asses the moral status of the verbal behavior of the missionary. It is at the very least insensitive, but potentially an instance of racism.

The feminist perspective provides an opportunity in which a deeper understanding of the case is possible. We know from the case that this missionary is (1) a female, (2) educated, (3) unmarried (4) long-serving in the field. It is also reasonable to assume that her 35 years were spent in a world with radically different gender attitudes than that in which she was raised. It is well-known that gender attitudes and roles are significantly more traditional outside the developed world than inside. Hence it is reasonable to assume that this missionary was tasked with a goal in a social environment with significant cultural obstacles presented to a woman who happens to be the one entrusted to meet it.

Therefore, regardless of what one thinks of her verbal behavior, it can be helpful to understand the forces which have operated in her life which cause her to behave this way. These forces may or may not excuse. But they will explain. And furthermore, they will help NGOs to better think about how they train potential new labor for long-term service in the field.

Later That Evening, in the Same Town

This case presents a classic clash of two cultural systems over the issue of appropriate dress in public. Here we find female NGO workers dressed in a manner that is completely inoffensive in the west but which in this nation is considered inappropriate or even sexually suggestive. Are the female NGO workers wrong for dressing in this manner?

Many times, discussions along these lines become at least as pragmatic as they are moral. It is probably impossible to defend the view that dressing in a western manner is intrinsically immoral (or moral). But this does not imply that decisions regarding how to dress is an unweighty choice. In this case, it is clear that the way in which the aid workers are dressed attracts the attention of males in the town who perceive their manner of dress as a sign of sexual promiscuity. This situation invokes many potentially dangerous situations.

NGO responses to this reality vary. Some "hold the line" and make no attempt to articulate dress standards for their staff or volunteers. Such NGOs must understand that while visitor politeness entails that the GO/NGO will not be confronted by locals for their policy (or lack thereof) that this will not prevent its being the case that locals won't notice. In some cases, residents will take a positively dim view of the NGO (or GO) in question and consequently resist its programs. That is both a moral and a pragmatic problem.

NGOs that articulate a policy for appropriate dress, however, find themselves in the unenviable position of articulating different behavioral rules on the basis of one's gender. Faith-based entities typically do not have a problem with this, but non faith-based NGOs are very reticent to do this.

Consequently, the moral issue to be discussed in this case, whether from a utilitarian or Kantian perspective, is in regards to whether one is comfortable with the compromises that one must make on this issue.

Nurturing African Entrepreneurs

Those who discuss this case or others like it would do well to consult David Maranz's book *African Friends and Money Matters* (Maranz, 2001). This ethnography of money in sub-saharan Africa offers significant insights into the most commonly shared norms regarding the identification and use of money. Several passages are of relevance, but this observation is particularly apt:

> Resources are to be used, not hoarded. It is a general rule that people expect that money and commodities will be used or spent as soon as they are available. If the possessor does not have immediate need to spend or use the resource, relatives and friends certainly do. To have resources and not use them is hoarding, which is considered to be unsocial. (Maranz, 2001, p. 16)

Of equal use, but less accessible to the anglophone, is Mwamba Cabakulu's *Dictionnaire des Proberbes Africaines* (Cabakulu, 1992). This work collects sayings and aphorisms of Central and West African people groups and serves as a marvelous tool to understand the moral, political and spiritual landscape of the many peoples that inhabit the region. Cabakulu organizes the proverb by number with the people group in parenthesis as well as the name of the country they lived in at the time of publication. Here is a sampling (my translation in italics below each):

> 174. Si tu es riches et que tu n' es pas généreux, c'est comme si tu n'avais rien. (Bassar: Togo) (Cabakulu, 1992, p. 33)
> *174. If you're rich but not generous, you may as well have nothing (Bassar: Togo)*

> 1024. À la grande saison sèche, même l'oiseau fait des cadeaux à sa belle-mère. (Cabakulu, 1992, p. 119)

1024. *At the height of the dry season, even the birds give gifts to their mother-in-law.*

2308. On vous invite à accompagner à la chasse parce-ce que on a vu vos filles (Ntomba: Zaire) (Cabakulu, 1992, p. 253)
2308. *They [only] invited you to join them on the hunt because they saw your daughters.*

It is probably a safe bet that the organizers of the entrepreneurship competition neither consulted an ethnography of money nor meditated upon the meanings of African proverbs. As the case reads, they appear to have extracted an artifact of American pop culture (televised entrepreneurship reality television shows) and placed that artifact into West African culture. But they did not anticipate the inability of that artifact to survive translation.

It would be useful to organize a discussion among participants which attempts to better understand the situation in which Florence, as contest winner, finds her self. What are the values that Florence has, and how are those values in tension with the unstated presuppositions of the competition organizers? Moreover, are the words shared by the American corporation's CSR division with Chris on-target or off-base?

The Successful West African Recycling Entrepreneur

This case has been used in entrepreneurship trainings in francophone West Africa. Unlike other analyses in this section which are geared toward a "solution," this author will collect his own summary of reactions to the case based upon these experiences. A French version of the case follows.

1. Many discussion participants were keen to know whether or not Ousmane was treating his employees fairly. And in many cases participants were unwilling to discuss the other moral issues of the case until this issue was resolved with clarity. An early draft of this case stipulated that Ousmane was hiring teenagers in his company, but the author was forced to edit this detail out since discussion participants were uniformly skeptical that an older man would treat teenage employees fairly.
2. The question as to whether Ousmane "should" help his family with expenses is often taken to be a mathematical question. That is, case discussion participants typically first investigate whether or not it is possible to extract the capital from the business. And if it is *possible*, then Ousmane *should* do so. Only if it is *not possible* should it not be extracted. This

implies that family obligations have a propensity to override business needs regardless of the effect upon the business.
3. The West African entrepreneurs I spoke with, when pointed out the fact that giving this money to friends or family could ruin the business, feel a strong sense of tension. On the one hand they saw that helping family and friends was a strong moral obligation. But on the other hand, a course of action that destroyed the business would mean that all future help would cease since the revenue mechanism—the business itself—would be bankrupt.
4. When the case is modified and the 40,000 CFA is said to be for a medical emergency rather than a wedding, the sense of obligation to give is higher.
5. Female entrepreneurs disproportionately assert that they have no choice in this matter. Many have stated that no money that they being home is ultimately "theirs."
6. Some participants offered suggestions regarding how to hide their assets from the knowledge of their friends and community members. Others proposed ways to hire family members in need of funds rather than to just give them funds.
7. Discussing this case with west Africans is tricky and requires significant cultural competence on the part of the discussion leader. I very strongly encourage discussion leaders to not take a position regarding what Ousmane should or should not do.

Here is a French version of the case:

Ousmane a lancé une entreprise de recyclage de plastiques dans son village il y a deux ans. Il a découvert qu'une usine de recyclage lui paierait 1,000 CFA pour chaque sac de plastique qu'il leur apporterait. Ousmane a appris qu'il devait être extrêmement prudent pour s'assurer que le plastique qu'il apportait était propre. Toute pierre ou saleté dans le plastique signifierait que l'usine rejetterait toute la caution. Et cela signifierait qu'ils pourraient ne pas lui prendre de futures sacs.

Au début, il pouvait livrer deux sacs par jour à l'usine. Puis il s'est rendu compte que les gens de sa ville aimeraient avoir un emploi, et que cela l'aiderait à développer son entreprise. Alors il a commencé à embaucher des gens de sa ville pour l'aider. Chacun de ses employés recevrait le prix de 500 CFA pour chaque sac de plastique qu'ils lui donneraient. Ousmane chargeait ensuite le plastique sur son camion et le conduisait à l'usine de recyclage.

Désormais, il est capable de livrer en moyenne dix sacs par jour à l'usine de recyclage. Il croit qu'il peut offrir bien plus que cela à l'avenir. Mais il n'a pas le bon camion pour pouvoir mettre des sacs supplémentaires.

Table 6 Le buget d'Ousmane

Dépenses		Semaine	Annuelle
	Carburant	CFA 17,000.00	CFA 850,000.00
Revenue			
	Sacs de plastique	CFA 35,000.00	CFA 1,750,000.00
Revenue Net		**CFA 18,000.00**	**CFA 900,000.00**

Voici comment Ousmane a budgétisé son entreprise (Table 6).

Les gens du village d'Ousmane ont d'abord pensé qu'il était fou de ramasser les ordures. Mais quand ils ont vu qu'il gagnait de l'argent et que les gens de la ville travaillaient, ils ont commencé à admirer Ousmane. Il était considéré comme un homme de succès avec une entreprise rentable. C'est alors que les demandes de sa famille et de ses amis ont commencé à arriver. Son frère se mariait et a demandé à Ousmane 40,000 CFA pour l'aider à payer le mariage. Sa sœur lui a demandé 20,000 CFA pour l'aider à payer les uniformes scolaires de ses enfants. Et les gens de sa ville lui demandaient constamment de petites sommes d'argent pour répondre à leurs nombreux besoins.

À Discuter:

1. Ousmane établit-il correctement son budget? Y a-t-il des choses qu'il oublie d'ajouter à son budget?
2. Ousmane devrait-il aider son frère à payer le mariage?
3. Comment Ousmane peut-il aider son frère et sa sœur sans nuire à l'entreprise?

The Protective Guardian

In this case, we are asked to consider whether "spiritual development" should be included as a criterion for decisions regarding the placement of minors in child-protective services. This issue is sure to occur (and recur) in state-run child-protective services agencies as child-welfare issues happen to be one that is historically supported by religious communities. Those working in the sector should understand that such sectarian communities are allies, not adversaries.

Note that this case does not portray Maren's religious underpinnings as being in any way objectionable. The analysis of this case would change dramatically were this not so.

Nevertheless, in most countries such services are organized by the state, and most states do not organize their governments theocratically. State-originated funding rarely (probably never) *mention* the issue of spiritual formation or spiritual "rights."

My advice to discussion leaders is to not broach the issue of whether states *should* include such language. Such a discussion invites polarized discussion that generates more heat than light. Rather, the issue discussed should relate to whether or not a child's spiritual formation has any place in the state's decision regarding continued placement.

Dealing with Noncompliance in Syracuse

Discussion participants may need to understand the program terminology present in this case. "Compliance" refers to program participants' following the rules or guidelines of the program. "Noncompliance" refers to program participants' not following the rules or procedures of the program. So, for example, a vaccine drive's "compliant" participants are those who become vaccinated, and the "uncompliant" are those who decide not to be vaccinated.

At issue in this case is whether or not the program has a high rate of noncompliance and whether the results of the program reveal that the program was a failure.

It is common for program directors and those who implement ground operations to expect one result but to observe something very different. Under such circumstances it is tempting to conclude that the program failed. And under some circumstances this conclusion is justified. But a fair-minded reading of this case might reveal that it was a success in other ways. Perhaps those who left the program came to believe that their planned marriage was a mistake, and perhaps the low marriage rate of those who finished the program was attributable to the same rationale.

That is, it is probably hasty to assert that the program was a failure. It may have been a success in ways that were not anticipated.

Putting Nationals in Harm's Way

A recent trend among NGOs is the increased inclusion of nationals in their operations. This is highly desirable for a great many reasons. But from time-to-time this also creates situations in which the nationals are placed in risky situations which they would not have been subject to absent their work with the NGO. This case relates to the need for ground crew to transport cargo to and from an airport, but this scenario is mirrored in a myriad of ways at other NGOs performing different kinds of work.

Participants will be unable to effectively consider the moral facet of this case without knowledge of transportation hazards in the developing world. In the best of times, road transportation in undeveloped locations will constitute the single greatest safety and security risk. And transportation during a time of political or social crisis even more so. This does not even begin to address the serious consequences that take place when the rule of law breaks-down.

This case invokes at once a need to consider the Kantian means-end principle as well as the dangers of egoism.

It is clear that there is a threat of using the ground crew as a means toward the end of fulfilling a contract. But recall that the principle asserts that it is wrong to use people as "mere" means. Discussion participants should consider whether the ground crew is being treated as a *mere* means to the end of fulfilling a contract.

Relatedly, it is worth pursuing whether the director of the flight company would consider placing his non-national staff in a position of doing the ground transport during a crisis.

It is likewise important to consider why the flight company may feel pressure to continue operations. If this pressure is purely financial, then the wrong of the case occurred when the contract was written up, not just on the day in which the NGO deliberated about whether to place nationals in harm's way.

Another Feeding Program Begins

This case presents a classic utilitarian dilemma. On the one hand the person creating this program is to be commended for their self-sacrificial zeal. But on the other hand the energy and resources exerted in the case could bring about much greater good if directed toward professionals already working in the area.

Those who work in food-resources initiatives will recognize facets of this case from their own experience. It may be helpful to let group participants share vignettes of their experiences with new, ill-conceived programs and the effects that those programs had (or didn't have) upon the participants.

A deeper question presented is whether a utilitarian analysis should prevail. To say that this person ought not undertake their program because that program fails to maximize benefit easily implies that no one else, for any other program whatsoever, should do so either. This implies that a great many social services programs are immoral since they fail to deliver less-than-the-best results.

Expanding on this line of thought, there are probably a great many things that most persons do which, if only done differently (or not at all) would result in greater overall happiness. Taking one's kids to the zoo expends resources that could have been used for poverty alleviation, after all. If we judge that this person ought not engage in this program, should we likewise tell parents that they should not fund outings with their children?

What Could Go Wrong?

This case presents the opportunity to discuss an instance of a dangerous program implemented through passionate ignorance. The most pressing moral issue is *not* whether it is permissible for a person to pursue a passion project.

Discussion participants may not have significant experience with field operations in child trafficking initiatives despite this issue's recent popularity among the NGO and NFP community. As you organize your discussion, keep in mind the following known features of such a phenomena:

1. Not all trafficked children are orphans. Those with living relatives (including parents) are frequently sold by their own family members due to economic hardship. Should the child be returned the chances that they would be sold again are high.
2. It is more expensive and time consuming to house and nurture a child than it is to "rescue" a child. But rescuing without restoration is irresponsible.
3. Those engaged in trafficking are committing more crimes than just the crime of trafficking. These including violent crimes. To act so as to thwart their operation is to invite violence.
4. In many nations, trafficking schemes are fostered by political and security forces. Counteracting trafficking can therefore attract corrupt attention, some of whom are earning significant money via bribery from the traffickers.
5. It is common for trafficked children who are rescued to be trafficked again.

It is also worth pursuing whether those who demonstrate passion for this issue are attracted to the notion of fostering the interests of imperiled children, or whether they are attracted to the romantic notion of being their savior. The former is noble, but the latter is self-centeredness.

Land Title Woes in Sub-Saharan Africa

This case demonstrates the failure of entities (in this case, a for-profit business) to adequately understand the business environment that exists in other nations. In every nation, whether developed or undeveloped, the line between cultural values and business practices is blurred. It is not just a quirk of Western culture that land title is a constant of their legal fabric. Rather, land title is an expression of an individualism known to permeate the west (especially, though not limited to, the United States).

But this case does not take place in a region with such a tradition. Discussion leaders may be interested in the work of Hernando de Soto whose economic analyses specifically link the policy mechanisms of land title with macroeconomic trends (De Soto, 2003).

Many features of this case are hardly subject to debate. It is wrong to "shoot people off the land." Likewise, it is wrong to confiscate property and it is wrong to deprive the poor the right to assets.

A better discussion relates to what sorts of perspectives and expertise must be present in order for initiatives to be successful in the developing world. Participants would do well to consider drawing up a list of what (unintentional) false steps the investor group took when they embarked on the project.

Additionally, participants should know that many corporations have "redlined" entire nations due to these issues. This is what is referenced when businesses decline to invest due to issues regarding "the rule of law." What needs to be changed in such countries for investment to become possible, to what extent should businesses feel a responsibility to invest, and what are the root causes of perennial economic instability?

Microfinance, Interest and Islam

Discussion leaders must understand that there is no *one* Islamic teaching on the issue of interest as a financial instrument for the Muslim. Some Islamic traditions have asserted that all forms of interest are intrinsically immoral while others have asserted that only those forms of interest which constitute usury are immoral. For a fair survey of the teaching refer to Hasan (Hasan et al., 2020). For a critical appraisal see Chong and Liu (Chong & Liu, 2009).

While a debate regarding the nature of Islamic finance is indeed fascinating, that debate is probably best left out of this book. What *is* germane is a discussion as to whether a Nobel Prize winning financial instrument (Yunus & Jolis, 2008) is intrinsically anti-Islamic. And on that note, it is worth pointing out that Yunus's invention of this financial instrument *began* in an Islamic nation.

Discussion participants should be prepared to understand how to make a financial instrument be profitable and sustainable on both a cultural and financial level.

Indian Nationalism and the Foreign NGO

The world is currently witnessing a widespread counter reaction against NGOs (Brown, 2014). The reasons are many, and only partly related to the activities of NGOs. Such extraneous causes include the rise of populism, the increase of nationalism, tensions caused by migration, and increasing insecurity following the pandemic (Burlet, 1999).

But as referenced in this case, NGOs also have from time-to-time exasperated this problem. Many faith-based sects have intentionally undertaken a course of action which positively valorizes lying to government authorities in nations abroad (this began with the publication of *God's Smuggler* and continues to this day) (Brother Andrew & Sherrill, 1967). It is currently common for the faith-based sector to create shell companies for the purpose of gaining business visas with no intention of performing any work other than sectarian religious work. This causes great problems for the entire NGO industry.

It would be a most illuminating exercise to request that discussion participants find current news articles regarding Delhi's reaction to foreign-run NGOs in India. Such research will go a long way toward understanding the background history that gives rise to this case.

Lying to the Police

Human Rights Watch has compiled a fair assessment of the *talibé* issue (Human Rights Watch, 2018). Their research article fairly encompasses the problem. Although since publication my anecdotal information leads me to believe that the problem has accelerated.

Henriette must decide whether to lie to the police. Each perspective covered in chapter one of this book bears scrutiny in this case. Here is the briefest of ideas regarding each theory:

Egoism: What exactly *is* Henriette's interest in this case? Lying or telling the truth?

Utilitarianism: Does the consequence of lying justify the lie?
Kant: Lying is almost always wrong for Kant, and the only counterexamples to this position are somewhat contorted. Is this evidence of a defect within Kantian ethics?
Virtue Ethics: Is a lie an instance of lack-of-virtue, or is it the defense of other virtues?
Feminism: What gender imbalances are present in the case as described?

Closing the Orphanage

This case is woefully common and quite real.

On the one hand it is included in this book because uncovering the existence of such ad hoc social services is common. Africans and westerners often create poorly funded programs which have both noble goals and noble results. But their precarious undercapitalization makes them vulnerable to socioeconomic turmoil.

Additionally, it is common for westerners who witness the self-sacrificial service of the ground crew to lionize them. It is not unusual, for example, for short-term teams to return to their nation of origin speaking impressively of the moral or spiritual character of the nationals who they visited.

But this comes at a price, as this case shows.

Therefore, this case is best discussed among those who are working among small, financially perilous NGO operations. Such operations place nationals in a precarious situation in which a potential collapse is very real. It is essential that such persons ask the tough questions regrading whether their actions, or inactions, are a contributing cause.

Professorial Malfeasance Abroad?

This case illustrates those considerations that motivate the "post" theories discussed at the beginning of this section. Here we find financially interested university researchers failing to fulfill their ethical duties in the field all the while reporting success to funders. Suffice to say, this is immoral.

A more interesting question is in regards to what the subject of the case must do. Here we must implement the insights of the "post" theories. Wealthy westerners must understand that they work in an environment of not only lesser wealth, but lesser privilege and freedom. This creates a situation in which it becomes possible, and from time-to-time tempting, to underperform. And since those in a position to detect this ruse lack freedom and privilege, they will be powerless to react.

Given this insight, it will now be helpful for discussion participants to evaluate the decision of the third party who discovered this instance of malfeasance.

Archiving a Nation's Text Messages

The Medical Ethics system will be of use in discussing this case. Again, those four values are:

1. Nonmaleficence
2. Beneficence
3. Autonomy
4. Justice

What we see in this case is that the staff of the telecom company are being asked to perform an action (or series of actions) with competing (possible) consequences. For this case, it would be helpful to go through this list and to identify the ways in which each of those four values bears upon the analysis. Here is a first pass, but by no means an exhaustive pass:

1. Nonmaleficence: Government may use the data to harm the interests of minority communities.
2. Beneficence: This initiative will quickly detect outbreaks.
3. Autonomy: No user of the telecom system is being asked to opt-in. This is a violation of autonomy.
4. Justice: It is unfair that rural residents have poor healthcare options and this program addresses this fact. But it is also unfair that those communities are disproportionately targeted by government authorities.

Where There Are No Government-Issued IDs

This case asks the reader to consider the ethics of storing identity credentials of persons in developing nations. The case is tricky because most such nations have no cyber-laws at all, and where they exist they are almost completely unused and ignored. Indeed, government entities (e.g., embassy workers) will routinely enforce strict cellphone use policies upon the (evidence-informed) assumption that foreign governments *will* be collecting information.

This matters, since one default position relates to an appeal to the well-known position that when two systems compete, default to the one that is more stringent. While there may be no HIPPA law in the nation in question, there is one in the west. This principle therefore implies that one must follow HIPPA while abroad.

But the problem with this is that this medical information is being stored *within* a government system abroad which does *not* enforce the same confidentiality measures in its own data.

Political Disinformation, Community Outreach and Vaccine Drives

While the locus of this case pertains to the Covid-19 vaccine, the issue at root extends far beyond this particular issue. The broader issue is the increased incidence of online sources of varying degrees of credibility influencing the decisions of persons.

Responding to this case is a creative endeavor. Discussion participants should think of means which they can undertake to instill confidence in a known-effective therapy within an environment of low-confidence and great fear.

Election Season and Viral Online Videos

The crisis of confidence in traditional information sources is a significant moral (and political) issue. And while this issue is much discussed by residents of the developed nation, the issue much more pressing in undeveloped nations. Many such nations have never had a free press for the entirety of their histories. In others a free press exists but is itself highly ideologically driven. It is worth having discussion participants reflect upon the implications of this. For example, when Americans want to know how a vote in congress turned out, they read a news article. But how does a person in an undeveloped nation have any reliable understanding of what happened in their legislature when no sources are trusted?

This phenomena causes significant violence, unrest and instability in many nations.

It would be wrong to blame Juan for not consulting "reliable" sources when it is quite possible that no such sources exist. Nevertheless, even if they do exist, it is ill-informed to think that Juan is behaving differently than any other rational peer within his nation. Increasingly, informal online sources are *the way* that information is transmitted.

A harder issue to resolve is whether any steps should be undertaken to speak with Juan and what policies must be in-place for public communications and private social-media account usage.

Finally, there are simple exercises which can be undertaken which help discussion participants to experience the frustration of dealing with impartial or biased news sources. Choose a country with which you the discussion leader have some familiarity and to request that discussion participants report on a current issue regarding which there is significant ideological division. Selecting an issue regarding which you know in advance there exists contradictory information is most helpful. Then let participants report upon what they found. This exercise will help to offer participants the experience of attempting to decipher truth when presented with unreliable sources. Here are some examples:

1. Assign one student to use Egyptian sources to understand the impact of the Grand Renaissance Dam, while another to use Ethiopian sources to do the same.
2. Assign a student to report upon the attitudes of Hondurans to the presidency of Xiomara Castro.
3. Assign a participant to report on farmer land confiscation schemes in Zimbabwe.
4. Assign a student to report on the rationale of Ivorian Cacao national pricing schemes.

Each of these will provide discussion participants the opportunity to experience the contradictions and confusions of unreliable or ideologically-driven information sources.

Revealing the Location of Vulnerable Women

This case illustrates how the failure to both *have* and to *follow* policy can cause significant moral peril.

The case offers no reason to think that the services offered the women are in any way deficient or that any form of abuse or manipulation occurs within the NGO compound. That is, on a programmatic level we have no reason to think that the NGO has failed any of its moral obligations.

However, one of the revenue streams of the NGO—short-term visitors—has proven to unintentionally cause a serious security issue.

It would be a wonderful exercise with real-world payoff to articulate a social-media policy for such an NGO.

It will become obvious in such a discussion that an "onboarding" training is necessary for all visitors. Using your discussion time to design such a training would be most helpful. But be mindful that the nature of this case is such that the cause of the problem (the visitors' use of social media) is not physically present at the foreign NGO office during the time in which pre-entry training should occur. It is common for small NGOs to rely upon the training of a foreign, unaffiliated friend or partner (typically, the foreign visitor organizing the excursion) to perform this training. This is dangerous, as such persons are often not associated with the pressing needs of daily security issues in NFP operations.

Child Porn, Revenge Porn and Non-Fungible Tokens

Blockchain is an invention which, like packaging tape and synthetic rubber, has so many applications that it would be impossible to list them all or predict which ones will become most significant. And while talk of the widespread use of NFTs is currently significant, it has yet to be seen whether this will translate to lasting market-power (Cohney et al., 2019).

This case presents an issue which has been discussed on-again and off-again in several public circles: ought victims be given NFT rights over the video or photographic evidence of the crime?

Respondents to the case should consider to the reasonings that are provided in the case, as the reasonings presented are those most often cited in debates on the issue.

On the one hand, implementing NFT ownership schemes satisfies our desire for justice to deprive victimizers of "intellectual property" related to the crime. But on the other hand this remedy is a potential new form of trauma. The act of giving a victim this "property" *just is* to give them evidence of their victimization.

This case, perhaps more than any other in this book, is permissive of creative thinking and problem-solving.

Bibliography

Abbascia, D., & Poggi, G. (2012). *Cote D'Ivoire Election Crisis & Aftermath.* Hauppauge, NY: Nova Science Publications.

Association of Fundraising Professionals. (2022, August 11). *Code of Ethical Standards.* Retrieved from The Association of Fundraising Professionals: https://afpglobal.org/ethicsmain/code-ethical-standards.

Association of Fundraising Professionals. (2022, August 12). *Donor Bill of Rights.* Retrieved from Association of Fundraising Professionals: https://afpglobal.org/donor-bill-rights.

Austin, J. L. (1962). *How to Do Things with Words* (2nd ed.). Cambridge, MA: Harvard University Press.

Avolio, B. J., & Yammarino, F. J. (2013). *Transformational and Charismatic Leadership: The Road Ahead 10th Anniversary Edition.* Bingley, UK: Emerald.

Barbou, A. (1882). *Victor Hugo and His Time.* New York, NY: Harper and Brothers.

Barna Research Group. (2022, August 9). *Barna Research Group.* Retrieved from Barna Research Group: https://www.barna.com/research/.

Batts, M. E. (2017). *Nonprofit Financial Oversight: The Concise and Complete Guide for Boards and Finance Committees.* Orlando, FL: Accountability Press.

Beauchamp, T. L., & Childress, J. F. (2019). *Principles of Biomedical Ethics* (8th ed.). Oxford, UK: Oxford University Press.

Behnke, A. (2001, March). Grand Theory in the Age of Its Impossibility. *Cooperation and Conflict, 36*(1), 121–134.

Bentham, J. (1988). *Bentham: A Fragment on Government.* Cambridge, UK: Cambridge University Press.

Bernard, G. (2019). *Talibé: enfant des rues Roman.* Paris, FR: L'Harmattan.

Bialy, B. (2017, Summer). Social Media—From Social Exchange to Battlefield. *The Cyber Defense Review, 2*(2), 69–90.

Boardsource. (2010). *The Handbook of Nonprofit Governance.* San Francisco: Jossey-Bass.

Bragg, S. M. (2020). *Nonprofit Accounting: A Practitioner's Guide.* Centennial, CO: AccountingTools, Inc.

Brother Andrew, & Sherrill, J. (1967). *God's Smuggler.* Grand Rapids, MI: Zondervan.

Brown, T. (2014, February). Negotiating the NGO/Social Movement Dichotomy: Evidence from Punjab, India. *Voluntas: International Journal of Voluntary and Nonprofit Organizations, 25*(1), 46–66.

Burlet, S. (1999, March). Gender Relations, 'Hindu' Nationalism, and NGO Responses in India. *Gender and Development, 7*(1), 40–47.

Cabakulu, M. (1992). *Dictionnaire des Proberbes Africains.* Paris, FR: L'Harmattan.

Césaire, A. (2000). *Discourse on Colonialism.* New York, NY: Monthly Review Press.

Chong, B. S., & Liu, M.-H. (2009). Islamic Banking: Interest-Free or Interest-Based? *Pacific-Basin Finance Journal, 17*(1), 125–144.

Ciconte, B. L., & Jacob, J. (2009). *Fundraising Basics: A Complete Guide* (2nd ed.). Burlington, VT: Jones and Bartlett Learning.

Cohney, S., Hoffman, D., Skarloff, J., & Wishnick, D. (2019, April). Coin-Operated Capitalism. *Columbia Law Review, 119*(3), 591–676.

Compassion International. (2022, August 8). *Child Sponsorship FAQ.* Retrieved from Compassion International: https://www.compassion.com/sponsor_a_child/sponsorship-faq.htm.

De Soto, H. (2003). *The Mystery of Capital Why Capitalism Succeeds in the West and Fails Everywhere Else.* New York, NY: Basic Books.

Fischer, M. (2000). *Ethical Decision Making in Fundraising.* New York, NY: Wiley.

Frye, M. (1983). *Politics of Reality: Essays in Feminist Theory.* Berkeley, CA: Crossing Press.

Hanson, C. (2022). The Ethics of Commission in Fundraising: A Defense. *The International Journal of Community and Social Development, 4*(2), 216–225.

Harpool, D. (1996, Fall). The Sibley Hospital Case: Trustees and Their Loyalty to the Institution. *Journal of College and University law, 23*(2), 255–283.

Hasan, M., Shaikh, S. A., & Kayhan, S. (2020). *Introduction to Islamic Banking and Finance: An Economic Analysis.* Singapore: World Scientific.

Hester, D. M. (2022). *Guidance for Healthcare Ethics Committees* (2nd ed.). New York, NY: Cambridge University Press.

Hobbes, T., & Curley, E. (1994). *Leviathan: With Selected Variants from the Latin Edition of 1668.* Indianapolis, IN: Hackett Press.

Hoschild, A. (1999). *King Leopold's Ghost: A Story of Greed, Terror, and Heroism in Colonial Africa.* Boston, MA: Houghton Mifflin Harcourt.

Human Rights Watch. (2018). *"These Children Don't Belong in the Streets": A Roadmap for Ending Exploitation, Abuse of Talibés in Senegal.* New York: Human Rights Watch.

Hurley, E. (2012). *A Concise Introduction to Logic*. Boston, MA: Cengage Learning.
IRS. (2022, August 6). *Disciplinary Sanctions—Internal Revenue Bulletin*. Retrieved from irs.gov: https://www.irs.gov/tax-professionals/disciplinary-sanctions-internal-revenue-bulletin
Kruger, D. (2020). *Levelling Up Our Communities:: Proposals for a New Social Covenant*. London, UK: The Parliament of the United Kingdom.
Lindemann, H. (2019). *An Invitation to Feminist Ethics* (2nd ed.). Oxford, UK: Oxford University Press.
Livingston, S. (2011). *Africa's Evolving Infosystems: A Pathway to Security and Stability*. Washington, DC: Africa Center for Strategic Studies.
MacAskill, W. (2015). *Doing Good Better: How Effective Altruism Can Help You Make a Difference*. New York, NY: Gothan Books.
MacIntyre, A. (2007). *After Virtue: A Study in Moral Theory* (3rd ed.). South Bend, IN: Notre Dame Press.
Maranz, D. (2001). *African Friends and Money Matters: Observations from Africa*. Dallas, TX: International Academic Bookstore.
Marx, K., & Engels, F. (2015). *The Communist Manifesto*. New York, NY: Penguin Classics.
Mukenge, T. (2002). *Culture and Customs of the Congo*. Westport, CN: Greenwood Press.
Nolan, K. (2022, August 8). *Please Continue to Not Sponsor This Child*. Retrieved from The New Internationalist: https://newint.org/features/2022/04/04/feature-please-continue-not-sponsor-child.
Nussbaum, M. (2016). Judging Other Cultures: The Case of Genital Mutilation. In L. May & J. Delston, *Applied Ethics* (6th ed., pp. xxii–xlii). New York, NY: Routledge.
Occupational Health and Safety Administration. (2022, August 19). *Mandatory Vaccination Policy Template*. Retrieved from Occupational Health and Safety Administration: https://www.google.com/url?sa=t&rct=j&q=&esrc=s&source=web&cd=&ved=2ahUKEwiAgpLilNP5AhXfTDABHeF6CjwQFnoECA4QAQ&url=https%3A%2F%2Fwww.osha.gov%2Fsites%2Fdefault%2Ffiles%2Fcovid-19-ets2-sample-mandatory-vaccination-policy.docx.
Petty, J. G. (2013). *Nonprofit Fundraising Strategy: A Guide to Ethical Decision Making and Regulation for Nonprofit Organizations* (2nd ed.). New York, NY: Wiley.
Praykash, G. (1994). Subaltern Studies as Postcolonial Criticism. *American Historical Review, 99*, 1475–1490.
Rachels, J., & Rachels, S. (2018). *The Elements of Moral Philosophy* (9th ed.). Dubuque, IA: McGraw-Hill.
Ricardo, D. (2004). *The Principles of Political Economy and Taxation*. Mineola, NY: Dover Publications.
Rist, G. (2019). *The History of Development* (4th ed.). London, UK: Zed Books.
Sargeant, A., & George, J. (2021). *Fundraising Management: Analysis, Planning and Practice*. New York, NY: Routledge.

Scharf, K., & Tonin, M. (2018). *Economics of Philanthropy: Donations and Fundraising.* Cambridge, UK: The M.I.T. Press.

Schuck, P. H. (2002). Affirmative Action: Past, Present, and Future. *Yale Law & Policy Review, 20*(1), 1–96.

Scott, E. D. (2005). The Ethics of Human Resources Management. In J. W. Budd & J. G. Scoville, *The Ethics of Human Resources and Industrial Relations (LERA Research Volume)* (pp. 173–201). Champaign, IL: Labor and Employment Relations Association.

Singer, P. (1994). *Ethics.* Oxford, UK: Oxford University Press.

Smith, A. (2003). *The Wealth of Nations.* New York, NY: Bantham Dell.

Subsommittee on the Constitution of the Committee on the Judiciary. (2001, June 7). *Constitutional Role of Faith-Based Organizations in Competitions for Federal Social Service Funds.* United States Senate. Washington: Committee of the Judiciary.

The Center for Disease Control and Prevention. (2022, August 19). *Workplace Vaccination Program.* Retrieved from The Center for Disease Control and Prevention: https://www.cdc.gov/coronavirus/2019-ncov/vaccines/recommendations/essentialworker/workplace-vaccination-program.html.

The Food and Drug Administration. (2022, August 11). *COVID-19 Vaccines.* Retrieved from The Food and Drug Administration: https://www.fda.gov/emergency-preparedness-and-response/coronavirus-disease-2019-covid-19/covid-19-vaccines.

Timmons, M. (2021). *Moral Theory: An Introduction* (2nd ed.). London, UK: Dev Publishers & Distributors.

Todaro, M., & Smith, S. (2020). *Economic Development* (13th ed.). Harlow, UK: Pearson.

U.S. Department of State Bureau of Consular Affairs. (2022, August 12). *International Country Information Page—Senegal.* Retrieved from United States Department of State: https://travel.state.gov/content/travel/en/international-travel/International-Travel-Country-Information-Pages/Senegal.html.

U.S. Department of Treasury. (2022, August 13). *Specially Designated Nationals And Blocked Persons List (SDN) Human Readable Lists.* Retrieved from U.S. Department of Treasury: https://home.treasury.gov/policy-issues/financial-sanctions/specially-designated-nationals-and-blocked-persons-list-sdn-human-readable-lists.

Vasu, N., Ang, B., Teo, T.-A., Jayakumar, S., Faizal, M., & Ahuja, J. (2017). *Fake News: National Security in a Post-Truth Era.* Singapore: Rajaratnam School of International Studies.

Watts, L. L., Medeiros, K., McIntosh, T., & Mulhearn, T. (2021). *Ethics Training for Managers: Best Practices and Techniques.* Abingdon, UK: Routledge.

Worth, M. J. (2020). *Nonprofit Management: Principles and Practice* (Vol. 6th). Los Angeles, CA: CQ Press.

Yunus, M., & Jolis, A. (2008). *Banker to the Poor: Micro-Lending and the Battle Against World Poverty.* Philadelphia, PA: PublicAffairs.

Zack, N. (2022). *Thinking About Race* (2nd ed.). Belmont, CA: Cengage.

Zinsmeister, K. (2016). *The Almanac of American Philanthropy.* Washington, DC: The Philanthropy Roundtable.

Index

A

administrative cost rates 105, 237
African Entrepreneurs 151, 254
Argumentum ad Baculum 208
Argumentum ad Misericordiam 208
Argumentum ad Populum 209
Argumentun Ad Hominem 209
Assigned Positions 200
Autonomy 16, 44, 45, 128, 221, 247, 249, 264

B

Begging the Question 210
Beneficence 16, 44, 45, 128, 228, 247, 249, 264
Biomedical ethics 44
Board
   volunteerism 59
Boards and oversight 51, 53, 55, 57, 59, 61, 63, 65, 67, 69, 71, 73, 75, 77
Bribery 241

C

Categorical imperative 10, 37, 224
Child porn 192, 267
Child sponsorship 90, 232
Complex Question 210
Corruption
   Public 112
crisis response plan 238
Cross-cultural ethics 127
crypto donations 92
Cultural relativism 5
Cutting vital services 84
Cyber ethics 181

D

Deontological ethics 7
Discussion Guides 219
Discussion-Leader Tips 197
Disinformation 187, 265
diversity 142

E

Egoism 13, 14, 33, 47, 221, 230, 239, 262
Entrepreneur 153
Equivocation 210
Ethics committees 155
Ethics Vs Law 27
Evaluating Ethics Argumentation 203
Events 239
  Accounting 110
Executive leadership 79, 81, 83, 85, 87, 89, 91, 93, 95, 97, 99
exploitation 95, 234

F

False Cause 210
False Dichotomy 210
feeding program 162
Feminist ethics 17, 40
Finance 101, 103, 105, 107, 109, 111, 113, 115, 117, 119, 121, 123, 125
finder's fee 114, 243
Frye, Marilyn 19

G

Governance 60, 222
Graft 97, 235
guardian 158

H

Hasty Generalization 209
Hippocrates 2
HR 156
Hume, David 3

I

IDs 185
Ignoratio Elenchi 209

Indian nationalism 170, 262
Individual relativism 5
Is-Ought Problem 4

J

job descriptions 87, 231
Justice 16

K

Kant, Immanuel 12, 37

L

laicité 9
Land title 165
Leader-Guided Discussion 200
Lying to the Police 171, 262

M

MacIntyre, Alisdaire 17
major gifts officer 72, 74, 121, 227
Means-end principle 10, 37, 225, 235
medical ethics 15
Mergers 116, 244
Microfinance 168, 261
Misallocation 70, 104, 226, 236

N

Niave vs. Nuanced Ethics 3
noncompliance 160, 258
Non-Fungible Tokens 192, 267
Nonmaleficence 16, 44, 128, 223, 247, 249, 264

O

Obedience (Board Mission) 54
Organized Debates 200
Outsider discussion leader 200

Index

P
Participant-Led Discussion 200
Personnel Management 75
pet project 68, 225
Posterior Written Responses 199
PR crisis response 108
Prior Written Responses 199
Program operations 155, 157, 159, 161, 163, 165, 167, 169, 171, 173, 175, 177, 179

R
Red Herring 209
Relativism 5
Religion-based ethics 7
Religious ethics 46
Research papers 201
Revenge porn 192, 267

S
Short-termer 137
Slippery Slope 210
Social Enterprise 65, 225
Staff-Training 157
Straw Man 209
sub-Saharan Africa 165, 261

T
Teleology 12
Text messages 183
Theft 111
Threaded Discussions 200

U
Utilitarianism 15, 34, 47, 221, 230, 239, 263

V
Vaccine drives 187
Vaccine policy 57, 219
Vaccine resistance 144, 252
Virtue ethics 17, 42
Vulnerable Women 266
    right to privacy 190

W
Weak Analogy 210
White savior 93, 234
Wills and Bequests 121

Printed in the United States
by Baker & Taylor Publisher Services